Mindprints

Mindprints

THOREAU'S MATERIAL WORLDS

Ivan Gaskell

THE UNIVERSITY OF CHICAGO PRESS
CHICAGO AND LONDON

The University of Chicago Press, Chicago 60637
The University of Chicago Press, Ltd., London
© 2024 by The University of Chicago
All rights reserved. No part of this book may be used or reproduced in any manner whatsoever without written permission, except in the case of brief quotations in critical articles and reviews. For more information, contact the University of Chicago Press, 1427 E. 60th St., Chicago, IL 60637.
Published 2024
Printed in the United States of America

The author has asserted his moral rights.

33 32 31 30 29 28 27 26 25 24   1 2 3 4 5

ISBN-13: 978-0-226-83607-2 (cloth)
ISBN-13: 978-0-226-83619-5 (e-book)
DOI: https://doi.org/10.7208/chicago/9780226836195.001.0001

Library of Congress Cataloging-in-Publication Data

Names: Gaskell, Ivan, author.
Title: Mindprints : Thoreau's material worlds / Ivan Gaskell.
Other titles: Thoreau's material worlds
Description: Chicago : The University of Chicago Press, 2024. | Includes bibliographical references and index.
Identifiers: LCCN 2024009353 | ISBN 9780226836072 (cloth) | ISBN 9780226836195 (ebook)
Subjects: LCSH: Thoreau, Henry David, 1817–1862. | Material culture—Philosophy. | Object (Aesthetics) | Object (Philosophy) | Aesthetics.
Classification: LCC B931.T44 G37 2024 | DDC 306.4/601—dc23/eng/20240315
LC record available at https://lccn.loc.gov/2024009353

♾ This paper meets the requirements of ANSI/NISO Z39.48-1992 (Permanence of Paper).

Not till we are lost, in other words not till we have lost the world, do we begin to find ourselves, and realize where we are and the infinite extent of our relations.

Thoreau

Contents

List of Illustrations ix
Preface xi

CHAPTER ONE
Worlds · 1

CHAPTER TWO
Migrants · 11

CHAPTER THREE
Buildings · 32

CHAPTER FOUR
Shelter · 54

CHAPTER FIVE
Artistry · 80

CHAPTER SIX
Collections · 106

CHAPTER SEVEN
Sounds · 137

CHAPTER EIGHT
Conclusion · 154

Acknowledgments 157
Notes 159
Index 209

Illustrations

Fig. 1. Herbert W. Gleason, *Map of Concord, Mass. Showing Localities Mentioned by Thoreau in His Journals*, 1906. 11

Fig. 2. Replica of Thoreau's house at Walden Pond by Roland Wells Robbins and assistants, 1985. 55

Fig. 3. Richardson and Cox after Richards, *Alcott's Summer House*, wood engraving. From *Homes of American Authors*, 1853. 65

Fig. 4. Title page of Henry David Thoreau, *Walden; or, Life in the Woods*, stereotyped woodcut by William Jay Baker and John Andrew after Sophia Thoreau, 1854. 68

Fig. 5. Jean Jacques Aliamet after Charles Eisen, frontispiece engraving, in Marc-Antoine Laugier, *Essai sur l'architecture*, 2nd ed., 1755. 70

Fig. 6. Raphael Morghen after Guido Reni, *Aurora*, 1787, engraving. 85

Fig. 7. Precontact Native American bird's-head pestle, stone, Concord, Massachusetts, collected by H. D. Thoreau. 103

Fig. 8. Precontact Native American clam-shell opener, stone, Concord, Massachusetts, collected by H. D. Thoreau. 118

Fig. 9. Blanding's Turtle (*Emydoidea blandingii*), collected by H. D. Thoreau. 126

Fig. 10. Precontact Native American winged atlatl weight, stone, Concord, Massachusetts, collected by H. D. Thoreau. 134

Preface

He who eats the fruit, should at least plant the seed.

Thoreau

In a world of scholarship in which adherence to a field of study within a single discipline commands the greatest respect, my mode of proceeding has never been orthodox. Yet for all the apparent shifts of attention among fields and disciplines in my writing, there is an underlying consistency of purpose in an avowedly transdisciplinary body of work.

When pursuing the most intractable inquiries in apparently varied but actually subtly interconnected fields, I have found myself consistently appealing to two thinkers in particular. I almost always find succor and guidance in the works of Ludwig Wittgenstein and Henry David Thoreau. These philosophers are rarely, if ever, paired—for good reason. Yet both were strenuous thinkers who—although neither isolated nor reclusive, but rather social creatures who shared ideas with others—beat unique mental paths in manners similar to Wordsworth's Newton, "forever voyaging through strange seas of thought, alone."[1]

Thoreau is sometimes dismissed as no more than one of a small group of transcendentalists, inspired by German idealism, whose intellectual leader was the Sage of Concord, Ralph Waldo Emerson. If Thoreau was ever in intellectual thrall to Emerson, as well as obliged to him for occasional material support—most consequentially the site of his house at Walden Pond—in maturity he distinctly became his own man in every sense, including in the realm of ideas.[2] Although they remained close right up to Thoreau's death, the younger man at times resented the older man's guidance. In a journal entry in January 1852, Thoreau writes, "I should value E's praise more which is always so discriminating, if there were not some alloy of patronage & hence of flattery about [it]."[3] By then a genuine difference had arisen between the two thinkers, in part because, rather than adhering for the most part to deductions from general principles, Thoreau developed a determined commitment to the observation and examination of the phenomenal world in all its variety and complexity. He conducted this most consistently on his doorstep but also on occasional tours farther afield. As literary scholar F. O. Matthiesson observed, Thoreau "had a more dogged respect for the thing than any of his companions."[4] Herein lies an intriguing connection with the thought of Wittgenstein, who also insisted not only on the importance of general principles but on a commitment to the character of particularities. A further point of intellectual congruence in their work may appear paradoxical, for Thoreau strove for certainties in ethics, and, by extension, in the political sphere. Yet elsewhere, most particularly in his reflections on his observations of the natural world, he sought clarity, which is the very quality that Wittgenstein values when in the *Tractatus Logico-Philosophicus* he states, "The object of philosophy aims at the logical clarification of thoughts" followed immediately by "philosophy is not a theory but an activity."[5] This—an activity—is what philosophy clearly was for Thoreau as an experimental philosopher. I shall not strain to identify further points of intellectual sympathy in their thought as we know it through their writings and those of their intimates. That would be pointless. Instead, in this book I shall focus on some aspects of Thoreau's thought as I understand it in order to address puzzles I have identified myself, most particularly the constitution of *worlds* by *mindprints*, as I define these terms in the first chapter.

Thoreau is best known, of course, for *Walden; or, Life in the Woods*, published in 1854. This is his account of his sojourn between July 1845 and September 1847 in a small house of his own making near Walden Pond in Concord, Massachusetts. In his short life—he died of tuberculosis at the age of forty-four, in 1862—he published other texts, including the book *A Week on the Concord and Merrimack Rivers* (1849) and a number of magazine articles, often without a byline.[6] His sister, Sophia, assembled various of his writings for publication after his death, and from the later nineteenth century onward scholars have prepared editions of his works, culminating in the monumental though as yet unfinished Princeton edition.[7] Thoreau's constantly reworked journals, written regularly between 1837 and 1861, constitute one of the richest documents of observation and reflection in American letters and beyond. I find myself turning most consistently to the journals as much if not more than to *Walden* and Thoreau's other published writings.[8]

I readily admit that there is a geographical as well as a philosophical reason for my turn to both Wittgenstein and Thoreau. Wittgenstein lived a significant part of his life in Cambridge, England. He submitted his famously challenging *Tractatus Logico-Philosophicus* as his doctoral dissertation to the university in 1929 and spent key periods of his career there as a professor.[9] He died and was buried in the city in 1951. I lived in Cambridge between

1983 and 1991, walking the same streets as Wittgenstein. As something of a ghostly presence in those places, he regularly haunted my thoughts in much the same way as I imagine Newton haunting Wordsworth's, although there is no marble index of the philosopher in the college of which both he and Newton were fellows, Trinity.[10] I was fortunate enough to spend an evening in the Trinity College rooms where Wittgenstein had lived—usually inaccessible—when a friend from America, a guest of the college, was staying in them.

My sense of Thoreau's spectral presence in Concord and its environs is even stronger, for since 1992 I have lived within a few miles of the country through which Thoreau rambled daily. I, too, have regularly swum in Walden Pond, and I have followed in Thoreau's footsteps and boat wake on local trails and rivers. There is nothing mystical about this sense of their presence in the respective haunts of Wittgenstein and Thoreau. I simply follow Edward Gibbon in acknowledging the importance of experiencing a place firsthand for an appreciation of what transpired in it.[11] Once again, this sensibility is a matter of attention to particularities.

Although leading contemporary scholars have engaged seriously with Thoreau's thought, a great deal of his appeal is to amateurs.[12] This strikes me as ideal, for it seems a sign of strength in ideas that they should appeal to a thinking readership well beyond the confines of professional literary studies and philosophy. I count myself an intermediary between these two camps.

I first came across Thoreau's thought while living in Cambridge, England, through *Walden*, read with compelling sensitivity and compassion on BBC radio by the storyteller and author Garrison Keillor.[13] I was hooked, just as I was a little later by reading Ray Monk's enthralling intellectual biography, *Wittgenstein: The Duty of Genius*.[14] My wife, Jane Whitehead, gave me a fat single volume of a selection of Thoreau's works. The philosopher Anne Eaton gave me a copy of the *Philosophical Investigations* with the German text and English translation on facing pages.[15] I treasure both, and both have seen hard though affectionate service. If the *Philosophical Investigations* is the "Key to all Mythologies," *Walden*, as Thomas Wentworth Higginson put it, is "the only book yet written in America, to my thinking, that bears an annual perusal."[16]

[CHAPTER ONE]

Worlds

Henry David Thoreau called on his fellow mortals to "simplify, simplify."[1] The bare facts of Thoreau's life can be summarized simply enough. He was born in 1817 in Concord, Massachusetts, where his father later became a pencil manufacturer. Thoreau attended Harvard College, graduating in 1837. Thereafter he led a somewhat improvised life, at times teaching, land surveying, and improving processes in his father's pencil works. He was close to his family: his parents, John and Cynthia; his sisters, Helen and Sophia; and most especially, his elder brother, John, whose death from tetanus at the age of twenty-six, in 1842, affected Thoreau profoundly.[2] Encouraged by the Sage of Concord, Ralph Waldo Emerson, who was his mentor and lifelong interlocutor, thinking and writing were at the core of Thoreau's activities. Natural history and the human condition were his major concerns, notably human relationships with the natural world. Most people familiar with at least some of his work recognize him principally as a naturalist and as an ethicist concerned with both personal conduct and social justice. He is best known for his reflections derived from his sojourn in a one-room house he built about fifty yards north of the shore of Walden Pond, just south of the village of Concord, between 1845 and 1847, published as *Walden; or, Life in the Woods* (1854). Yet the heart of his writing is his journal, which he kept for some twenty-four years, until shortly before his death from tuberculosis in 1862, at the age of forty-four.

To denote the material traces "of the oldest men," Thoreau coined the word *mindprint*.[3] There are many such traces. For Thoreau, a trace "is no single inscription on a particular rock, but a footprint—rather a mindprint—left everywhere."[4] He specifies the products of Native Americans and ancient Assyrians, but by extension the term applies to all sensually apprehensible items with which humans interact. How do mindprints—material items from Native American arrowheads to Thoreau's own house beside Walden Pond—constitute worlds amenable to philosophical and historical examination? I specify *worlds* in the plural, sensitive to the implication of

Thoreau's question in *Walden*: "Why do precisely these objects which we behold make a world?"⁵ Thoreau was exactingly precise in his language, especially in texts prepared for publication, so I take his use of the indefinite rather than the definite article before "world" to be deliberate. This has far-reaching implications. Furthermore, Thoreau himself wrote of "worlds, of realm on realm," alluding to the variety of creation. Soon after moving into his house at Walden Pond, he asked: "Who knows who his neighbors are? We seem to lead our human lives amid a concentric system of worlds, of realm on realm, close bordering on each other, where dwell the unknown and the imagined races, as various in degree as our own thoughts are,—a system of invisible partitions more infinite in number and more inconceivable in intricacy than the starry one which science has penetrated."⁶ By "imagined races" Thoreau means not solely humans but all living things that he subsequently describes in the "Brute Neighbors" chapter of *Walden*, asking immediately afterward: "Why do precisely these objects which we behold make a world? Why has man just these species of animals for his neighbors; as if nothing but a mouse could have filled this crevice?"⁷ Each creature, even each mindprint, constitutes a world that is itself part of a "concentric system." This thought certainly contains the germ of what would later become ecology but goes far beyond to contain phenomenal worlds of every kind, initially as encompassed by a transcendental concept of symbolism exemplified in Emerson's thinking, but later developed into a conception of phenomena wholly Thoreau's own. Speaking of things constitutive of the world in his 1837 address at Harvard's commencement, Emerson claimed that if you "show me the sublime presence of the highest spiritual cause lurking, as always it does bristling with the polarity that ranges it instantly on an eternal law," then "the world lies no longer a dull miscellany and lumber-room, but has form and order; there is no trifle, there is no puzzle, but one design unites and animates the farthest pinnacle and the lowest trench."⁸ In contrast, Thoreau, growing far more circumspect than his interlocutor, rather than proposing "one design" preserves multiplicity when considering how material items constitute *worlds*.

What might be the context of the exploration I offer? Working within the disciplinary frameworks of both philosophy and history, I have long been concerned with human beings' relationships with the material items they make and use and with their relations with one another mediated by those items. Most especially, I am concerned with relations across not only space but also time as humans attempt to grasp ever-changing pasts and the ever-changing present in relation to one another, in terms of what the peoples of Europe and its diaspora conceive of as *history*. History is what humans at any given present moment make of pasts.

The material items to which I appeal vary widely across space and time in terms of modes of making, designation, adaptation, and use. Made items are artifacts that humans have fashioned. Designated items can be naturally occurring, ranging in size from bacteria to heavenly bodies, adopted by humans through a cognitive process. Adapted items are either artifacts or designated items that humans modify physically or conceptually or both. Use concerns the ways in which humans deploy all these items. Because these processes entail change, history is essential when seeking to describe and explain them; but I have long found myself also using the resources of two further distinct disciplines, art history and anthropology, to grapple with the character of certain kinds of material items. Furthermore, to attempt to grasp the mechanisms of these various relationships as consistently, parsimoniously, and accurately as possible, I appeal to the resources of philosophy, most often of the analytical kind. History and philosophy are overlapping and equal frames of reference in my inquiry.

The philosophical thread that runs through these selective studies of Thoreau's thought is best captured in the philosophical term *aesthetics*. I use aesthetics to bind with a single thread all the themes I address: not an aesthetics of beauty and sublimity alone, but one that concerns the properties of material items subject to judgment more broadly. Thoreau certainly discusses beauty in respect to various phenomena, from fine art—he considers William Gilpin's *Essays* at length in his journal—to apples.[9] Indeed, one section of his essay "Wild Apples" is headed "Their Beauty," and he describes apples—trees, blossoms, and fruit—in terms of beauty throughout the essay.[10] Yet when considering what is beautiful, Thoreau is especially attracted to those phenomena that most people overlook. For instance, in his journal he writes admiringly of an "uncommonly fair" sunset he observed on September 18, 1858, wondering at its resemblance to "an Orient city" and "a world of enchantment." But then he reports turning toward "the sober-colored but fine-grained Clamshell Hills, about which there was no glitter." He continues, "I was inclined to think that the truest beauty was that which surrounded us but which we failed to discern, that the forms and colors which adorn our daily life, not seen afar in the horizon, are our fairest jewelry."[11] As this passage suggests, his center of aesthetic attention is the apparently ordinary, whether phenomena in nature or the material items of many kinds that humans use, often oblivious to their aesthetic resonances. We can best gather all these instances under the term *everyday aesthetics*, as defined by Yuriko Saito and others, and *environmental aesthetics*, as discussed by Ronald Hepburn, Allen Carlson, and Arnold Berleant, among others.[12] Thoreau's aesthetics largely operates, broadly speaking, within these realms.

Literary scholars have appealed to aesthetics when considering Thoreau's thought in respect of language and literature; he did, after all, write verse. Among philosophers, though, attention to aesthetics as the wellspring of Thoreau's thinking is rare. Rick Anthony Furtak persuasively argues that on Thoreau's account our perception of reality "depends on how we are oriented in the world," suggesting that a "sense of reality" can be transformed by "affective receptivity"—an aesthetic capacity—as it was in Thoreau's case. Furtak concludes that Thoreau navigated between the "extremes of dogmatic realism and subjective idealism," holding: "The world's beauty is not fabricated by the eye of the beholder, but it does require the right kind of eyewitness in order to be seen."[13] John Kaag points to what he describes as Thoreau's "poetic renderings of the emergence and complexity of the natural world," perceptively suggesting that Thoreau conceived of the natural world as "continuous with human creativity."[14] Citing Thoreau's query in "The Bean Field" in *Walden*—"What shall I learn from beans or beans from me?"—Kaag proposes that Thoreau's preferred cognitive process depended on a well-functioning aesthetic imagination based in nature, as opposed to the "'civilized' conception of the aesthetic imagination . . . characterized by stultified ways of thinking and acting" exemplified by museums, concert halls, and salons.[15] Although he does not develop his insight regarding the importance of aesthetics to Thoreau's thinking, Kaag helpfully opens the way to further inquiry, particularly with regard to the place of material items—including artifacts—in Thoreau's thought and actions. This is not to say that Thoreau's artifacts have received no attention. The work of David Wood on Thoreau's personal possessions is exemplary.[16]

Meanwhile, the attention of philosophers to Thoreau as a philosopher, as opposed to as a writer of fine literature, dwells for the most part on his ethics. (His metaphysics seems to be beyond the pale for philosophers.)[17] Thoreau is clearly an ethicist, at times sententiously so. His work and behavior exhibit a streak of self-righteousness that even those closest to him—Emerson, for instance—could scarcely condone, though Emerson never once, to my knowledge, expressed doubts concerning the integrity that underlay even the most rebarbative aspects of Thoreau's behavior. No one who studies his thought seriously can evade Thoreau's insistence on his own definitions of ethical imperatives. Thoreau's aesthetics was admittedly entangled with his ethics. "The perception of beauty is a moral test," he proclaims.[18] Yet ethics need not be the exclusive focus of attention. So although far from absent, ethics is not central to this study. Furthermore, Thoreau is often charged with being a mystic. Some make this claim admiringly, others with derision. I suspect that what at times appears mystical is more accurately a product of aesthetic thinking, if one accepts a definition of aesthetics as concerning far more than the character of, principally, beauty, as rather a theory of sensibility—that is, perception by feeling involving the emotions.[19] I shall make the case that aesthetics lies at the heart of Thoreau's work, including aesthetics of nature, of human conduct, and of everyday life.[20] This is a principle that he expresses clearly in *A Week on the Concord and Merrimack Rivers*, in which in the "Sunday" episode he notes that he and his brother John passed two men in a skiff. He describes the sight as "a beautiful and successful experiment in natural philosophy," and continues, "It reminded us how much fairer and nobler all the actions of man might be, and that our life in its whole economy might be as beautiful as the fairest works of art or nature."[21]

Much more than I shall ever read has been written about Thoreau and his works. Many Americans have had to read *Walden* as a high school text, some resentfully; but many others have become converts to what they take in their various ways to be what he stood for, whether social justice or environmental sensitivity, or self-sufficiency and congenial sobriety. These are among his worlds.

As much as anyone in nineteenth-century America, Thoreau led the classical philosophers' ideal of the examined life, but for inspiration he relied as much on Hindu scriptures—principally the *Bhagavad Gita*—as on Greek philosophy.[22] As much as anything, though, he appealed to his observations of the natural world, prompted, we can be confident, by the teaching of his Harvard College instructor in natural history, Thaddeus William Harris, whom Thoreau visited regularly until Harris's death in 1856.[23]

Not for Thoreau the impersonal attempt at objectivity that many philosophers—not all (think of Nietzsche!)—adopt. He cogently reminds his readers that it is always the first person—*I*—who is speaking in a text, a point I hope never to forget.[24] The observer and the observed, the collector and the collected, are invariably in a relationship of mutual dependence, the one on the other, if either is to attract and sustain the attention of others. I am not suggesting that Thoreau anticipated the ideas of William James, nor yet Bruno Latour's actor network theory, Karen Barad's agential realism, Nicholas Thomas's theory of entanglement, or Lambros Malafouris's material engagement theory. That would be culpably anachronistic. Yet Thoreau's reflections on minds and bodies immersed in the observation of things both natural and human-made and their capacity for mutual influence point to a sensitivity to uncertainties regarding divisions between humans and nature, and between nature and artifice in relation to one another and to humans, with strong contemporary philosophical resonance and pertinence. This consideration evokes not a world that is open to inspection and eventually finite definition, but *worlds* oscillating in perpetual flux among actants among which humans are but one disparate and disjointed party.[25]

What follows is necessarily a highly selective series of discrete moments of attention to just a handful of issues raised by a small selection of Thoreau's doings as reported by his friends and by his writings. Although not necessarily always readily apparent, my attention is on a paired register of history and philosophical aesthetics. What one can infer of Thoreau's attitude to history (I repeat, history is what humans in any given present make of pasts) suggests a lack of concern to discriminate other than casually among periods of human existence in North America over many thousands of years. For Thoreau, the value of the deep human past is that it is invariably present through mindprints, which, even if "altogether illegible" in any literal sense, as he states, nonetheless remain "a perpetual reminder to the generations that come after."[26] That such things should be immediately evocative of human minds and, in Thoreau's words, "subtle spirits that ... are not far off" is an aesthetic understanding that pervades Thoreau's thinking on many matters, including on the "objects which we behold" that "make a world."[27]

In the previous sentence I used the word *objects* because this is the term that Thoreau employs on the occasion to which I allude. This prompts me to offer a note for the sake of clarity on my usage of certain terms referring to material worlds. I do not use terms such as *object*, *thing*, and *item* interchangeably. *Thing* refers to an item to which adheres the possibility, likelihood, or certainty that it is or might be vested with the living, sacred status and personhood of, for instance, an ancestor or deity. *Object* refers to an item divested of, or never invested with, sacred or animate status or personhood, so far as I am aware. *Item* is a term I intend to be indeterminate. An item can be a thing or an object. Some things can become objects, and some objects can become things, depending on their ritual treatment. Some things and some objects can never change status, whether in principle or in practice. All things and objects are items, and I do not intend any disrespect, whether to things themselves or to their constituencies, by the use of the latter term. Such definitions and scruples may seem irrelevant to some philosophers and other readers, but the respect I intend to convey through this practice is of the utmost importance to many communities. The explicit or implicit disrespectful belittling or ignoring of the standpoints of others by numbers of Eurocentric philosophers is a source of constant frustration and pain.

The chapter that follows immediately, "Migrants," is not about judgments according to aesthetic criteria to the same extent as the chapters that come after. It concerns ethics, but as moral responsibility in social terms rather than as principally individual obligations. The chapter addresses the ethics of relations among peoples of different racial and ethnic identities inhabiting the same place—Concord, Massachusetts—and aspects of Thoreau's place, socially, intellectually, and affectively, in that network of relations. Thoreau himself was the grandson of Jean Thoreau, an immigrant from the Channel Island of Jersey. Throughout his life he encountered other immigrants and their offspring, whether they had arrived involuntarily in what they called and continue to call *North America*, such as those of African ancestry; were fleeing starvation and colonial oppression, such as the Irish who came in large numbers, mostly between 1842 and 1852; or were privileged Europeans, such as the Swiss scientist Louis Agassiz (discussed in the chapter "Collections"). Thoreau implicitly considered all these newcomers, himself included, in relation to the Indigenous inhabitants of the old world to which they or their forebears had come. He was aware that, as he put it, "if you hold a thing unjustly,"—the lands of that old world—"there will surely be the devil to pay at last."[28]

One of the most significant mindprints associated with Thoreau—even though it now only exists in the form of a print after his sister Sophia's drawing, and as replicas—is his one-room house at Walden Pond. But before we can examine it in any detail, we must endeavor to place it within a schema of buildings more broadly. To do that appropriately, we must set aside *sedentist assumptions*. Sedentist assumptions follow from the prejudice that sedentary lifeways are inherently superior to nomadic or peripatetic lifeways.[29] This prejudice underlies most discussions of the built environment and is related in a complicated manner to racist assumptions about the superiority of urban cultures. If we are to be truly open to Thoreau's lessons about what a responsible way of life might be on an overheating planet imperiled by human greed, poisoned by hypercapitalist throwaway values, and grossly polluted by the petrochemical products of fossil fuel extraction, we should examine the largely unacknowledged prejudices that lead to such claims as those of the economist Edward Glaeser that cities are "our greatest invention" and make "us richer, smarter, greener, healthier, happier."[30]

If the chapter "Buildings" offers a historical taxonomy of building types with some of Thoreau's thoughts on the limitations of architecture, the chapter that follows it, "Shelter," directly considers Thoreau's ideas about the second of what he identifies in *Walden* as the four "necessaries of life for man in this climate": the "several heads of Food, Shelter, Clothing, and Fuel." He avers that "not until we have secured these are we prepared to entertain the true problems of life with freedom and a prospect of success."[31] Thoreau's thoughts on shelter are complex, and he put certain of them under experimental pressure during the two years and two months he lived in the house he built in 1845 near Walden Pond. I argue that an aesthetic understanding of both the environment (perhaps misleadingly signaled by the term *nature*) and everyday items and routines, including walking, decisively informs Thoreau's claims about shelter. The house was a mindprint for Thoreau even as he unsentimentally abandoned it. He chose his sister's drawing of it to combine with the text of the title page of *Walden* to create an *emblem*, in the European Renaissance sense that epitomizes the ideas he presents in his book. The mindprint of Thoreau's house continues to resonate in replicas and analogs to this day.

The fifth chapter, "Artistry," discusses Thoreau's reliance on aesthetics in his examination of worlds by looking at phenomena subject to aesthetic attention on a spectrum of material items from fine art to the everyday. *Artistry* characterizes material products of human ingenuity on this spectrum. This chapter also considers natural occurrences beyond this spectrum. It begins with an outline of the use of the term *aesthetics* by Thoreau's contemporaries before examining how Thoreau and members of his circle approached such fine art as was available in the Boston area. I also discuss Thoreau's engagement with writings on fine art. There is an unresolved tension between Thoreau's intuition that fine art can be of value in promoting the cultural armature that can support philosophical experiments in living, such as his own, and his conviction that art must be eclipsed by nature as an object of aesthetic and moral contemplation and inspiration. I then turn to Thoreau's ideas about *useful arts*. For Thoreau, humans must avoid becoming what he calls "tools of their tools," but he recognizes that accomplishments and satisfactions can attend the exercise of craft skills. He particularly values what he terms "a step beyond pure utility." He is reluctant to dissociate the two characteristics of useful items and fine art items—utility and purposelessness—aesthetically. Items that combine beauty and utility that are apprehensible in terms of everyday aesthetics can be a mindprint; he claims that "each one yields me a thought." His aesthetic system is expressive, embracing the natural art of the "Artist" or "Creator" and the imitative art that mortals make.

The chapter "Collections" looks at those items that Thoreau assembled for study and contemplation. One way in which Thoreau set about addressing his core question—"Why do precisely these objects which we behold make a world?"—was by forming collections. These comprised botanical and mineralogical specimens; birds' eggs, nests, and skins; and ancient North American Indigenous artifacts. He arranged for most of them to go to a museum after his death. Museums existed in creative tension with private collections, as both sought to identify and categorize material items of many kinds. This chapter contrasts Thoreau's pursuit of natural history through collecting with emerging practices of methodical science. Thoreau complemented his speculative and generalizing form of aesthetic historical understanding with another that depended on what his friend and first biographer, Ellery Channing, epitomized as the "particular and definite": particular facts that Thoreau explicitly sought to "trap." A certain irony attends recent claims from the field of science studies that have undermined notions of scientific objectivity, when contrasted with the observation that Thoreau's methodical though poetically—aesthetically—inspired procedures now yield data vital to contemporary climate science.[32] Thoreau became increasingly tolerant of museums, and he bequeathed all but two modest groups of items to the museum of the Boston Society of Natural History. Thoreau sought to represent the material worlds that he perceived "realm on realm" by means of his collections. He constituted all of them in terms of the aesthetics of the natural environment and of everyday life.

The penultimate chapter, "Sounds," extends the notion of material culture and its worlds to sonic realms. European thinking going back to antiquity lends privilege to sight. For a settler of European origin, schooled in the works of Greek and Roman antiquity, Thoreau was unusually sensitive to sounds. His increasingly attentive contacts with Native Americans, culminating, though not ending, in his travels in the backwoods of Maine in 1857 with Panawáhpskewi (Penobscot) leader Joseph Polis, likely enhanced his attentiveness to the importance of hearing as a way of fathoming worlds.[33] Already in 1853, on his second journey to the Maine woods, he had realized that the words spoken by his Aln8bak (Abenaki) companions among themselves "were the sounds that issued from the wigwams of this country before Columbus was born; they have not yet died away."[34] Those Indigenous voices were the aural equivalent of lithic artifacts as mindprints, in Thoreau's formulation. By the time Thoreau made that ear-opening visit to the Maine backwoods, he already believed human voices to be constitutive of human society.

That includes song. Thoreau's consideration of music is complex. He counts music a subset of sound, holding that the value of music is in the sound, not the tune. A child, Thoreau asserts, delights in striking a tin pan because "it detects the finest music in the sound, at which all Nature assists."[35] For Thoreau, the goal of the adult should be to recover the child's sensibility to become "a soul in health," "mistress of herself," attuned to a huge variety of simple natural and human-made sounds discerned through engagement with the aesthetics of the environment and everyday aesthetics.[36] On Thoreau's account, those simple sounds, discerned by the soul in health, directly afford transcendence.

It is not my purpose to offer a comprehensive account of Thoreau's philosophy, much less of his thinking in other registers, in this text. All I can hope to do, by means of a conjoint philosophical and historical discussion, is to alert readers to the part aesthetics plays in aspects of his thinking and how mindprints play a role in Thoreau's conceptions of the worlds he inhabited and examined so assiduously.

[CHAPTER TWO]

Migrants

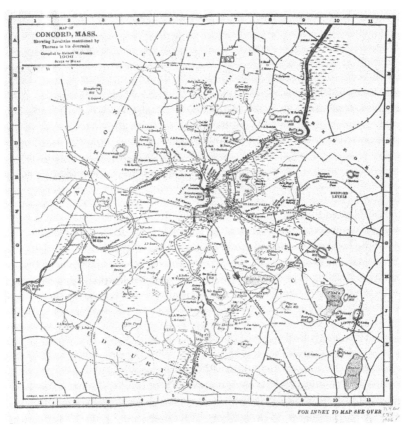

FIGURE 1. Herbert W. Gleason, *Map of Concord, Mass. Showing Localities Mentioned by Thoreau in His Journals*, 1906. Beinecke Rare Book & Manuscript Library, Yale University.

To explore some of the material worlds that Thoreau examined in broadly aesthetic terms, we might best proceed by gaining a sense of human presence in relation to material items in the place where Thoreau was born and lived longest, and which he knew best. This is the town of Concord in eastern Massachusetts (see figure 1). Concord in Thoreau's day was the home, whether temporary or long term, to a number of distinct social groups. This chapter looks in turn at four constituent groups in what was once Musketaquid, beginning with the oldest known, Native peoples, followed by European, initially English, settlers, who claimed the land from 1635 onward; then enslaved and formerly enslaved people of African origin and their descendants; and finally Irish immigrants, recently arrived when Thoreau lived there. Each social group with its distinctive material culture constitutes a world of human movement and settlement.

This choice of focus entails some simplification about migration in the Concord area. The historian Robert Gross has shown that during Thoreau's lifetime, Concord's population changed dramatically. Concord had a population in flux from at least the 1830s through the 1850s. Country dwellers from Massachusetts and New Hampshire arrived and left in waves; by 1835 two out of every three male adults had come from elsewhere. From 1844, the railroad brought increasing numbers of foreign immigrants, while locals left. By 1855, 20 percent of Concord's 2,250 inhabitants were immigrants.[1] In addition to the Irish, there were considerable numbers of Canadians from Nova Scotia and Quebec.[2] Many of the immigrant men remained landless day laborers or mechanics, their numbers rising in 1850 to 419, or 69 percent of the adult male population of taxpayers, up from 42 percent in 1801.[3] These were the local migrant conditions within which Thoreau lived and worked.

Human movement and settlement concerns at once large numbers of people changing location, whether temporarily or for the long term, and individual transits, alone or aggregated, from one place to another. The movement of people, whether en masse or individually, usually leads to encounters with other people, because for at least twenty thousand years few parts of the globe—Antarctica is the exception—have been uninhabited by humans. People who move meet others whose cultures are unfamiliar to them. What follows may be benign mutual incomprehension or the growth of shared understandings that lead to exchanges of things and people. Alternatively, encounters can lead to conflict, even resulting in the apparent extinction of one people through destruction or cultural absorption.

Most societies craft elaborate material things, whether portable, as in the case of nomadic peoples, or immovable, in the form of fixed abodes of varying size and complexity. Few peoples leave no material traces. At the very least, they leave fire hearths and middens. All these things, from palaces to dumps, play roles in defining the cultures of the societies that created and, in many cases, inherited them, whether intact and in continuous, if changing, use, or excavated following abandonment and burial. Insofar as an article of clothing or a building type is distinctive, it is a marker of cultural community that permits identification and the acceptance or exclusion of those who conform or differ in their usages.

What might be the consequences for relations among social groups of this general observation regarding identification, acceptance, and exclusion based on the making and use of material things of many kinds? These are temporal relationships—they take place over time—and so are marked by instability and are properly subjects of history. My choice of Concord assumes that Thoreau's hometown can act not only as a lens to focus on his own aesthetic (and other) apprehensions of his circumstances, but also as an example, however peculiar, of a community within a large, complex society that changed through human movement on an enormous scale in a very short period of time: the movement of peoples to North America from Europe and Africa between the sixteenth and nineteenth centuries.[4] Although English colonists incorporated Concord in 1635 within the Massachusetts Bay Colony, chartered in 1629, this was a relatively late date in the history of human occupation of the grassy plain and low hills at the confluence of what came to be called the Sudbury and Assabet Rivers to form the Concord River. That this was so was only too well known to Thoreau.

As a white person, Thoreau was a descendant of recent arrivals in that patch of North America its settlers called New England. Although he may have shared at least some of the assumptions regarding the relative standing of various ethnic and cultural groups held by many of his contemporaries, somewhat unusually for a white man, he was conscious of the equivocal position he and his fellow settlers occupied. This can be seen, for instance, in his idiosyncratic take on the myth of the Pilgrim Fathers, found in his account of his walking tours of Cape Cod, the large peninsula to the south of Massachusetts Bay where the Pilgrims first landed in 1620. They subsequently founded Plymouth Plantation on the mainland opposite Cape Cod and soon expanded their settlement. Writing about the acquisition of the lands north of the area at the top of the lower cape settled by the inhabitants of Plymouth in 1644 as Eastham, Thoreau expressed his skeptical attitude:

> When the committee from Plymouth had purchased the territory of Eastham of the Indians, "it was demanded, who laid claim to Billingsgate?" which was understood to be all that part of the Cape north of what they had purchased. "The answer was, there was not any who owned

it. 'Then,' said the committee, 'that land is ours.' The Indians answered, that it was." This was a remarkable assertion and admission. The Pilgrims appear to have regarded themselves as Not Any's representatives. Perhaps this was the first instance of that quiet way of "speaking for" a place not yet occupied, or at least not improved as much as it may be, which their descendants have practised, and are still practising so extensively. Not Any seems to have been the sole proprietor of all America before the Yankees. But history says that, when the Pilgrims had held the lands of Billingsgate many years, at length "appeared an Indian, who styled himself Lieutenant Anthony," who laid claim to them, and of him they bought them. Who knows but a Lieutenant Anthony may be knocking at the door of the White House some day? At any rate, I know that if you hold a thing unjustly, there will surely be the devil to pay at last.[5]

The circumstances of the founding of Concord were equally open to question. They were readily available to Thoreau and his fellow townsfolk in the version told by the historian and publisher Lemuel Shattuck in *History of the Town of Concord* (1835).[6] Drawing on sources that include the records of the General Court (the legislative body of the colony) and the journal of the early governor of the colony, John Winthrop (1587/88–1649), Shattuck mentions the devastation of the Native population by smallpox; the ostensible Indigenous name of the place, Musketaquid; the allegiance of its inhabitants to the widow of the Muhsachuweesut (Massachusett or Massachuset) sachem Nanepashemet; and the local sachem, Tahatawan, when the English arrived. "Both assented to the sale of Musketaquid," asserts Shattuck. The sale of some or possibly all of the land took place in 1637, it having been incorporated by act of the General Court in New-Town (Cambridge) in September 1635.[7] These circumstances gave rise to the notion that the new name, Concord, specified in the 1635 act, commemorated its peaceful purchase, though Shattuck doubts this explanation. He plausibly prefers the idea that it refers to the ideal of harmony among the English settlers.[8] Further, he notes how prosperous Musketaquid had been, its lands highly suitable for the agrarian cultivation practiced by the Native inhabitants, as well as hunting and fishing. These advantages clearly made it desirable to the English settlers, too. But for Thoreau, the Native people have an inextinguishable moral claim to this land and these waters. On the very first page of his first book, *A Week on the Concord and Merrimack Rivers* (1849), Thoreau gives the English translation of Musketaquid as Grass-ground River and makes the point that "it will be Grass-ground River as long as grass grows and water runs here; it will be Concord River only while men lead peaceable lives on its banks."[9]

Archaeological evidence confirms the prosperity of Native peoples in Musketaquid over a long period. As one might expect, there were considerable changes in Native populations, lifeways, and natural resources over the more than ten thousand years of human habitation prior to the arrival of English settlers.[10] In the earliest period, big game satisfied human needs, but after its disappearance the human presence apparently declined. By eight thousand years before the present, oak-dominated forest had become established, and the inhabitants lived on nuts, small game such as deer and turkey, and river mussels and turtles. Bivalve, bone, and turtle remains at sites such as that beside the Sudbury River known as Clamshell Bluff, a place familiar to both Shattuck and Thoreau, suggest elements of the culture that endured until about three thousand years before the present.[11] After a period of apparent dearth, increased usage of coastal shellfish, such as clams, helped to sustain the population while they developed ceramic vessels for wild grain storage. A warming climate allowed the development of horticulture—corn, beans, and squash—from about one thousand years before the present onward, leading to a denser population than existed previously. Concord was just far enough south to sustain horticulture.[12]

At the beginning of the seventeenth century the center of gravity of the people who came to be known to settlers as the Pawtuckets was likely at the juncture, rich in fish, of the Concord (Musketaquid) and Merrimack Rivers. Their winter villages were most likely distributed along the Merrimack and the several rivers feeding it. Environmental historian Brian Donahue suggests that as many as five hundred Native people are likely to have lived on the banks of the Musketaquid River at the time of the acquisition of six square miles of land by the English.[13] Shattuck notes that the principal English negotiators who led the settlement were the religious leader Peter Bulkeley and the merchant and army officer Simon Willard. They induced new colonists to leave England for Concord, then the first English settlement beyond tidal waters and, at the time of the purchase, still entirely surrounded by lands still under Native control. The major commercial attraction was the availability of beaver pelts, traded by the Native inhabitants for metal, woolen, and linen items.[14]

Shattuck wrote of the continuing Native presence, though it diminished steadily, and at times precipitously, as a result of English incursions. Ever-increasing numbers of mainly English colonists wanted land. They pressed westward, creating new settlements. They brought diseases with them to which the Native inhabitants had no resistance, causing devastation. The beaver population was overhunted and declined wherever Native peoples trapped these animals and traded their pelts to the colonists. Religious conversion efforts led by the Puritan missionary John Eliot and others acculturated—at least in part—those Algonquian communities that converted to Christianity and inhabited the towns of "Praying Indians." Most destructive were the wars, notably that between various colonies with their Native allies and the Pequots between 1634 and 1638, and—most far-reaching of all—the mutually devastating conflict known as King Philip's War, between 1675 and 1678.[15] The early predominant Algonquian peoples' strategy of allying with the various groups of settlers on the New England littoral to support them in their intercommunal hostilities gave way to what turned out to be a climactic fight for survival. The wars led not only to the deaths of many of the Native inhabitants of southern New England but also to the enslavement and deportation to the West Indian colonies of many of the survivors. It is important to state, though, that the Indigenous presence in Massachusetts, although diminished, was never expunged.

In Shattuck's day, the Indigenous presence as an independent cultural entity in southern New England, though not absent, was growing increasingly difficult to discern. The impact of the European colonists on Native lifeways had been all but overwhelming, at least on the surface. A continuing Native presence in Massachusetts was limited in the eyes of most settlers to a few small communities. Those Native peoples who did not move northward or westward were to a greater or lesser extent acculturated. A report to the governor of Massachusetts in 1861 recorded that the population of "Indians and Indian-descendants" was 1,610 persons.[16] Most were members of ten recognized groups with lands, funds, or government support, though not all inhabited Native enclaves. Some lived in or near coastal ports.[17] The settler authorities regarded them as wards of the state. In 1869 the Massachusetts Enfranchisement Act extended citizenship to its Native inhabitants. Although apparently a progressive move, this had a further acculturating consequence, for it led to the sale of most of the remaining communally owned Native lands. In the words of the historians who have studied the act and its consequences: "Ironically, the offer of full citizenship carried the price of relinquishing Indian identity—Indian 'peculiarity.'"[18]

Indigenous peoples in Massachusetts may have seemed to "vanish" in the decades following the 1869 act, but their resurgence in recent decades suggests otherwise. One measure of resurgence is the acquisition by Native communities of federal government recognition as self-governing, sovereign tribal nations through an arduous administrative process. As of January 2020 there are 574 federally recognized tribal entities in the United States.[19] In Massachusetts, the Wampanoag Tribe of Gay Head (Aquinnah) on the island of Noepe (called by settlers Martha's Vineyard) gained federal recognition in 1987, and the Mashpee Wampanoag Tribe acquired federal recognition in 2007. In addition, four further Wampanoag bands and two

Nipmuc bands have gained Massachusetts, though not federal, recognition. There are also organized but governmentally unrecognized groups that assert Muhsachuweesut (Massachusett or Massachuset) or Praying Indian identity.[20] Casino gambling has fueled a huge change in the fortunes of federally recognized sovereign tribal nations in states where gaming is permitted. None of the three recently licensed casinos in Massachusetts is a Native American enterprise, but in neighboring Connecticut, well-established casino gambling has led to the spectacular economic resuscitation of the Mashantucket Pequot Tribal Nation and the Mohegan Indian Tribe thanks to their respective casinos, Foxwoods and Mohegan Sun.

Another measure of resurgence is language recovery, exemplified by the Wôpanâak Language Reclamation Project. Wôpanâak is the language of the Wampanoag peoples of southeastern New England, which until recently was dormant. The revival of the spoken as well as written language since 1993, as a result of the work of Mashpee Wampanoag tribal member Jesse Little Doe Baird, represents a determination not to acquiesce in the submergence of Native cultural identity in that of the dominant society.[21]

Along with resurgence come challenges to white versions of the past. The Mashantucket Pequot have expended considerable resources on revising history through the Mashantucket Pequot Museum and Research Center, challenging white stereotypes and assumptions, especially with regard to Indigenous survival after the conflicts in the seventeenth century. The example of this institution for research and public education prompts the question of what should become of the plethora of material culture items, many of them archaeological, acquired by generations of settlers and their descendants, large numbers of which are to be found in settler institutions, including the vast majority of American museums. Among them is the greater part of the collection of Indigenous artifacts acquired, mostly during his habitual walks in Concord, by Henry David Thoreau. I shall discuss this collection in greater detail in the chapter "Collections."

Thoreau was well aware that the inhabitants of Concord who were of European descent were newcomers.[22] Referring to land, we have seen him state his belief that "if you hold a thing unjustly, there will surely be the devil to pay at last." In 1835 Shattuck had brought the antiquity of human habitation to his readers' attention with a certain admiration: "Many hatchets, pipes, chisels, arrow-heads, and other rude specimens of their art, curiously wrought from stone, are still frequently discovered near these spots, an evidence of the existence and skill of the original inhabitants."[23] Thoreau, too, was consistently aware of how the land he walked had been inhabited by Native people for many generations. In 1842, echoing Shattuck, he wrote in his journal:

> When I walk in the fields of Concord and meditate on the destiny of this prosperous slip of the Saxon *family*—the unexhausted energies of this new country—I forget that which is now Concord was once Musketaquid and that the *American race* has had its destiny also. Everywhere in the fields—in the corn and grain land—the earth is strewn with the relics of a race which has vanished as completely as if trodden in with the earth.
>
> I find it good to remember the eternity behind me as well as the eternity before. Where ever I go I tread in the tracks of the Indian—I pick up the bolt which he has but just dropped at my feet. And if I consider destiny I am on his trail. I scatter his hearth stones with my feet, and pick out of the embers of his fire the simple but enduring implements of the wigwam and the chase—In planting my corn in the same furrow which yielded its increase to his support so long—I displace some memorial of him.[24]

Writing about his bean field in *Walden* (1854), he states, "In the course of the summer it appeared by the arrow-heads which I turned up in hoeing, that an extinct nation had anciently dwelled here and planted corn and beans ere white men came to clear the land."[25]

Although most of the Indigenous artifacts Thoreau gathered were chance surface finds, he knew the value of digging. He conducted no proto-archaeological investigations of the kind made famous by Thomas Jefferson, who reported on his excavation of an Indigenous burial mound on the south bank of the Rivanna River in *Notes on the State of Virginia* (1785).[26] However, Thoreau did occasionally dig. His friend and early, though not always reliable, biographer, Franklin Sanborn, reports him finding an Indigenous hearth site during one of his many expeditions with his students when, between 1838 and 1842, he ran a school in Concord with his brother, John. Drawing on an account told to him many years later by one of the students, Henry Warren, Sanborn relates that the school party had observed a place on the bank of the Concord River from their boat where Thoreau thought Native peoples might have lived. They returned the following week with a spade.

> Then, moving inland a little further, and looking carefully about, he [Thoreau] struck his spade several times, without result. Presently, when the boys began to think their young teacher and guide was mistaken, his spade struck a stone. Moving forward a foot or two, he set his spade in again, struck another stone, and began to dig in a circle. He soon uncovered the red, fire-marked stones of the long-disused Indian fireplace; thus proving that he had been right in his conjecture. Having settled the point,

he carefully covered up his find and replaced the turf,—not wishing to have the domestic altar of the aborigines profaned by mere curiosity.[27]

The last observation—perhaps stressed by Warren to Sanborn—if reliable, reveals an attitude on Thoreau's part that is wholly in character. Thoreau was consistently reluctant to be intrusive, whether observing humans, their traces, or the natural world. Even as a young man, he would seem to have placed a human value on the ancient Indigenous hearth and taken care to see it honored.

Thoreau's curiosity about the long-term inhabitants of New England led him beyond their material remains. He took pains to gather information firsthand from such Native people as he met. One example occurred during a visit to his friend Daniel Ricketson in New Bedford, Massachusetts, in June 1856.[28] The two men "heard of, and sought out, the hut of Martha Simons, the only pure-blooded Indian left about New Bedford," as he recorded in his journal.[29] Alluding to his house at Walden Pond, where he had lived between 1845 and 1847, he describes in searching detail their visit to her in her "little hut not so big as mine" near the shore. He describes her appearance and her "peculiarly vacant expression" as she answered their questions "listlessly," though he attributes this not to stupidity but to cultural habit. He writes a dispassionate account of an elderly woman who has lost her language. He reports that her grandfather, who had lived on the same spot, was the last who could speak the Native tongue, and that she had heard him praying but could only understand "Jesus Christ." She had gone out to service at the age of seven and now lived alone with only a "miserable tortoiseshell kitten." However, she identified the specimen of *Aletris* that Thoreau had collected as "husk-root . . . good to put into bitters for a weak stomach," thereby demonstrating her herbal knowledge. This is an unusual description of a cross-cultural encounter—from the white point of view only, of course—between a Native person and a third-generation immigrant. While Martha Simons's grandfather had come from that very same spot on the south coast of Massachusetts, Thoreau's grandfather, Jean Thoreau, had emigrated to America from the Channel Island of Jersey as recently as 1773.[30] From an Indigenous perspective, Thoreau, like all whites, was a newcomer.

There are many other instances of Thoreau's questioning of Indigenous people, for instance in the course of his visits to the northern Maine wilderness in 1846, as well as with Panawáhpskewi (Penobscot) guides in 1853 and 1857, and during a visit to the Dakȟóta (Dakota) peoples in Minnesota in 1861.[31] Between 1850 and 1861 he compiled a series of twelve manuscript notebooks containing extracts from his extensive reading on Native

Americans and other observations, totaling just under three thousand pages.[32] Called by Thoreau the "Indian Books" or "Indian book," they are now in the J. Pierpont Morgan Library and Museum, New York.[33] Franklin Sanborn surmised that he may have compiled them with a book in mind that he did not live to write.[34] Literary scholar Robert Sayre pointed out that whatever may have been his intention in this regard, Thoreau made extensive use in other writings of the materials he so diligently gathered.[35]

What Thoreau's mature beliefs about the character and future of Native peoples in America might have been is a matter of controversy. However, it seems likely that he shared at least some of the emerging ethnological assumptions that Native people were for the most part unwilling or unable to adjust to the new circumstances that had been introduced by settlers, and they were fated to disappear, as he believed they had all but done in New England ("a race which has vanished as completely as if trodden in with the earth").[36] However, his extensive readings, epitomized in the "Indian Books," and in particular his intimate encounters with Panawáhpskewi (Penobscot) and other Native people during his travels in backwoods Maine in 1853 and 1857, appear to have prompted him to move beyond the "savagism" espoused by most of his settler contemporaries.[37] His experiences opened his ears and eyes to the enduring presence of Native peoples and prompted a certain admiration, reinforced by his visit to Minnesota in 1861.

Nonetheless, the equivocal character of Thoreau's stance toward Indigenous peoples is readily apparent in his writings. Adherence to prejudices regarding the relative status of the "savage" and the "civilized," prevalent in contemporaneous American society, colors a number of Thoreau's statements about Indigenous people, including those whom he met. For instance, Thoreau's many reflections on his and Edward Hoar's Panawáhpskewi (Penobscot) guide, Joseph Polis, during their journey in Polis's birchbark canoe on the Allagash River in Maine in 1857 are equivocal at best, incorporating stereotypes of taciturnity and childishness.[38] But he also expresses admiration for Polis's canoeing, hunting, and wayfinding skills. His attempt to describe cultural difference leads him to acknowledge: "Often, when an Indian says, 'I don't know,' in regard to the route he is to take, he does not mean what a white man would by those words, for his Indian instinct may tell him still as much as the most confident white man knows."[39] Unfortunately, some contemporary writers are prepared to chide Thoreau by charging him with racism, as though he were a contemporary of theirs (or ours). Referring to Joseph Polis by a condescending abbreviation of his given name ("Joe"), a disappointed Ben Shattuck writes that Thoreau "was surprisingly *of* his time here in his description of Joe, of the blandly cruel racism, and many levels of social decision-making in the nineteenth century."[40] Yet no one is not of their own time. People in any given community may well hold a wide variety of beliefs and act in a variety of ways, some admirable and some odious by the conventions of any given era. Some beliefs and actions that were admirable in a past time may also be so in the present, and the same applies to heinousness; but the most compelling ethical judgments available to those in the present are not necessarily entirely coincident with those applicable to a past time. To assume an absolute uniformity of ethical imperatives across time is to abandon historical understanding. If to establish grounds for judgment is among the duties of the philosopher, among those of the historian is to ensure that none should be too comfortable in its exercise.[41] Thoreau's attitude to Native peoples was complex and is not justifiably epitomized as racist in the same sense that we might apply the term to contemporaries in the twenty-first century. Nonetheless, we can recognize that Thoreau was not free from the taint of ethnological racism, according to which contemporaneous white thinkers were writing Indigenous peoples out of history and relocating them within an emerging anthropological schema in which they were described in terms of unchanging ethnicities tied to the natural world.[42] Worth noting is that Franklin Sanborn reports that Emerson, in his funeral eulogy, stated, "Three persons made a profound impression on Thoreau in these later years,—John Brown, Joe Polis, his Indian guide, and *another person not known to this audience*" (emphasis in original).[43] Thoreau declined to publish his account of his third journey to the Maine backwoods during his lifetime, to guard Polis's privacy. As Robert Sayre wrote, "In this sensitivity, as also in the amount that Thoreau learned from Polis, he clearly honored him."[44]

If Thoreau was keenly aware that "an extinct nation had anciently dwelled here," and that that nation was not entirely extinct, he was also keenly aware of his own status, and that of all other white people in New England, as relative newcomers. But as Thoreau acknowledged, not all newcomers were white.

Prior to the Revolutionary War (1775–83), Massachusetts had been a slave colony. Unlike in the Caribbean and southern plantations, most enslaved people from Africa or of African descent in Massachusetts lived and worked individually in farming or artisanal households.[45] The numerous Black slaves kept at his estate in Medford, Massachusetts, by Isaac Royall, the wealthiest man in the colony before independence, were an exception, being in this respect a cultural extension of his family's plantation in Antigua.[46] Historian Elise Lemire has given a detailed account of slavery and its aftermath in Concord in her book *Black Walden*.[47] She shows that the end of slavery in Massachusetts was confused and uncertain. It turned on several factors: abandonment by owners (sometimes engineered by enslaved people themselves), military service in the Patriot cause by the enslaved, and the interpretation by the Massachusetts Superior Court of the 1780 Massachusetts Constitution. This document does not mention slavery explicitly and asserts at the beginning of its first article: "All men are born free and equal." Lemire demonstrates how abandoned, self-manumitted, and other formerly enslaved Blacks and their descendants continued to live in Concord. If slavery in Massachusetts ended during the turbulent times of the Revolutionary War, the plight of those once enslaved did not. Until 1793, when the practice was prohibited by the Massachusetts General Court, "warning out," by which strangers who might become a charge on the public purse could be expelled from towns to which they tried to move, ensured that many formerly enslaved people, unable to leave their own towns, continued to work in much the same way they had previously.[48] They either endured domestic or farm service, which was little better than the formal slavery that the change of government tacitly and gradually ended, or they lived independently on marginal land that they acquired or on which they squatted with the permission of the owner. Others elsewhere in New England ignored the prohibitions and returned repeatedly to those places from which they had been expelled despite punishment, as the increase in the numbers of landless and more readily transient people undermined the assumption that inhabitants would remain in one place throughout their lives.[49]

Thoreau was one of many active abolitionists in Concord at a time of rising tension between free soil and slave states in the Union that would lead to the Civil War in 1861, the year before his death. He expressed his antislavery stance in speeches that were later published, notably "Resistance to Civil Government" (1849; better known as "Civil Disobedience"), "Slavery in Massachusetts" (1854), and "A Plea for Captain John Brown" (1860).[50] In *Walden*, Thoreau evokes the memory of former enslaved people: "For human society I was obliged to conjure up the former occupants of these woods."[51] Historian Robert Gross has established that as many as fifteen people of color lived in Walden woods through the 1820s.[52] Thoreau's choice of words, with their associations of ghostly invocation, is quite deliberate. He describes one Black woman, who lived independently by making baskets and spinning linen for over forty years in a small hut near the site of Thoreau's own, in witch-like terms: "One old frequenter of these woods remembers, that as he passed her house one noon he heard her muttering to herself over her gurgling pot,—'Ye are all bones, bones!'"[53] Thoreau identifies her as Zilpha, though her name was Zilpah White, formerly the pretended property of John White Sr. of Spencer, Massachusetts. She had come to Concord from Spencer. She died in old age in 1820.[54]

Thoreau also evokes Brister Freeman and his "hospitable wife, Fenda, who told fortunes, yet pleasantly."[55] Freeman had been enslaved in the service of the wealthy John Cuming. Rather than continue in service tantamount to slavery after his military service in the Revolutionary War, Freeman broke away to live independently on a small lot he purchased with a fellow veteran near Walden Pond, having chosen his name deliberately when he reenlisted for military service in 1779.[56] He was a beneficiary of Cuming's will, but the bequest was administered by Concord's selectmen, who used the money in trust to purchase part of his land to cover delinquent taxes. This left him with just half an acre and an unreliable income from the trust for the support of himself, Fenda, and their three children.[57] Freeman died in 1822.[58] Thoreau mentions his obscure grave marker, on which he is described, in Thoreau's scathing words, as "'a man of color,' as if he were discolored."[59] A third former enslaved person whom Thoreau mentions who had lived nearby was Cato Ingraham, who had been abandoned by his former master, Duncan Ingraham, when in 1795 Cato married Phyllis, the daughter of another formerly enslaved person.[60]

Lemire surmises that these inhabitants may well have been following African precedents in clustering small dwellings together.[61] By Thoreau's time, few traces of their former existence were extant. He notes that "Cato's half-obliterated cellar hole still remains, though known to few, being concealed from the traveller by a fringe of pines."[62] Brister Freeman's property was marked only by the "apple trees which Brister planted and tended; large old trees now."[63] Thoreau neither explicitly suggests nor denies that by choosing to live in a small cabin on marginal land long associated with impoverished Blacks he was presenting himself as little better, as his fellow townsfolk might believe, than his Black predecessors at the site. Yet by conjuring up these former occupants, Thoreau was implicitly identifying as their successor, thereby laying himself open to such an accusation by his many suspicious or hostile contemporaries in Concord. And—as I suggest in the chapter "Shelter"—he was also indicting his fellow town dwellers for their failure to adequately shelter those who had suffered enslavement.[64]

One of the most significant migrations of the mid-nineteenth century in North America was the movement of escaped enslaved people of African origin or descent from the southern states of the United States to Canada following the enactment of the abolition of slavery in the British Empire in 1834.[65] Numerous fugitives traveled north, often aided by formerly enslaved people, as well as by abolitionists, both before and after the passage of the federal Fugitive Slave Act in 1850. The arrangements for offering aid to escapees on their way to Canada (and also to Mexico and the Caribbean islands)—passing from safe house to safe house—were known collectively as the Underground Railroad.⁶⁶

The Thoreau family was firmly abolitionist. Thoreau's mother, Cynthia, and his two sisters, Helen and Sophia, were supporters of William Lloyd Garrison, a founder of the American Anti-Slavery Society and editor of the prominent Boston abolitionist newspaper the *Liberator*. As participants in the Underground Railroad, the Thoreau family provided shelter to fugitives fleeing slavery in the southern states. On August 1, 1846, the Female Anti-Slavery Society in Concord organized an antislavery event on behalf of the Massachusetts Anti-Slavery Society on Emerson's property beside Walden Pond, where Thoreau was then living in the house he had built the previous year. The event was a picnic, with four featured speakers who addressed the gathering from the threshold of Thoreau's house. One of the speakers was Emerson himself, but the last was Lewis Hayden, a young Black man who had escaped slavery in Kentucky two years earlier and had spent time in Canada and Detroit before settling in Boston in 1846. His words are not recorded, but he would soon become an agent—that is, a traveling speaker—for the *Liberator*. If Thoreau was present—whether he was is uncertain but seems likely—Hayden's words would surely have brought home to him at firsthand the reality of migration to escape slavery.⁶⁷

Because aiding fugitives from slavery was illegal and was particularly perilous after the passage of the Fugitive Slave Act in 1850, recorded specific instances of Thoreau giving aid through participation in the Underground Railroad are necessarily few and cryptic. In *Walden*, he describes:

> Men of almost every degree of wit called on me in the migrating season. Some who had more wits than they knew what to do with; runaway slaves with plantation manners, who listened from time to time, like the fox in the fable, as if they heard hounds a-braying on their track, and looked at me beseechingly, as much as to say,—
>
> "O Christian, will you send me back?"
>
> One real runaway slave, among the rest, whom I helped to forward toward the north star.⁶⁸

In his journal, the only place Thoreau incautiously gives an account of helping a fugitive is in the entry for 5:00 p.m. on October 1, 1851, which begins: "Just put a fugitive slave, who has taken the name of Henry Williams, into the cars for Canada." This man had been in hiding in Boston since the previous October but was alerted that a writ had been issued and that the Boston authorities were looking for him. Carrying letters from Cambridge and Boston abolitionists, he fled to Concord on foot, where the Thoreaus sheltered him overnight and gathered funds for him. Henry Thoreau took him to the depot, intending to buy him a ticket to Burlington, Vermont, but "saw one at the Depot who looked & behaved so much like a Boston policeman, that I did not venture that time."[69] Thoreau presumably took Williams farther up the line to catch the train.

As Laura Dassow Walls notes, the Virginia abolitionist Moncure Conway recorded one further incident. Conway was lodging in Concord for the summer of 1853 and met Thoreau, his parents, and his sister, Sophia, through Emerson. His account is worth quoting in full, for it gives an impression of what it meant to Thoreau to give shelter to one in the very process of a perilous migration:

> He [Thoreau] invited me to come next day for a walk, but in the morning I found the Thoreaus agitated by the arrival of a coloured fugitive from Virginia, who had come to their door at daybreak. Thoreau took me to the room where his excellent sister Sophia was ministering to the fugitive, who recognised me as one he had seen. He was alarmed, but his fears passed into delight when after talking with him about our country I certified his genuineness. I observed the tender and lowly devotion of Thoreau to the African. He now and then drew near to the trembling man, and with a cheerful voice bade him feel at home, and have no fear that any power should again wrong him. That whole day he mounted guard over the fugitive, for it was a slave-hunting time. But the guard had no weapon, and probably there was no such thing in the house. The next day the fugitive was got off to Canada, and I enjoyed my first walk with Thoreau.[70]

Until recently, Concord, an almost wholly white and increasingly wealthy town, has paid little attention to its African and African American past. I know of no archaeological excavations of sites associated with former enslaved inhabitants and their descendants. However, the Drinking Gourd Project, a charitable organization dedicated to raising awareness of Concord's African, African American, and antislavery history, was able to rescue a house that had been built in the early nineteenth century by a formerly enslaved person, Caesar Robbins. It had originally stood on marginal land to the north of Concord village but had been moved to another site in the late nineteenth century. In 2009 it was threatened with demolition, but it was saved thanks to pressure from the Drinking Gourd Project and others, with the financial support of the Town of Concord Community Preservation Fund. In 2010 the house was moved to a site near the Old North Bridge, where it has been restored as the Robbins House Interpretive Center.[71] It now draws the attention of the many visitors to this section of the Minute

Man National Historical Park to African American history in Concord.[72] Although scarcely an archaeological undertaking, the rescue of the Caesar Robbins House demonstrates the value of another layer of long-ignored immigrant history in Concord: that of enslaved Africans as involuntary immigrants and their descendants, whose existence—even as "human society" to be "conjured up"—Thoreau was one of the few to acknowledge. Thoreau was among those who drew attention to the African American presence in his town, a presence that, despite considerable local support for abolitionism, was even then being progressively expunged from communal memory and the received historical record.

If Thoreau was aware of himself and his fellow whites as immigrants and descendants of immigrants in relation to the Algonquian peoples whom they had for the most part displaced, and of the descendants of enslaved Africans as another category of relative newcomer, he was also well aware of the most recent immigrant group with its own distinctive culture to have arrived in the Boston area from the 1840s onward, Roman Catholic Irish. While many Irish women worked in domestic service—including with the Thoreau family—Irish men found employment in Concord as farm laborers; wood and ice cutters; ditch diggers; and most notably, railroad construction workers on the Fitchburg Railroad, laid through Concord between 1842 and 1844. Fleeing oppression and starvation in Ireland, they arrived in considerable numbers, prompting hostility on the part of some existing inhabitants that found expression in stereotypes of the Irish as feckless, dirty, illiterate, and prone to excessive drinking. Although Thoreau clearly had sympathetic relationships with several Irish immigrants, literary scholar Helen Lojek has argued convincingly that he "shared, apparently without thought, most of his society's prevailing anti-Irish sentiments," though more by acquiescing in and repeating accusations of thoughtlessness and squalid living than by active hostility.[73]

In the discussion in "Shelter" we shall see that in April 1845, when the work on the Fitchburg Railroad had moved on from Concord, Thoreau bought for $4.25 what he describes as the "shanty" that an Irish railroad worker, James Collins, and his family were about to leave behind.[74] In his description of the hut as inhabited by the Collins family, Thoreau contrasts its "dirt floor for the most part dank, clammy, and aguish" with what he implies were unnecessary luxury possessions within: "a silk parasol, gilt-framed looking glass, and a patent new coffee-mill nailed to an oak sapling."[75] The Collins family took these items with them. Thoreau used the former dwelling as a source of boards for the small house he was building on Emerson's wood lot beside Walden Pond. Adhering to another pair of stereotypes about Irish immigrants, he reports being "informed treacherously by a young Patrick" that a neighbor and compatriot of Collins was stealing usable nails from boards from the disassembled cabin while Thoreau was off carting others away.[76]

At the end of his residence at Walden Pond, in 1847, Thoreau consigned his house to Emerson, who in turn sold it to his gardener, Hugh Whelan, an Irish immigrant. Whelan removed it to the nearby site of Thoreau's bean field, planning to add an extension.[77] We shall see in "Shelter" how Whelan dug a new cellar for the extension too close to the original house, causing one end of it to collapse. Thoreau further reported in a letter to Emerson, then in England, that Whelan, although a gardener, had been unable to raise a crop in the sandy soil near the pond. Revealing his own prejudice, in the light not only of these failures but of Whelan's reputation as a drinker and his flight from Concord, leaving his wife behind, Thoreau criticizes Whelan's behavior as "Irish-like."[78]

In the fall of 1853, Concord farmer Abiel Wheeler cheated his Irish immigrant employee, Michael Flannery, out of his $4 winnings from a spading contest at the Middlesex County Fair. Thoreau acted to raise not only the money to recompense Flannery but also the $50 required for the passage of Flannery's wife and children from Ireland.[79] He describes in his journal going from door to door to raise a subscription for the purpose, revealing various attitudes toward Irish immigrants on the part of his neighbors. He writes:

> Today I have had the experience of borrowing money—for a poor Irishman who wishes to get his family to this country—One will never know his neighbors till he has carried a subscription paper among them—Ah it reveals many & sad facts to stand in this relation to them—To hear the selfish & cowardly excuses some make—that *if* they help any they must help the Irishman who lives with them—& him they are sure never to help—Others with whom public opinion weighs will think of it—trusting you never will raise the sum & so they will not be called on again—who give stingily after all—What a satire in the fact that are much more inclined to call on a certain slighted & so-called crazy woman in moderate circumstances rather than on the president of the bank. But some are generous & save the town from the distinction which threatened it—And *some* even who do not lend plainly would if they could.[80]

He made up the deficit himself.[81] Flannery's family arrived in 1854 and lived in the Thoreau household until they were settled.[82]

In the following year Thoreau published an article on an Irish tragedy that must have been on his mind when helping Flannery to write the letter to his wife about the passage they were about to take. This article would subsequently constitute the first chapter of his book *Cape Cod*, published posthumously in 1865 and edited by his sister, Sophia.[83] Both the article and the book have a bearing on Irish immigration when that huge movement of people contributed to a radical reshaping of the political landscape of Massachusetts and beyond. Thoreau's article was published with the title "Cape Cod" in *Putnam's Monthly* in June 1855.[84] Its first section deals directly with the fate of Irish immigrants lost in a shipwreck during a storm just off the coast of Massachusetts on October 7, 1849. When, two days later, Thoreau and Channing visited Cohasset, the coastal town south of Boston near where the disaster had occurred, up to twenty-eight bodies had been recovered. Many anxious Irish relatives of the vessel's passengers were on the same train as Thoreau and Channing, who were bound for Cape Cod. The sea would continue to throw up bodies for weeks afterward. Some ninety-nine lives were lost, many of passengers from County Galway and County Clare in the west of Ireland. The British brig *St. John*, which had been bound for Boston from Galway, was a typical "famine vessel," its passengers fleeing from starvation. Many were women, "who probably had intended to go out to service in some American family," as Thoreau surmised when describing one female corpse he saw.[85] His firsthand descriptions of the dead are vivid but all the more affecting for being dispassionate. Of the corpses in makeshift coffins laid on the ground near the beach, he writes:

> Sometimes there were two or more children, or a parent and child, in the same box, and on the lid would perhaps be written with red chalk, "Bridget such-a-one, and sister's child." The surrounding sward was covered with bits of sails and clothing. I have since heard, from one who lives by this beach, that a woman who had come over before, but had left her infant behind for her sister to bring, came and looked into these boxes, and saw in one,—probably the same whose superscription I have quoted,—her child in her sister's arms, as if the sister had meant to be found thus; and within three days after, the mother died from the effect of that sight.[86]

Thoreau made two particular points. First was that the dead had "emigrated to a newer world than ever Columbus dreamed of, yet one of whose existence we believe that there is far more universal and convincing evidence—though it has not yet been discovered by science—than Columbus had of this";[87] second was that local inhabitants did not scruple to gather the seaweed cast up by the storm for manure, regardless of the tragedy: "This shipwreck had not produced a visible vibration in the fabric of society."[88]

Yet a great deal happened to engender a visible vibration in the fabric of American society—notably in Massachusetts—between the loss of the *St. John* in 1849 and the publication of *Walden* in 1854 and "Cape Cod" in 1855. The huge influx of Irish Roman Catholic immigrants had contributed to the sudden growth of what historians usually describe as nativist sentiment among established settlers: an anti-immigrant wave of hostility on the part of large numbers of American-born Protestants. Fraternal societies espousing nativism that were vehemently anti-Catholic as well as antislavery sprang up. They maintained strict secrecy, their members being instructed, if questioned, to respond, "I know nothing." These Know Nothings, as they swiftly came to be called, soon organized politically as the Native American Party (from 1855, the American Party), and in 1854 they had their greatest success in Massachusetts, where they swept the elections for governor, the commonwealth legislature, and the US House of Representatives, winning all eleven electoral districts.[89] It was in these political circumstances that Thoreau's comments on Irish immigrants appeared in print. Indeed, *Putnam's Monthly*, in which Thoreau published his account of the wreck of the *St. John*, took a decidedly anti–Know Nothing line concerning immigration. Associate editor Parke Godwin published denunciations of Know Nothing hostility to immigrants in the January and May 1855 issues, the second of which also appeared in his *Political Essays*, published the following year.[90] Nationally, the Know Nothings were to split along sectional lines, North and South, and be overtaken by events as immigration declined dramatically in the second half of the decade, while the issue of slavery—on which Thoreau took a strong stance, as we have seen—came inexorably to the fore.[91]

The United States is often described as a nation of immigrants, but this is only partly the case. The cultural values of the dominant immigrant group—whites of European origin—generally prevail, only selectively accommodating the cultural values of other immigrant groups. Thoreau recognized this immigrant group—the "prosperous slip of the Saxon *family*"—as having a destiny associated with the "unexhausted energies of this new country," though he stressed that the "*American race*" that it had displaced had had its own destiny too.[92] From the perspective of that "American race," though, all those who have arrived from elsewhere since the sixteenth century, whether voluntarily or by compulsion, are recent arrivals. By assembling a large collection of ancient stone implements made by Native peoples in an area recently settled by waves of newcomers—English, other Europeans (such as Thoreau's Channel Islander grandfather), Africans (involuntarily), and Irish (fleeing starvation and oppression)—Thoreau provides a benchmark by which to measure the incidence of human arrival in a part of the world often misperceived as "new."

Migration in the Musketaquid-Concord area and beyond, on which Thoreau reflected, clearly has ethical implications. I look here at some ethical ramifications of the cases of Native peoples, Americans of African ancestry, and Americans of Irish ancestry in turn.

The treatment by settler societies over many generations of the Native inhabitants of North America is clearly shameful and the cause of continuing resentments that have led to occasional violent confrontations.[93] In 2007 the prime minister of Canada, Stephen Harper, formally apologized for the abuse of Native peoples, specifically the abduction of tens of thousands of children for acculturation in residential schools. Justice Murray Sinclair (Anishinaabe [Ojibwa]; born Mizanay [Mizhana] Gheezhik), chair of the Truth and Reconciliation Commission of Canada (TRC) that was set up to investigate First Nations residential schools, called this policy an act of cultural genocide.[94] The TRC issued its final report in December 2015.[95] Many in Canada believe that more action should follow. The United States has been even more hesitant than Canada to express remorse for its shameful conduct toward Native peoples within its borders. In 1993 a joint resolution of the US Congress acknowledged US complicity in the overthrow of the Hawai'ian monarchy one hundred years previously and the unlawful US annexation of Nā Mokupuni o Hawai'i (the Hawaiian Islands) in 1898.[96] Buried in the Department of Defense Appropriations Act of 2010, which was signed into law by President Barack Obama in December 2009, is the first "apology to Native Peoples of the United States" for "years of official depredations, ill-conceived policies, and the breaking of covenants by the Federal Government regarding Indian tribes," as well as "for the many instances of violence, maltreatment, and neglect inflicted on Native Peoples by citizens of the United States." However, the text specifically states that this admission is not intended to support any legal claims against the government.[97]

If the ethical state of affairs regarding relations between Native and settler peoples remains at best equivocal in both Canada and the United States, the same can be said of slavery in the United States. The Thirteenth Amendment to the Constitution, which abolished slavery (in most circumstances), may have been ratified in 1865, but the consequences of slavery resonate to the present. The House of Representatives and the Senate passed different resolutions apologizing for slavery in the United States, in 2008 and 2009 respectively, but they have not been reconciled and signed by the president. Advocates regularly and prominently make a strong case for reparations.[98] One wonders whether the majority of the people of the United States will ever fully face the ethical implications of their ancestors' actions or their own individual and communal responsibilities regarding either Native or African American fellow citizens.

The case of the Irish is somewhat different. Although members of the majority US population have discriminated against Roman Catholic Irish immigrants since at least the days of the Know Nothings, most Americans see the United States as a haven to which many oppressed and starving colonial subjects fled. It was not for any US president to apologize to the Irish, but for a British prime minister to do so. In 1997 Prime Minister Tony Blair expressed regret for Britain's role in the famine that killed over a million people between 1845 and 1852, in a letter to the organizers of an event commemorating its 150th anniversary, but stopped short of apologizing.[99] Commemoration of the famine has grown in US cities in recent years, at times not without controversy. An early example of a memorial is a large Celtic cross dedicated in 1914 to the victims of the *St. John* disaster in Cohasset Central Cemetery by the Ancient Order of Hibernians, a fraternal organization of Roman Catholics of Irish birth or descent. A more recent example is the Irish Hunger Memorial, completed in lower Manhattan in 2002, designed by artist Brian Tolle and landscape architect Gail Wittwer-Laird.[100] Entertainment for popular consumption, though, continues to perpetuate the stereotype of Irish immigrant propensity to gang violence and political corruption from the mid-nineteenth century to the present, as can be seen in such American movies as *Gangs of New York* (2002) and *Black Mass* (2015).

All too often, the established members of the settler majority—which includes enculturated members of minorities—perpetuate distrust or outright hostility, whether subtly or crudely, toward Native peoples or toward other immigrants and their descendants. The cultural values of the settler majority may predominate, but we can appeal to Thoreau's own practices to evoke an alternative view of immigration in Musketaquid-Concord and beyond. If we are not to be too comfortable in the exercise of our ethical judgment with regard to migration, we might take notice of the long-term view prompted by a consideration of Thoreau's observation that new immigrants, from wherever they may have come, from the seventeenth century onward are just that: newcomers to a very old world.

[CHAPTER THREE]

Buildings

Having identified some of the intersecting social worlds that Thoreau inhabited or knew in his hometown of Concord, I now turn to one extremely varied species of material creation: buildings. I offer what I term a *historical taxonomy* of buildings in the belief that only a discussion that addresses categorization based on historical contingency is likely to account for Thoreau's views on shelter, which I shall discuss in detail in the next chapter. Although this discussion of buildings in general may not focus on Thoreau's ideas quite so directly as the subsequent chapters, it sets the scene for his philosophical experiment in living lightly on the land at Walden Pond. The form of living that Thoreau followed at Walden Pond challenges conventional notions of architecture. His relinquishment of his house after a relatively short time implicitly casts doubt on the culturally dominant value among his contemporaries of permanence, or at least longevity, as a building ideal.

In the following discussion of buildings, I use the term *historical taxonomy*—likely unfamiliar in philosophy—to distinguish a form of categorization that takes historical contingency and the inconveniences of particular instances into account at the expense of absolute order. This distinction opens the way for possible confusion, so it is worth elaborating on it briefly. In contrast to taxonomy in the field of, for example, biology, historical taxonomy does not aim for, much less produce, discrete categories ordered into neat hierarchies. Historical taxonomy addresses the history, function, and use of entities rather than their formal features alone. Furthermore, it addresses contingent human uses and conceptions of entities expressed in social conventions, rather than attempting to define an absolute, universally applicable order. An example of a historical taxonomy in conflict with a biological taxonomy is the 1818 New York case *Maurice v. Judd*. At odds were two conceptions of whales: Are whales fish or mammals? The popular, biblically sanctioned view that whales are fish prevailed over the biological view that they are mammals. For government inspection purposes, the jury found whale oil to be fish oil.[1]

Although I would not describe Thoreau's adoption and adaptation of taxonomic classifications of entities in the natural world as historical taxonomies, neither do they correspond exactly with the taxa that zoologists and botanists known to Thoreau were developing at Harvard during his lifetime. Although Thoreau increasingly used binomial Latin designations for species, he could also contrast his aesthetic sensibility toward nature—acknowledging the role of metaphor in the language of description—with a scientific language that he objected to as "a parcel of dry technical terms."[2] When corresponding about specimens he supplied in 1847 to the Harvard scientist Louis Agassiz, Thoreau teasingly and irreverently writes of "*Roach* or *Chiverin, Leuciscus pulchellus, argenteus,* or what not."[3] Thoreau is firm that "observation—to be interesting i.e. to be significant must be *subjective*."[4] Historical taxonomy is not subjective in Thoreau's sense, but it does have to accommodate the successive subjectivities of those who categorize phenomena variously across time and cultures.

My historical taxonomic investigation focuses on built structures, including but not initially limited to those built to provide shelter. When considering shelter, Thoreau places himself, his own experiences, and his preferences at the center of his considerations. Echoing his claim in *Walden* that "the necessaries of life for man in this climate may, accurately enough, be distributed under the several heads of Food, Shelter, Clothing, and Fuel," he writes in his journal entry for October 20, 1855: "I like best the bread which I have baked—the garment which I have made—the shelter which I have constructed—the fuel which I have gathered."[5] The solipsistic precision of this statement reveals Thoreau's *sedentism*. In contrast to Thoreau, I shall examine shelter from a standpoint that I hope differs from that of sedentism, which is the espousal or even the assumption that a sedentary lifeway is and ought to be the human norm. Although Thoreau was used to sleeping either outside or in temporary shelters when traveling on foot or by small boat, he was a sedentist in that he assumed a need for a fixed structure, however modest, for long-term dwelling. As such, Thoreau unsurprisingly conformed to a nineteenth-century New England standard. Even the remaining Native inhabitants, including the Panawáhpskewi (Penobscot) guides whom Thoreau and his companions (George Thatcher and Edward Hoar, respectively) employed during their visits to backcountry Maine in 1853 and 1857, lived sedentary lives despite frequent forays into the wilderness. Those Native inhabitants of Massachusetts who lived near towns were equally settled, such as the Narragansett "Martha Simons, the only pure-blooded Indian left about New Bedford," whom as we have seen Thoreau and his friend Daniel Ricketson visited in "her little hut not so big as mine" in June 1856.[6] Thoreau's was an overwhelmingly and predominantly sedentary society that fostered sedentist values to which Thoreau himself adhered. Thoreau's sedentism, though, was not so uncompromising as that of many of his fellow settlers, for he valued regular peripatetic forays with no more than flimsy shelter, if any, and he expressed no known regret at the impermanence of his Walden Pond dwelling.

Within a set of sedentist assumptions and values, most minority world societies from at least the eighteenth century onward have placed a particularly high value on forms of shelter—and other forms of building—that they describe as *architecture*, even though architecture is a tiny fraction of the built environment. (By *minority world societies*, I refer to those hegemonic societies and strata of societies that enjoy advantages of power, status, and command of resources in contradistinction to, and often at the expense of, other societies and strata of societies that constitute *majority world societies*.) In their accounts of building as a human activity, minority world philosophers, no less than architectural and even cultural historians, generally ignore most of the structures that humans create. Is there a justification for this exclusion? Is the emphasis on the tiny proportion of human-made structures described as architecture a matter, in the first instance, not only of cultural but rather of racial prejudice? Or is the mutual antagonism between those who value not only architecture but long-term building generally and those who use temporary or movable structures even more fundamental than racial prejudice? Inspired by Thoreau's attention to shelter as a human need, I offer a sketch of a historical taxonomy of shelter types that can serve as a first step in analyzing a set of circumstances in which the values of sedentary peoples, including Thoreau, overwhelm and obscure those of others. I also argue that the contempt of sedentary peoples for others, whether explicit or implicit, is as fundamental a form of human group antagonism as is that of members of one perceived *race* for another.

If architecture and urbanism go together, it would seem that discrimination between architecture and other built things is not principally a matter of racial prejudice, because scholars in the minority world now credit the Fertile Crescent of West Asia, the Indus Valley of northern India, the Yellow River valley of China, Mesoamerica, and the Peruvian littoral as the birthplaces of urban societies.[7] Although some sedentist communities predated the establishment of agriculture during the so-called Neolithic Revolution (a term introduced by the archaeologist V. Gordon Childe in the 1930s), urban development accelerated thereafter.[8] All five of these regions are non-European and non-Western. The dominant European tradition, though, has placed Greek and then Roman urban settlement practice—the *polis* and its successors—at the heart of the development of civilization. Civilized urban settlement existed in the Mediterranean peoples' scheme of things in contradistinction to the supposed barbarism of nomadic peoples beyond their borders. From at least the time of Herodotus in the fifth century BCE, the settled peoples of the Mediterranean regarded the nomadic Scythians of the western steppes of the Eurasian landmass as their "Other" par excellence. Even those who sought to discredit Thoreau's experiment in living in his house at Walden Pond, by comparing him unfavorably with the *pithos* or barrel-dwelling Greek philosopher Diogenes, implicitly preserved him, like Diogenes, within the sedentist agora rather than banishing him to nomadic barbarism.[9]

Adherence to the values of settled peoples has long been a mark of civilization in the minority world. In consequence, apologists for various majority world societies have claimed the social status deriving from urban development. Scholars anxious to promote the equal status of the peoples of sub-Saharan Africa have pointed out the Black African role in the growth of ancient Egyptian culture, as well as the sophistication of sub-Saharan urban sites that include brick or stone buildings from the eleventh century onward, such as Djenné, Mapungubwe, and Great Zimbabwe, in present-day Mali, South Africa, and Zimbabwe, respectively.[10] Received opinion suggests that Europeans had to deny the capacity of Black Africans to develop urban societies in order, in part, to justify their racist projects of slavery and colonialism. Demonstrating that some Black Africans, at least, had created complex built structures from durable materials shows some apologists for Black African societies acquiescing in the European claim that the attainment of civilization is dependent on urban settlement. This assumption, nurtured by European archaeologists, anthropologists, geographers, and historians from at least the nineteenth century onward, remains dominant in minority world ideology. As a widely held, scarcely questioned assumption, the claim is part of minority world orthodoxy.

The modern minority world notion of social evolution—describing progress from savagery (marked by the use of the bow, fire, and pottery), through barbarism (characterized by agriculture, the domestication of animals, and metalworking), to civilization (which alone employs writing)—derives from the work of the American historian and anthropologist Lewis H. Morgan, whose *Ancient Society* was published in 1877.[11] This work has colored popular and academic thinking about human social organization ever since. Although many people may avoid explicit talk of social evolution, it nonetheless colors much thinking, both academic and popular, about the built environment. "Cities are birthplaces of civilization; centers of culture, trade, and progress; cauldrons of opportunity," states the web page for real estate developer Jonathan Rose's book *The Well-Tempered City* (2016). "The Answer is Urban" is the title of his introduction.[12] Harvard economist Edward Glaeser, who writes that to wander large cities "is to study nothing less than human progress," proclaims an ideological creed as the subtitle of his 2011 book *Triumph of the City: How Our Greatest Invention Makes Us Richer, Smarter, Greener, Healthier, Happier*.[13] He goes so far as to misrepresent *Homo sapiens* as "our urban species."[14] Looking no further than the "Solitude" chapter of *Walden*, Glaeser selectively quotes Thoreau, whom he snidely dubs the "Patron Saint of American environmentalism," to suggest that as an "antiurbanite" he was antisocial.[15]

It is not my purpose to take issue with such wrong-headed claims regarding the potency of cities. Neither is it my purpose to argue in favor of other ways of life as either desirable or practicable now or in the foreseeable future for the majority of humankind on a planet with a population of over eight billion people.[16] I simply want to draw attention to the long-sustained, pervasive opinion that urbanism—indeed, settlement more generally—affords the best conditions for high civilization and is inherently superior to other ways of life. It seems to me to be gross prejudice to project such a belief in the inevitable superiority of the settled life backward in time and to assume that urban life—indeed, all forms of sedentary life—is and always has been inherently superior to other ways of life. I am not alone in questioning the assumptions of those who believe in the superiority of sedentism and urbanism; the political scientist James C. Scott has eloquently taken issue with such assumptions, drawing on archaeological scholarship focused on ancient Mesopotamia.[17]

Various of Thoreau's contemporaries questioned the assumption that urbanism was superior, if not to nomadism, at least to what Charles Lane—cofounder, with Thoreau's friend Bronson Alcott, in 1843 of the Fruitlands experiment in "consociate" living—called "woodland life." Lane used the term in an article titled "Life in the Woods," published in the transcendentalist magazine the *Dial* in April 1844.[18] Thoreau had published his essay, "A Winter Walk," in the *Dial* the previous October.[19] The second line of the title Thoreau chose for his 1854 book, *Walden; or, Life in the Woods*, is presumably an allusion to Lane's essay. However, whereas Lane surmised that "the first wigwam was probably erected more as a defence from the assaults of man against his brother, than from the assaults of uncongenial weather," and that "the thought of erecting a house grew not out of human necessity so much as out of human rapacity,"[20] Thoreau stresses the origin of sheltering structures as among the "necessaries of life for man in this climate."[21] When he wrote "Life in the Woods," Lane, an Englishman, was not yet familiar with the winter climate of New England, having only arrived in Massachusetts with Alcott in October 1842, although if he was considering it at all when forming his theory, to describe the New England winter as "uncongenial weather" might be a characteristically English ironic understatement.²²

Although a sedentist, Thoreau was clearly curious about those who still led a partly or wholly nomadic life. The temporary or movable shelters of nomadic peoples lie lightly on the land, whether in woodland or elsewhere.

In the summer of 1861, in the hope of acquiring relief from the tuberculosis that was killing him, Thoreau traveled to Minnesota. Had he not been curious about nomadic people, he would scarcely have made a round trip of some five hundred miles up the Minnesota River from St. Paul to the Redwood Agency by river boat. He accompanied the governor of the state, Alexander Ramsey. The occasion was the payment of annuities to the Dakȟóta (Dakota), who in 1858 had relinquished lands north of the upper Minnesota River. The still nomadic Dakȟóta came in large numbers to the agency. Thoreau describes what he saw in a letter to Franklin Sanborn: "A regular council was held with the Indians, who had come in on their ponies, and speeches were made on both sides thro' an interpreter, quite in the described mode; the Indians, as usual, having the advantage in point of truth and earnestness, and therefore of eloquence. The most prominent chief was named Little Crow. They were quite dissatisfied with the white man's treatment of them & probably have reason to be so."²³ Thoreau was observant regarding the dissatisfaction of the Indigenous people whose nomadic way of life was threatened by encroaching sedentist settlers. The following year the Bdewékhaŋthuŋwaŋ Dakȟóta (Mdewakanton Dakota) leader Thaóyate Dúta, whom Thoreau saw and mentions by name—Little Crow—would assume leadership of the Native resisters in a war that resulted in the defeat of the Dakȟóta, the notorious mass execution of thirty-eight Native prisoners, and the killing of Thaóyate Dúta in 1863.²⁴

In order to grasp the tensions between peoples that spring from fundamental aspects of their lifeways—placing an emphasis on human built structures—the first step must be to propose a basic historical taxonomy, appealing to fundamental formal features of those structures in relation to their functions. Certain basic questions offer a starting point: Can the histories, functions, and usages that serve to situate a consideration of material and formal characteristics of built things help inquirers to sort out distinctions among a wide variety of such things in all parts of the world throughout history? Are inquirers justified in excluding the majority of the structures people make from any account of building as a human activity, whether in terms of philosophy or history? If not, what might the consequences for aesthetics and history be?

I use the term *building* (as a noun) in the broadest possible sense to encompass structures made by humans, rather than in the sense in which many sedentary people use it to denote fixity and permanence. Sedentary people tend to use different terms to distinguish implicitly between fixed structures, which they think of as *built*, and temporary or movable structures, which they think of as *set up* or *erected*. For reasons that I hope will become apparent, I shall not hold to this culturally contingent distinction.

The distinctions I make are not so much dependent on materials, modes of construction, or duration in a given place as on function. Following Thoreau's lead and bearing in mind Thoreau's concern (looked at in detail in the next chapter), my principal functional focus is shelter. Few peoples live without shelter, in the first instance from the elements, whether precipitation, wind, cold, or the heat of the sun. Shelter is almost as widespread a human need as those others specified by Thoreau—food, clothing, and fuel—to which one might add sleep and water.[25]

Although much building is about the provision of shelter, it is important to recognize that some buildings articulate space for other purposes. For instance, there are processional ways in various parts of the world, such as the sixth-century BCE route leading to the Ishtar Gate in Babylon. Walls do not necessarily support roofs. Humans also build walls to impede progress, such as the Ming dynasty–era Great Wall of China, rebuilt and extended between the fourteenth and the sixteenth centuries. On a smaller scale, humans build walls or stockades designed to provide more local defense, such as settler forts throughout nineteenth-century northern and western North America. Walls might be said to provide a form of shelter—shelter for those behind them from the unwanted attentions of those who might seek to breach them, whether animal, human, or supernatural—but in writing of shelter here, although this sense may be applicable, it is not foremost in my consideration. As well as making enclosed structures sheltering those within from the elements, humans also make open-air structures. Among those built by peoples in the past are henges (circular or elliptical earthworks) in the British Isles; stone circles, predominantly in Europe and West Asia; stone pyramids in Mesoamerica; and stone platforms (*marae, malae, malaʻe, meʻae, ahu*) in Oceania. The modern and contemporary world has seen the building of many examples of open-air structures, such as parade grounds. There is none currently more ubiquitous than the sports stadium.

Another kind of nonsheltering structure is designed to span obstacles, often water, as bridges in many parts of the world attest. They range from cordage pedestrian walkways in Tawantinsuyu (the former Inka empire in South America), to wooden ritual structures in east Asia, to arched stone bridges on piers in the Roman world and its successor polities, to steel constructions using girder or suspension technology in the contemporary world. People on foot, people on horseback, pack animals, vehicles drawn by draft animals, railroad trains, and motor vehicles all require appropriate bridges. Some timber-truss bridges have been built with their roadways fully sheltered in parts of China, Switzerland, and North America, but these shelters are intended to preserve the wooden structural parts, to prevent the accumulation of snow on the roadway, and to forestall shying by mounts and draft and pack animals, rather than to shelter people crossing them from the elements.

Other forms of travel have occasioned the building of suitable structures that may or may not incorporate sheltering elements, though shelter is rarely fundamental to their core functions. These include accommodations on shores and harbors for waterborne travelers and goods, railroad stations from the nineteenth century, and airports, from the twentieth century onward. Humans also construct buildings for storage, beginning with agricultural products and subsequently for manufactures of all kinds. Last in this far from comprehensive list of human buildings by purpose, there are built structures of many kinds for the disposal of the dead, from enormous stone monuments and mausolea, such as the pyramids at Giza, Egypt, and the tombs of Mughal India (the mid-seventeenth-century Taj Mahal, Agra, being the most famous), to the stone *dakhmas* (towers of silence) used for the aerial exposure of the dead by the Parsi in Mumbai, India, and Karachi, Pakistan, to the wooden scaffolds for the dead of various North American Native peoples. Other structures exist for the cremation of the dead, whether the burning ghats of India, among which those in Varanasi are best known, or the modern crematoria of western Europe and North America, where reformers advocated cremation from the 1870s onward. But because my concern is with Thoreau's philosophical experiment at Walden Pond and his thinking more widely, especially in relation to aesthetics, my focus is on human-made structures that provide shelter for the living as their core purpose.

The European tradition of thought about shelter is unusual in that a kind of shelter making has grown up to which many within that tradition lend a particular kind of privilege under the heading *architecture*. Architecture can encompass nonsheltering structures, but sheltering ones predominate. Specialist, privileged practitioners are called *architects*, in contradistinction to builders or, from the nineteenth century onward, engineers.

Architects, who plan their building designs for others to execute, emerged as a distinct type in fifteenth-century Europe, looking back to the forms inherited from Greece and Rome in emulation of Vitruvius, the first-century BCE author of the treatise *De architectura*, of which the first known printed edition was published in 1486.[26] These Renaissance building designers (architects)—Leon Battista Alberti, Donato Bramante, and

Filippo Brunelleschi prominent among them—claimed that aesthetic and intellectual components, notably mathematics, characterized their invention of shelters. Alberti set the precedent with *De re aedificatoria*, written between 1443 and 1452, which was the first book printed on architecture, in 1485.[27] Alberti based architecture on mathematics. In the sixteenth century this mathematical basis led to the claim that architecture was the highest visual art form, epitomized by the works of Michelangelo Buonarroti, most famously his staircase vestibule for the Laurentian Library in Florence, first designed in 1524 but not opened until 1571, and his design for the Piazza del Campidoglio and its surrounding palaces in Rome, from 1536 onward.[28] In this account, architecture is an abstract rather than a practical pursuit, according privilege to the work of the mind rather than the hands and expressed, in the first instance, in drawing. In the extended European world, architecture has been professionalized as an intellectual activity, with admission to the body of architects strictly controlled. This is a familiar story. What is not so familiar to those who live unquestioningly in the extended European world is that in terms of the totality of human shelter making, architecture—including architecture as discussed by Thoreau and his circle—is an aberration.

To describe a wide range of building practice as architecture—from the Parthenon in Athens, built under the supervision of Phidias between 447 and 431 BCE, to the expansions of the Clark Art Institute in Williamstown, Massachusetts, by Japanese architect Tadao Ando, built between 2001 and 2014 (an example chosen at random)—is appropriate but limited in its address of human-made shelter. The designation *architecture* emphasizes the contribution of a privileged individual as someone who conceives and plans rather than executes. This designation also lends privilege to forms of shelter that impose upon the land in a heavy, long-term manner. Such an imposition is part of the way of life of sedentary peoples, as opposed to that of those who move regularly, that is, nomadic peoples.

Members of sedentary communities dominate both scholarly and popular discussion. Their assumptions shape descriptions and debate. They accord the status of civilization to themselves and to other sedentary peoples selectively but denigrate nomadic peoples as undeveloped or primitive. Indeed, such is the disdain of many sedentary peoples for nomadic peoples that the former can quite literally write the achievements of the latter out of history. One egregious example is the want of recognition among settler historians until recently of the role played by Comanchería—the empire of the Nʉmʉnʉʉ (Comanche)—in shaping the movement and settlement of peoples in south central North America in the eighteenth and nineteenth centuries.²⁹ In the sedentary peoples' scheme of things, urbanism, not movement, characterizes high civilization, and urbanism depends on building for the long term. In this schema, building for the long term produces many nonarchitectural buildings, but as its superior achievement, it alone produces architecture. In contradistinction to many of his fellow townsmen and contemporaries more widely, Thoreau, although a sedentist, had a developed sense of what it was like to live lightly on the land as part of a human and natural ecology. Not only did he leave his house after a short sojourn without expressing regret, but in his own account, his house at Walden Pond had permeable boundaries that admitted other living beings, as he observes in the chapter "Brute Neighbors" and elsewhere in *Walden*.³⁰

Theorists, practitioners, and clients predominantly invest architecture with high social status. Architects design buildings for those at or toward the top of a social hierarchy comprising political, corporate, or religious entities, or wealthy and powerful individuals. Thoreau expresses disdain for architecture, characteristically intermingling aesthetic with ethical judgment:

> Consider the beauty of New York architecture—and there is no very material difference between this & Baalbec A vulgar adornment of what is vulgar—To what end pray is so much stone hammered? An insane ambition to perpetuate the memory of themselves by the amount of hammered stone they leave—... The grandeur of Thebes was a vulgar grandeur. She was not simple—& why should I be imposed on by the hundred gates of her prison. More sensible is a rod of stone wall that bounds an honest man's field than a hundred-gated Thebes that has mistaken the true end of life.—that places hammered marble before—honesty.³¹

In his condemnation of the architecture of grandeur, Thoreau damns it as "the luxury of princes," whether literally or metaphorically.³²

Places of work where people lower than literal or metaphorical princes on the social ladder predominate, such as workshops and factories, are usually not examples of architecture. Architectural historians habitually ignore factories, even in authoritative surveys. For instance, in the 948-page *Oxfordshire* volume of the *Buildings of England* (published in forty-six volumes between 1951 and 1974), Jennifer Sherwood and Nikolaus Pevsner discuss thousands of buildings, giving architects' names wherever possible.³³ Yet they make no mention of buildings that are among the most prominent in Oxford: the Morris Motors factory and the adjacent Pressed Steel factory (both part of British Leyland at the time of the publication of *Oxfordshire*;

now BMW Group Plant Oxford). Factories acknowledged as architecture are rare exceptions. One is the Fagus shoe last factory in Alfeld, Germany, designed by Walter Gropius and Adolf Meyer and built between 1911 and 1913, with additions completed in 1925.[34] Not only did Gropius and Meyer conceive of a complete façade for the first time in glass, leaving the corners open for glazing, but with great subtlety they placed the entire structure on a low plinth of deep red bricks to make it seem to float. They also gently inclined the brick piers between the window frames inward to subvert the appearance of pure verticals and horizontals. In contradistinction to many industrial buildings, the Fagus Werk is a factory as architecture. It derives this distinction not only from its physical characteristics, which are subtle, inventive, and extraordinary, but from the professional and social standing of its designers as architects.

Although often still associated with single creative figures, architecture is usually created by teams. For instance, even though the website of the architect of the Clark Art Institute's expansion, Tadao Ando Architect & Associates (founded in 1969 by Tadao Ando), focuses relentlessly on Ando himself, he works with a number of associates and employees that fluctuate over time, comprising no more than about twenty.[35] This is a small practice. Architecture is increasingly a multinational corporate activity. For instance, the American firm Gensler, responsible for the Shanghai Tower, the world's second tallest building (completed in 2015), employs more than five thousand people in fifty-two offices in seventeen countries.[36] Gensler also played a role in the Clark Art Institute's expansion, the New York office serving as architect of record to implement Tadao Ando Architect & Associates' designs for the Clark Center, which opened in 2014.

Just as commentators today ascribe the work of architectural teams to those individuals who lead them, such as Tadao Ando, so they project the assumption that an individual, whether identified or not, must be responsible for any structure from an earlier era or other culture accorded the dignity of architecture, regardless of how the structure concerned might actually have been made. For example, with no evidence whatsoever beyond the structure itself, architectural historian William MacDonald assumes that an individual architect must have been responsible for the Pantheon in Rome, built soon after 120 CE: "A thorough-going professional would have had to make drawings and models, calculate all the details of design and construction, and supervised the complicated, exacting work as it progressed."[37]

Those who subscribe to the idea that architecture is the most developed form of human building value the longevity of architectural structures, even if sustaining a given building entails its radical adaptation or the regular renewal of perishable parts. For instance, a significant part of the Clark Art

Institute project entailed renovating and adapting two existing buildings: the original 1955 white marble Museum Building and the 1973 red granite building that houses administrative offices, research and academic programs, and the library, which was renamed the Manton Research Center. The renovation was designed by Selldorf Architects, New York, led by Annabelle Selldorf. The Museum Building and the Manton Research Center at the Clark Art Institute are just two among many buildings worldwide that have changed over time. Such change can take many forms in various places for different purposes at various times. On occasion, a conversion can be a single major event, such as the adaptation of the Pantheon, Rome, built in the second century as a temple to the Roman gods and converted into a Christian church—the Basilica of St. Mary and the Martyrs—in about 609 CE.[38] In other instances, a building can be subject to repeated renewal, sometimes in the self-same form. An example is the seventh-century Shintō shrine complex, Ise Jingū, in Japan, rebuilt from new timber every twenty years.[39]

Even a long-term building that has succumbed to the elements or to the human propensity for destruction, outliving its original cultural circumstances, can retain cultural value in the eyes of sedentary peoples. The great pyramids at Giza, Egypt, and the Yuanming Yuan (Old Summer Palace) in Beijing, destroyed by a British and French punitive expedition in 1860, are examples of damaged edifices that retain cultural value even though that value is quite different from that which they had when first built. Even though it is not possible to identify all those responsible for the design of these long-term structures—the Italian Jesuit missionary Giuseppe Castiglione designed the Western Mansions of the Yuanming Yuan—they are canonical items in various sedentary peoples' schemas of world architecture.[40] Thoreau, though, had no time for such things, writing in June 1852, "All the stone a nation hammers goes toward its tomb only. It buries itself alive."[41]

One considerable change in sedentary building practice, including architectural practice, is the increasing incidence of expendability and even planned obsolescence. Architectural historian Daniel Abramson has pointed out the origins of the obsolescence of built structures in early twentieth-century America for real estate investment purposes. The federal income tax code, introduced in 1909, incorporated tax deductibility for building depreciation. The Department of the Treasury relied on the National Association of Building Owners and Managers to advise it on "reasonable rates." These were settled—to its members' own advantage—by 1930.[42] Building obsolescence for purely economic reasons—owners could realize a greater profit by demolishing and rebuilding than by retaining a structure—led to a decreasing lifespan for buildings, especially commercial buildings, in American cities from the early twentieth century onward. One can view this phenomenon—far from limited to the United States—as benefiting financially those who control real property by affording them repeated opportunities to commission architecture on the same site—a perverse form of permanence.

A prominent but by no means isolated example of obsolescence is the destruction in 1910 of the thirteen-year-old Gillender Building in New York, once the second tallest building in the world, to make way for a taller skyscraper.[43] While many building owners and investors continue to claim a right to demolish obsolescent structures, a growing contemporary concern with adaptability and green sustainability has challenged their relentless pursuit of profit by this means. Sustainability is complemented by preservation regulations, whereby buildings deemed historically and aesthetically notable are identified for protection in perpetuity. This is the case with the Bankers Trust Company Building (now called 14 Wall Street), which in 1912 succeeded the Gillender Building on the same lower Manhattan site and still stands, protected by historic landmark status conferred by the New York City Landmarks Preservation Commission in 1997.[44]

Whether demolished and replaced or sustainably renewed or protected, many such buildings are the work of architects, identifiable people accorded the status associated with their profession. The Gillender Building, completed in 1897, was designed by accredited architects, the partners Charles I. Berg and Edward H. Clark.[45] They limited their profuse decoration to the three lower floors but then reintroduced decorative elements higher up the building, which was surmounted by an ornate drum and cupola. This feature was derived from the pair of subordinate domes after Michelangelo's original design for St. Peter's Basilica, Rome, built from 1564 onward. The Bankers Trust Company Building, which replaced the Gillender Building in 1912, was designed by architect partners Samuel Beck Parkman Trowbridge and Goodhue Livingston. They worked on this project in a neoclassical style, topping it with a version of the Mausoleum of Halicarnassus, one of the seven wonders of the ancient world.[46] Formal analysis of architectural allusion reveals ambition: from 1913, the Bankers Trust Company adopted the mausoleum as its logo, advertised itself as the "Tower of Strength," and registered a rendering of the mausoleum as its trademark.[47] One can view this choice as ironically confirming Thoreau's opinion that "all the stone a nation hammers goes toward its tomb only."[48]

I want to draw back from architecture in order to establish the desirability of contrasting, in the first place, architecture, in the sense outlined above, with fixed buildings to which no one accords the dignity of architecture.

Then I propose to contrast fixed buildings, including architecture, with those temporary or movable structures associated with nomadic peoples. Only then will the contingent and extremely limited scope of architecture become apparent. I begin discussing nonarchitectural structures by drawing some categorical distinctions among them.

There are numerous instances of long-term, sedentary nonarchitectural structures. Nonarchitectural structures are buildings conceived by people other than architects. That they constitute by far the greater quotient of built structures in the settled world is obvious but usually ignored. In many jurisdictions the use of the term *architect* is strictly controlled, limited to those who have obtained state-recognized or state-granted licenses following professional examinations. Government boards or professional bodies regulate practice, investigate complaints, and discipline violators.[49] Contractors of various kinds who can design and build structures for third parties are usually themselves licensed, though they are legally prohibited from using the title *architect*.[50] Obviously this state of affairs is contingent and does not inhibit later commentators from retrospectively attempting to dignify as such building designers who may not have had social recognition as architects (or some equivalent, if such existed) in their own societies.

Structures designed and built by nonarchitects, including contractors, are sometimes termed *vernacular architecture* to lend them dignity. This designation covers a vast range within the built environment, comprising by far the majority of long-term human-made structures. In the United States, the Vernacular Architecture Forum is dedicated to the "appreciation and study of ordinary buildings and landscapes."[51] The scope of vernacular architecture worldwide is huge. It includes, but is not limited to, a vast range of domestic dwellings, from high-end residences to shanty towns, artisanal workshops, farm buildings, industrial plants, and log cabins of the kind Thoreau described in Maine.[52] Some are constructed for clients by qualified professionals (contractors) or by others who claim to have building skills. Some are painstakingly constructed, others jerry-built. Yet others are built by their occupiers themselves, such as Thoreau's house at Walden Pond. Many such structures are provisional, improvised by members of impoverished communities spurred by the ingenuity of desperation. Mid-nineteenth-century Irish immigrant railroad workers' "shanties," one of which Thoreau bought for its boards in April 1845, are prime examples.[53] The numerous refugee and displaced persons' encampments around the contemporary world are testaments to such needs and motivations.

Another form of vernacular architecture is the creative adaptation of architecturally designed buildings for new purposes. For instance, a palace designed by an architect can be turned into an improvised apartment building. Mackintosh Burn built Tagore Castle in 1896 in Kolkata, India, for the arts patron and philanthropist Maharaja Bahadur Sir Jatindramohan Tagore. He designed it with battlements, turrets, and a one-hundred-foot-tall castellated tower, reputedly meant to evoke Windsor Castle, the seat of Queen Victoria in England, who from 1877 also reigned as empress of India. It began as an architectural edifice. Although still owned by a member of the Tagore family and the subject of a long-running legal dispute with the principal tenant, it is now occupied by several hundred informal tenants. Over recent decades these occupants have divided the rooms, making their own modifications inside and out. The result is a radical change to the appearance of the building. Original features have degraded and been overlaid with improvised accretions so that the exterior now has an informal, haphazard appearance.[54] Such a designation may appear to blur ideal taxonomic boundaries by evoking an apparent paradox: an architectural structure (in the narrow sense) modified so as to cease to be one. But when considering an issue such as shelter, the tidy, ideally stable taxonomy of the philosopher and biologist must give way to the messy and frequently blurred taxonomy of the historian. This historical imperative is not without philosophical sanction: Ian Hacking contends that "what is confused is sometimes more useful than what has been clarified."[55]

From the standpoint of philosophical aesthetics, it seems important to note that vernacular, improvised, and informal buildings exhibit properties worthy of attention. These properties may differ from those of buildings accorded the status of architecture, which are the result of detailed planning to produce structures of harmonious integrity. The former frequently exhibit characteristics of the kind to which Yuriko Saito has drawn attention: informality, improvisation, and disunity that cannot be reduced to nor reconciled with the dominant aesthetics of architecture.[56]

Most architects occupy a position of professional privilege in all societies. So, too, do licensed contractors and other professionally recognized builders who work for clients, though most occupy a lower rung on the ladder of social privilege than architects. These are positions of relatively high status that architectural historians and other commentators can apply retrospectively to the actual and supposed builders of structures in order to validate them selectively. In contrast, the majority of—though far from all—building improvisers, usually creating or adapting structures for their own use, are relatively socially disadvantaged. Therefore, it is hardly surprising that the world's majority of building improvisers inhabit polities where building regulation is relatively lax or unenforced. They are predominantly, though far from exclusively, South and Southeast Asian, African and African diasporic, or Latin American.

All the sedentary building types examined here, whether formal architecture, vernacular architecture, or adaptations of the one to the other, depend on three factors common to all sedentary societies. The first concerns conceiving of land as real property over which a sovereign entity, tenant in chief, tenant, grantee, or proprietor exercises control in respect of occupation, heritability, assignment, or alienation. The second concerns conceiving of land as subject to regulation, whether observed or flouted, in terms of what can be built upon it and how such buildings might be used, including their modification or renewal. The third, closely related to the second, concerns conceiving of land, its produce, and buildings erected on it as subject to taxation by a governing authority and consequently subject to all applicable culturally specific means of registration and oversight. For instance, Thoreau built his house beside Walden Pond in 1845 on a lot to which Ralph Waldo Emerson, according to the settler polity, had good title. Emerson had purchased it the previous October from the potter Thomas Wyman.[57] Emerson described the circumstances in a letter to his brother, William.[58] He possessed title to that land and gave Thoreau permission to build on it.

Nomadic peoples conceive of land in quite different ways from sedentary peoples. They may acknowledge exclusive rights on the part of a clan or larger social unit to certain specific resources of a tract of land, while acknowledging the right of others to other resources on the same land. They may claim exclusive or partial use of a tract of land at one period of the year but not at others. They are unlikely to claim exclusive tenancy and occupation or the right to exploit all resources, subject to occupation or improvement, such as one finds among sedentary peoples.

These definitions still obtain if one acknowledges that all human use of land is about access to material and immaterial resources, whether water and food or the presence in particular places of ancestors or sacred beings. Furthermore, the same is true if one recognizes that notions of territory and tenure concern, in the first instance, relations among people rather than the character of any given tract of land.[59] Various communities conceive of those human relationships in different ways, expressed by different conceptions of land. Different conceptions of land use have caused innumerable disputes among peoples who adhere to their own particular conventions. These disputes have arisen between different communities of sedentary peoples no less than between communities of sedentary and nomadic peoples. The most conspicuous mutual misconceptions of the last five centuries have occurred and continue to occur in the context of European expansion and colonial settlement throughout the Americas, Oceania, Africa, South and Southeast Asia, Australia, and the central and northeastern portion of the Eurasian landmass within successive Russian polities.[60]

The key point to make before turning to the kinds of structures made and used by nomadic peoples is that nomadic and sedentary peoples often come into conflict when they encounter one another. Their respective interests over land are irreconcilable. The same land cannot be subject to settled agricultural or urban use and the needs of nomadic hunter-gatherers or pastoralists simultaneously. In the past, some nomadic peoples have seriously disrupted the lives of entire communities of sedentary peoples, sometimes over many centuries. For example, invasions and raids by successive nomadic peoples of the western steppes of Eurasia into Russia, the Balkans, and at times parts of western Europe, occurred regularly between the eighth century BCE and the fifteenth century CE. The sedentary peoples of Han China were overwhelmed in the course of the thirteenth century by then predominantly nomadic Mongols from the north and west.

The principal requirement of state formation is the imposition of taxation, initially on agricultural produce, to secure revenues reliably. As political scientist James C. Scott has shown, some communities take great pains to avoid absorption into tax-levying states.[61] (Individuals also—including most famously Thoreau, but also his friend Bronson Alcott—have sought to evade taxes [in their case poll taxes] raised for purposes they consider to be immoral.)[62] The discipline that states seek to impose, rather than the pretended conveniences of long-term shelter, may be the principal reason that nomadic peoples have tended to adopt sedentary habits, gradually or peremptorily, as a result of contact, whether cordial or antagonistic, with sedentary peoples. Over the course of human history, the long-term advantage has been with sedentary peoples, whose ways of life more readily permit the creation of complex social mechanisms leading to the sustenance of ever-increasing populations. In their encounters, sedentary peoples have usually attempted to convert nomadic peoples to their own ways of life, if exclusion, expulsion, or extermination either fail or are not viable options. Yet nomadic lifeways still exist, notably in parts of West Asia, South Asia, and Africa.[63] In these places and others, they are under long-term and increasing threat. For instance, the 313 recognized "nomadic tribes" and 198 "denotified tribes" in India have continued to exist under a stigma of imputed criminality since at least the passage of the Criminal Tribes Act in 1871 and subsequent legislation. The act was repealed in 1949 (leading to the tribes listed in it being "denotified") but was succeeded by the Habitual Offenders Act of 1952.[64] In 2007 the United Nations Committee on the Elimination of Racial Discrimination called on India to repeal the Habitual

Offenders Act because the "so-called denotified and nomadic tribes... continue to be stigmatized."[65]

The antagonism of sedentary peoples toward nomadic peoples can be extreme. One of the worst genocides of the twentieth century was committed by the Nazi regime of Germany against the Roma and Sinti. Estimates vary widely, but it is likely that at least 25 percent of the pre-1939 population of just under one million were murdered in the death camps and elsewhere.[66] This was the culmination of antagonism on the part of most of the sedentary population of western and central Europe toward the itinerant strangers who had first appeared there in the early fifteenth century, reportedly claiming to be pilgrims who had come from Egypt, although they were of Indian origin. Between 1420 and 1530 their status was reduced throughout western Europe from that of protected pilgrims to hated vagabonds.[67] They were subject to legal and extralegal persecution and remain so to this day. A major aim of most European states is to entice or to force Roma and Sinti to abandon their nomadic way of life and adopt sedentary habits.

In the case of the Roma and Sinti in Europe, as in that of the "nomadic" and "denotified" tribes of India, sedentary distrust of nomadic peoples largely coincides with racial discrimination. It is tempting to see the former as more fundamental than the latter; that is, although not necessarily a consequence of distrust between settled and nomadic communities, that distrust can give rise to racial antagonism. However, one should be cautious in the face of historical contingency. It seems quite likely that various factors—racial antagonism, distrust between settled and nomadic communities—can have different weights in different circumstances, so it is not possible to make a general claim about which of the two factors precedes the other when both are present. It seems likely, though, that in a case such as that of the Roma and Sinti in Europe, racial antagonism was a consequence of distrust between settled and nomadic communities, rather than an originating cause of that distrust.

With these dynamics no more than sketched, I turn to the built structures of nomadic peoples. The first type to be distinguished comprises those that are repeatable, made from new materials in each new place. On arrival, builders gather appropriate materials from the immediate surroundings and construct a shelter, which they leave behind when they depart. It may remain intact or reparable for repeat visits, or it may disintegrate relatively swiftly. Such structures are or were found among the Sámi of northern Scandinavia and northwest Russia, the Afar of Ethiopia, and various Indigenous Australian communities, among many others. Second, some nomadic peoples make repeatable structures wholly or in part from materials they carry with them for the purpose. They may use pack animals to carry made parts, such as textiles, exterior matting, prepared hides, and poles, which they integrate with locally found, replaceable materials. Such structures are usually more elaborate than the first kind of nomadic structure, being the result of considerable labor and investment of aesthetic care to produce the prepared parts. Such elaborate structures include Bedouin and Tuareg tents, matting-roofed shelters in the Horn of Africa, Plains Native American lodges, central Asian yurts, and Roma tents. For instance, the eminent European American historian Francis Parkman Jr. gives a vivid account of witnessing in 1846 the preparation, transportation, erection, and disassembly of lodges by the Oglála Lakȟóta (Oglala Lakota) in present-day Nebraska and Wyoming.[68] The Dakȟóta (Dakota) whom Thoreau encountered at the Redwood Agency in Minnesota in 1861, "who had come in on their ponies," presumably erected tipis during their visit to receive government payments, although he describes Redwood simply as "a mere locality, scarcely an Indian village—where there is a store & some houses have been built for them."[69] Third, it is worth considering movable structures that remain intact while on the move, thanks to technologies of transportation. These include houseboats of various kinds, such as those on lakes in Jammu and Kashmir, and horse- and automobile-drawn trailers, including Roma *vardos* (horse-drawn trailers) in Europe.

For added complication, it should be noted that sedentary peoples can in some instances move their buildings. In some parts of the world, some buildings that would seem to be rooted to the spot, often with basements and foundations, can be moved from one place to another. This is sometimes done to preserve historic houses threatened by new developments, and at other times simply to initiate a new settlement site. Thoreau and his parents moved a house from one site in Concord to another—a common practice in nineteenth-century New England—after John and Cynthia Thoreau had bought a lot in a newly laid-out street near the new railroad depot in 1844.[70]

We should now be in a better position to see how many distinctions in the characteristically European, sedentary, cultural schema serve to exclude entire categories of built structures from aesthetic and historical consideration. We only understand a practice such as architecture in implicit contradistinction to other kinds of building practice often excluded from philosophical aesthetic and historical discussion. These excluded practices encompass the work of professional builders or of amateurs and improvisers within the sedentary schema, as well as the work of nomadic peoples against whose cultural practices sedentary peoples harbor a deep prejudice. That prejudice can coincide with, or prompt, racial discrimination, but need not do so. Neither is racial discrimination clearly at the root of the frequently mutual antagonism of sedentary and nomadic peoples, whose respective interests in exploiting resources—principally those derived from the land—are often irreconcilable, although antagonism, whether one sided or mutual, can find expression in racist language and actions.

We see one clear example of this dynamic in the relations between local settler inhabitants and Irish immigrant laborers building railroads in the United States between the 1840s and the 1860s. Living in temporary huts, these workers and their families were the epitome of a nomadic people, yet nomadic not by long-term cultural affiliation—they came from sedentist communities—but by force of circumstance. When they had completed a stretch of line, they relinquished their dwellings. Surviving evidence of these temporary structures is rare, but a few photographs exist.[71] Local historian Mrs. R. P. Peabody gives an account of the building of the Grand Trunk Railroad through Shelburne, New Hampshire, which began in 1851, condescendingly suggesting that the dreadful conditions in which the workers lived were all they required: "Most of the workmen were Irishmen who camped along the way with their wives and children. They only required limited quarters. . . . The houses, or hovels, rather, which they made for themselves were simply four posts set in the ground, boarded over and banked up, often to the eaves, with earth. A barrel stuck in one side allowed some of the effluvia to escape."[72]

Irish immigrant laborers were responsible for building the Fitchburg Railroad through Concord between 1842 and 1845. Henry Thoreau bought a superior example of an Irish family's hut directly from railroad worker James Collins in April 1845 to furnish materials for his Walden Pond house.[73] His father, John Thoreau, bought two huts auctioned by the local tax collector, Sam Staples, from which to build a lean-to for his pencil-making business. The anti-Irish immigrant Native American Party (Know Nothings) exemplified established settler hostility toward Irish immigrants. As we saw in the chapter "Migrants," in 1854 the Know Nothings swept the elections for governor, the commonwealth legislature, and the US House of Representatives. Religious hostility—most Irish immigrants were Roman Catholic—distrust of immigrants, and the peripatetic nature of the work performed by many combined to fuel antipathy on the part of much of the existing population.

It should be noted that a taxonomy of exclusion not only dominates the province of building but applies to many areas of human making. Just as in the case of architecture, so painting in the European manner within the art world functions as a category of practice in contradistinction to other forms of painting excluded from the art world: certain kinds of religious paintings, "mall" paintings, handmade copies of art paintings made to order in Asia, amateur work, and so on.⁷⁴ Yet distinctions among types within different media of creativity most likely vary, so that there is unlikely to be a shared "aesthetic template" to which all practices susceptible of aesthetic consideration, including building design and painting, conform.

Even though historical taxonomy addresses the history, function, and use of entities rather than formal features alone, can formal properties help scholars to establish criteria of differentiation within all or any of these practices, including the conception and making of buildings? The consideration of formal properties in the study of architecture in the extended European section of the minority world is certainly sophisticated. An example is the apprehension and appreciation of different builders' uses of the classical orders.⁷⁵ Yet to confine our attention to such matters is cripplingly limiting, even though the prospect of extending formal analysis to built things in any comprehensive sense is forbiddingly daunting. Consider, for instance, the classical orders defined by Vitruvius in Roman antiquity and Giacomo (or Jacopo) Barozzi da Vignola (whose *Regola delle cinque ordini d'architettura* was first published in 1562) as stylized means of providing or implying vertical support.⁷⁶ More expansive attention would relate these orders to other instances of the provision of vertical support in other societies. Yet by what criteria might we consider means of vertical support in relation to one another, such as the classical orders; Māori house posts from Aotearoa, New Zealand; and Tuareg tent poles from the Sahara? I regret that I am in no position to answer this or any other question of this kind. Rather, I propose to begin by developing a postcolonial taxonomy of building based on function, use, and material specifics (which includes formal properties), all of which should be understood historically as well as philosophically. Historical taxonomy, itself a philosophical enterprise, should take precedence over more narrowly conceived philosophical attempts to define a universally applicable taxonomy of buildings. Such a postcolonial historical taxonomy should take into account as many different kinds of building as possible—those of both sedentary and nomadic peoples—without prejudice. In doing so, we might do well to bear in mind Thoreau's strictures about architecture and the construction of shelters more generally: "What of architectural beauty I now see, I know has gradually grown from within outward, out of the necessities and character of the indweller, who is the only builder,—out of some unconscious truthfulness, and nobleness, without ever a thought for the appearance; and whatever additional beauty of this kind is destined to be produced will be preceded by a like unconscious beauty of life."⁷⁷

Such an approach recognizes the roles of all who occupy buildings of whatever kind, from temple to tent, regardless of their lifeways, whether sedentary or nomadic. In the absence of a comprehensive historical taxonomy of buildings that takes Thoreau's indwellers into account, we are condemned to repeat existing limited analyses that exclude vast swathes of human creativity found among the ethnically varied peoples of the world. Such unreflective, selective promotion of a minority of sedentary peoples through approval of their buildings, and penalization of the majority of sedentary peoples as well as nomadic peoples through neglect of theirs, should have no place in our thinking.

With this schema in place, I now turn to Thoreau's discussions of shelter as a human need, clarifying how he engaged with buildings in both practical and aesthetic terms. A discussion that fails to acknowledge the role of historical taxonomy is likely to account inadequately for the complexities of Thoreau's aesthetically (and ethically) grounded views on shelter as expressed in his writings and, most particularly, in his experiment in practical philosophy at Walden Pond.

[CHAPTER FOUR]

Shelter

Following the exploration of a wide variety of building types highlighting the limitations of a focus on the long-term structures of sedentary communities and the tiny sliver of built entities that conform to a sedentist concept of architecture, I now turn to Thoreau's discussions of shelter as a human need. This chapter principally concerns Thoreau's own one-room house, its origins, and its afterlife. I focus on Thoreau's house at Walden Pond in relation to his claims about architecture and the proper way for the inhabitants of his part of the world, New England, to provide themselves with shelter.

In *Walden* we have seen Thoreau claim, "The necessaries of life for man in this climate may, accurately enough, be distributed under the several heads of Food, Shelter, Clothing, and Fuel"; he continues, "for not until we have secured these are we prepared to entertain the true problems of life with freedom and a prospect of success."[1] For Thoreau, therefore, shelter was one of the four antecedent challenges a philosopher must address before, or on the way to, tackling "the true problems of life." This is why, in a book devoted to Thoreau's interactions with material worlds, shelter, preceded by a discussion of buildings more generally, must itself precede examinations of human artistry and the gathering of a variety of material items for the purpose of conceiving of knowledge claims (discussed in the chapter "Collections").

As a human need, shelter is not principally an aesthetic matter. Yet aesthetics plays an important role in Thoreau's reflections on the various kinds of shelter he encountered in New England and beyond. He also reflects on architecture more generally and in *Walden* gives a detailed account of how he built the house near Walden Pond. In part these writings incorporate Thoreau's attention to commonly agreed aesthetic features of buildings—he abhorred ornament—but most of all, these writings attend to the readily overlooked everyday aesthetic character of those buildings that were founded on simplicity.

I consistently use the term *house* for Thoreau's dwelling at Walden Pond rather than the more frequently encountered *hut* or *cabin*, for, as the archaeologist Roland Wells Robbins—the discoverer and excavator of the house site in 1945—states, "Of the nearly one hundred references to his abode which he makes in *Walden*, eighty odd of the number are 'house' . . . and only on one occasion does he use the word 'hut'" (see figure 2).[2]

Many writers have discussed Thoreau's house, not always accurately. A common misconception arose, probably even during Thoreau's lifetime, or at any rate not long after his death, that his Walden Pond sojourn was a lonely retreat to a remote wilderness. In spite of early rebuttal by authors such as Thomas Wentworth Higginson, the persistence of this misconception overshadows architectural historian Barksdale Maynard's recent discussion of the place of Thoreau's house in architectural history, though he does not subscribe to this misunderstanding himself. Maynard established that Thoreau's Walden Pond project reflects widespread contemporaneous ideas and practices concerning fashionable summerhouses and temporary rural or suburban retreats, advocated by early nineteenth-century "villa books."[3] Maynard also drew attention to the wilderness housing that had

FIGURE 2. Replica of Thoreau's house at Walden Pond by Roland Wells Robbins and assistants, 1985. Walden Pond State Reservation, Concord, Massachusetts. Photo by author.

impressed Thoreau during his visit to the Catskill Mountains in the summer before he built his own house at Walden. Maynard made valid points regarding cultural context and precedent, but as an architectural historian, he was not concerned with addressing the philosophy underlying Thoreau's project. In contrast, in what follows I focus in a philosophical register on Thoreau's house at Walden Pond, in particular in relation to his claims about architecture and the proper way for the inhabitants of his part of the world to provide themselves with shelter. Thoreau's residence at Walden Pond was, above all, a philosophical retreat. Perhaps only Ludwig Wittgenstein's sojourns in 1914, 1931, and 1936–37—in an isolated, three-room house he designed and had built in 1914 near Skjolden, Norway, above a lake not much bigger than Walden Pond—carry a similar associational weight among philosophers.[4]

Thoreau describes building his house in the first chapter of *Walden*, titled "Economy." In order to satisfy the four human needs he identifies, Thoreau advocates dispensing with what he considered to be every kind of superfluity and distraction. He was harsh in his strictures on human ambitions to work unnecessarily and even go into debt to procure the consolatory comforts that in his opinion characterized most settler housing, even dwellings that others would consider modest farmhouses.

In his experiment, and in his account, Thoreau was testing and elaborating the position espoused by the editor and literary critic Margaret Fuller, whose younger sister, Ellen, was married to Thoreau's closest friend, the poet and subsequently Thoreau's first biographer, William Ellery Channing. Fuller, editor of the principal transcendentalist serial publication, the *Dial*, between 1840 and 1842, was a thinker as important to Thoreau as the Sage of Concord, Ralph Waldo Emerson.[5] One can judge Thoreau's dependence on certain of Fuller's ideas from remarks in her book *Summer on the Lakes, in 1843*, published in 1844, the year before Thoreau took up residence at Walden Pond. Of a "double log cabin" on the bank of the Rock River opposite the small town of Oregon, Illinois, she writes, "Then, with a very little money, a ducal estate may be purchased, and by a very little more, and moderate labor, a family be maintained upon it with raiment, food and shelter."[6] Thoreau's emphasis on "Food, Shelter, Clothing, and Fuel" directly echoes Fuller's statement. His inclusion of fuel recalls Fuller's assurance that the Illinois cabin's inhabitants can afford "immense fires" owing to its proximity to a forest.[7] Thoreau's emphasis in *Walden* on how the pursuit of material luxuries ruins the lives of those who work to pay for them reflects Fuller's opinion in her description of the Illinois log cabin that "luxurious and minute comforts of a city life are not yet to be had without effort disproportionate to their value."[8] Pointing out such intellectual antecedents for two of Thoreau's key ideas about shelter does not detract from his originality in refining and elaborating them to lend them a philosophical consistency to which Fuller's travel account makes no claim.

Thoreau certainly took an interest in log cabins in remote locations. While occupying his Walden Pond house in 1846, Thoreau journeyed to Maine in late summer to attempt to scale the highest peak in the state, the remote Mt. Katahdin, in company with George Thatcher. Thatcher was married to Thoreau's cousin, Rebecca Billings. He was a merchant in Bangor, Maine, who had timber interests in the hinterland. Thoreau and Thatcher traveled with guides by batteau (a flat-bottomed boat with raked bow and stern used by Maine settlers) and on foot.[9] Six years later, in the late summer of 1853, Thoreau returned to the Maine woods, again with Thatcher. Guided by the Panawáhpskewi (Penobscot) Joseph Aitteon, they traveled by birchbark canoe to Lake Chesuncook. In his accounts of these wilderness journeys, Thoreau carefully notes the materials and building techniques employed in year-round log cabins built by settlers and in camps inhabited seasonally by loggers.[10]

Log cabins, though, were not an economical option in Concord, Massachusetts, where the old growth timber with the girth necessary for their construction was no longer locally available. Indeed, Thoreau notes a number of times in his accounts of his visits to the Maine woods that the vast quantities of timber logged in that wilderness and floated downriver to sawmills closer to the coast provided the lumber for house frames, clapboard, and shingles used in the construction of the majority of New England houses. "The very timber and boards, and shingles, of which our houses are made, grew but yesterday in a wilderness where the Indian still hunts and the moose runs wild," he notes in "Ktaadn."[11] Lumber milled into thin, economical planks—in Thoreau's case supplementing small timber he had felled himself—was the only practical option for a builder in Concord. Yet Thoreau rejected settler housing of the contemporary, standard variety. He looked with favor, rather, on superseded settler housing, notably the Conant family house in the relatively remote area to the southwest of the village beside the Sudbury River that he called Conantum. He writes in his journal entry for September 28, 1851: "What honest homely—earth-loving unaspiring houses they used to live in. Take that on Conantum for instance—so low you can put your hand on the eaves behind—There are few whose pride could stoop to enter such a house to-day. & then the broad chimney built for comfort not for beauty—with no coping of bricks to catch the eye—no alto or basso relievo."[12] Thoreau places comfort above beauty in his assessment of the Conant house, but that assessment is itself aesthetically informed, though in terms of everyday aesthetics applied to a building rather than more familiar judgments of taste.

One might suppose that in his rejection of standard settler housing, Thoreau was attracted instead by the shelter solutions of the Native inhabitants of Massachusetts. Although his attitude to Native Americans was complicated and equivocal, Thoreau took a great interest in their lifeways and was inspired by what he and his contemporaries termed the *wigwam*. The word derives from various Algonquian languages.[13] It denotes a circular or elongated frame of arched and braced saplings covered with bark or rush matting. Construction is swift and straightforward and incurs little or no expense. The resulting structures are weatherproof and comfortable. Thoreau approvingly quotes the detailed description of wigwams in Massachusetts by Daniel Gookin. Gookin had been a prominent early settler, captain of the Cambridge Trained Band, and superintendent of the so-called Praying Indians, who in his 1674 manuscript account of relations between settlers and Native inhabitants concludes, "I have often lodged in their wigwams; and have found them as warm as the best English houses."[14] In 1841 Thoreau notes in his journal what he regards as the "charm of the Indian," for "he stands free and unconstrained in Nature, is her inhabitant and not her guest, and wears her easily and gracefully." He continues, "But the civilized man has the habits of the house. His house is a prison, in which he finds himself oppressed and confined, not sheltered and protected. He walks as if he sustained the roof—he carries his arms as if the walls would fall in and crush him—and his feet remember the cellar beneath. His muscles are never relaxed—It is rare that he overcomes the house, and learns to sit at home in it—and roof and floor—and walls support themselves—as the sky—and trees—and earth."[15] Maintaining his opinion on this topic, he states in his journal in May 1859 that the settler houses he can admire are "the houses of the poor, with simply a cool spring, a good deal of weather-stained wood, and a natural door-stone: a house standing somewhere in nature, and not merely in an atmosphere of art, on a measured lot; on a hillside, perchance, obviously not made by any gardener, amid rocks, not placed there by a landscape gardener for effect; with nothing 'pretty' about it, but life reduced to its lowest terms and yet found to be beautiful. This is a good foundation or board to spring from."[16]

This predominantly everyday aesthetic assessment—"life reduced to its lowest terms and yet found to be beautiful"—does not mean that Thoreau was blind to the "benefit of the improvements of centuries, spacious apartments, clean paint and paper, Rumford fireplace, back plastering, Venetian blinds, copper pump, spring lock, a commodious cellar, and many other things," as he admits.¹⁷ He acknowledges that "the poor civilized man secures an abode which is a palace compared with the savage's."¹⁸ However, echoing Margaret Fuller, he argues that the disadvantage of the costs of obtaining and maintaining these comforts is disproportionate to the advantages. Thoreau had a specific conception of cost: "The cost of a thing is the amount of what I will call life which is required to be exchanged for it, immediately or in the long run."¹⁹ He states, "I wish to show at what a sacrifice this advantage is at present obtained, and to suggest that we may possibly so live as to secure all the advantage without suffering any of the disadvantage."²⁰ His proposal, then, is not to adopt Native dwellings nor to inhabit one himself, but rather to build himself an extremely modest version of a characteristic New England settler house. He proposes to do so as a matter of practical philosophy in which to initiate and sustain a practical philosophical experiment.

To build a house securely, the person responsible has to have a legitimate claim to the land on which it stands, or at least to its use for that purpose. Establishing title in New England was a legal matter, although it ultimately rested on the dispossession of earlier, Native inhabitants. Thoreau was well aware of the history of the settlement of Concord from 1635 onward as the first colonial town in the interior of the Massachusetts Bay Colony beyond tidal waters. As we have seen in the chapter "Migrants," Thoreau was familiar with the *History of the Town of Concord* (1835) by Lemuel Shattuck.²¹ Claiming and apportioning Native Musketaquid as colonial Concord depended on accurate surveying of the land concerned. Furthermore, reliable building construction on that land depended thereafter on accurate land surveying. The importance of land surveying in the United States in Thoreau's lifetime derived in part from the growth, especially since independence, of a tendency to treat land not principally as a heritable sufficiency, but rather as a vehicle for investment and improvement and therefore ultimately as a fungible asset.²² Although Thoreau did not take up land surveying for hire consistently until 1849, he first mentions surveying on his own account in November 1840.²³ His intimate knowledge of the lay of the land in any instance surely informed his thoughts about the construction of buildings for shelter, whether for himself, his parents, or his fellow villagers, or in general philosophical terms.

In addition to his concern with the lay of the land itself, Thoreau was more than casually interested in settler houses, notably in surviving early examples. He attended to construction techniques, in part to understand the materials the builders used and how they worked them, and in part to trace the history of a given house through construction and modification. His most detailed examination of an early settler building in Concord was of a house, one of two on a property bought by his friend, the Concord farmer Edmund Hosmer, in 1852.[24] It was known as the Hunt house after the family that had owned it since acquiring it from Adam Winthrop, a grandson of Governor John Winthrop, in 1701.[25] Thoreau noted in his journal details of the construction of the house following a visit in April 1852.[26] Thoreau visited the Hunt house several times between 1852 and 1859, describing its construction in his journal. Hosmer decided to disassemble it. As he took the house apart, completing the job in 1859, Thoreau examined its components and tool marks to ascertain its complex building history. He meticulously notes its features in his journal, together with sketches and a floor plan.[27] Thoreau clearly already had a good working knowledge of timber frame house construction when he came to build his house at Walden Pond in 1845, and as his work on the Hunt house demonstrates, his fascination with its details never deserted him.[28]

The one-room settler house that Thoreau built at Walden Pond evoked, perhaps purposefully, not so much settler houses that he knew in Concord as those that he had seen during trips to remote places. Thoreau had visited more than one wilderness house even before he went to the Maine woods for the first time. As Maynard points out, the one Thoreau particularly recalled was high in the Catskill Mountains in New York State near two tarn-like ponds, North and South Lake, sixteen hundred feet above the Hudson River.[29] He had been there with his friend Ellery Channing in the summer of 1844, less than a year before he began building his house at Walden Pond. The Catskill house was that of Ira Scribner and his family. Thoreau recalled it specifically the day after he moved into his Walden Pond house, writing in his journal on July 5, 1845:

> Yesterday I came here to live. My house makes me think of some mountain houses I have seen, which seemed to have a fresher auroral atmosphere about them as I fancy of the halls of Olympus. I lodged at the house of a saw-miller last summer, on the Caatskills mountains, high up as Pine orchard in the blue-berry & raspberry region, where the quiet and cleanliness & coolness seemed to be all one, which had this ambrosial character. He was the miller of the Kaaterskill Falls. They were a clean & wholesome family inside and out—like their house. The latter was not plastered—only lathed and the inner doors were not hung. The house seemed high placed, airy, and perfumed, fit to entertain a travelling God. It was so high, indeed, that all the music, the broken strains, the waifs & accompaniments of tunes, that swept over the ridge of the Caatskills, passed through its aisles. Could not man be man in such an abode? And would he ever find out this grovelling life?[30]

Scribner's house was not a log cabin, but it was "not plastered, only lathed," as was Thoreau's own house when he moved in. Thoreau only completed the plastering in the fall. The elevation, relative isolation, and above all the prospect, all recommended Scribner's house to Thoreau. In May 1851 he notes in his journal, "I wonder that houses are not oftener located mainly that they may command particular rare prospects—every convenience yielding to this," and continues, "A site where you might avail yourself of the art of Nature for three thousand years Which could never be materially changed—or taken from you a noble inheritance for your children. The true sites for human dwellings are unimproved."[31] That prospect is one of the principal aesthetic recommendations of a house to Thoreau and is a value that accords with what is now called environmental aesthetics.

What was Thoreau's purpose in building and inhabiting his house at Walden Pond? He does not reveal in his writings precisely what prompted him, beyond lofty statements of general purpose fitting a philosopher. He may have conducted the experiment within the conventions, broadly speaking, of a temporary rural or suburban retreat advocated by early nineteenth-century "villa books" and with recollections of wilderness dwellings in mind, as suggested by Barksdale Maynard.[32] Whatever may have been Thoreau's sources of inspiration, in general terms the project conforms with his conception of what it is to be a philosopher: "To be a philosopher is not merely to have subtle thoughts, nor even to found a school, but so to love wisdom as to live according to its dictates, a life of simplicity, independence, magnanimity, and trust. It is to solve some of the problems of life, not merely theoretically, but practically."[33]

To pursue philosophy as practice was fundamental for Thoreau. That meant meeting the *facts of life*, as though Thoreau intuited what Wittgenstein was later to develop in claiming that "the world is the totality of facts, not of things," and "the world divides into facts."[34] Two days after moving into his house at Walden Pond, Thoreau states his purpose in his journal: "I wish to meet the facts of life—the vital facts, which are the phenomena or actuality the Gods meant to show us,—face to face, And so I came down here."[35] He revises his expression of lofty purpose in a frequently quoted passage in *Walden*: "I went to the woods because I wished to live deliberately, to front only the essentials of life, and see if I could not learn what it had to teach, and not, when I came to die, discover that I had not lived."[36] The heart of Thoreau's practical philosophy was his taking action to *live deliberately*, confronting the challenges of procuring "Food, Shelter, Clothing, and Fuel"—facts of life—in such ways as to retain independence as far as possible while acknowledging human interdependence with the rest of the natural world. For Thoreau, this imperative had an aesthetic as well as an ethical dimension. That being so, Thoreau's ambition regarding shelter had huge implications for his conception and execution of sheltering structures subsumed under the term *architecture*.

Thoreau's self-abnegation in living in his small house inevitably prompted contemporaries to compare him with the fourth-century BCE contemporary of Plato, Diogenes. One of Diogenes's affronts to Athenian society was to sleep in a large ceramic vessel (*pithos*) in the marketplace to demonstrate his disdain for worldly possessions. In subsequent retellings and representations, Diogenes's abode is rendered as a barrel, vat, or tub.[37] Different writers made the comparison between Thoreau and Diogenes either admiringly or disparagingly, depending on their responses to Thoreau's ideas. Abigail May Alcott, in a letter dated March 1, 1848, to Hannah Simonds Robbins, the cofounder of the Lexington Lyceum, wrote of Thoreau: "He may truly be called the 'Diogenes' of the 19th century—so humble—true and wise—His hut being literally a Tub with a roof—but so comfortable—rural and classic."[38] Others used the comparison to criticize Thoreau. For instance, a report on Thoreau's lecture to Boston's Twenty-Eighth Congregational Society on October 9, 1859, called Thoreau "a sort of Diogenes, to whom everything but nature appears to be just what it should not be."[39] Most damaging, though, was James Russell Lowell's chapter on Thoreau in his collection *My Study Window*, first published in 1871 and reprinted many times. Thoreau and Lowell—a poet, an editor, a scion of Boston's privileged elite, and a Harvard professor—had had a history of difficult relations. Lowell dismissed Thoreau's behavior and thought in his essay. He wrote, "His shanty-life was mere impossibility, so far as his own conception of it goes, as an entire independency of mankind. The tub of Diogenes had a sounder bottom."[40] This dismissal prompted a rebuttal from the Unitarian minister, radical abolitionist, women's rights campaigner, and literary champion of poet Emily Dickinson, Thomas Wentworth Higginson.[41] Higginson quotes Lowell's remark, given above, then continues:

> But what a man of straws is this that Lowell is constructing! A young man living in a country village and having a passion for the minute observation of nature, and a love for Greek and Oriental reading, takes it into his head to build himself a study, not in the garden or the orchard, but in the woods, by the side of a lake. Happening to be poor, and to live in a time when social experiments are in vogue at Brook Farm and elsewhere, he takes a whimsical satisfaction in seeing how cheaply he can erect his hut, and afterwards support himself by the labor of his hands. He is not really banished from the world, nor does he seek or profess banishment: indeed, his house is not two miles from his mother's door; and he goes to

the village every day or two, by his own showing, to hear the news. In this quiet abode he spends two years, varied by an occasional excursion into the deeper wilderness at a distance. He earns an honest living by gardening and land-surveying, makes more close and delicate observations on nature than any other American has ever made, and writes the only book yet written in America, to my thinking, that bears an annual perusal. Can it be really true that this is a life so wasted, so unpardonable?[42]

This passage encapsulates and refutes many commonly held misconceptions about Thoreau's project at Walden Pond.

If Thoreau was no latter-day Diogenes—he was, after all, anything but a Cynic, much less a misanthrope—nonetheless he admits that his first thought for how a person might shelter economically was "somewhat callous": "I used to see a large box by the railroad, six feet long by three wide, in which the laborers locked up their tools at night; and it suggested to me that every man who was hard pushed might get such a one for a dollar, and, having bored a few auger holes in it, to admit the air at least, get into it when it rained and at night, and hook down the lid, and so have freedom in his love, and in his soul be free."[43] "Somewhat callous," indeed; but he states, "I am far from jesting," for "many a man is harassed to death to pay the rent of a larger and more luxurious box who would not have frozen to death in such a box as this."[44] Yet his actual proposal—and the course of action he took—was not to live in a box drilled with auger holes or in a wigwam, but to build a small version of a settler house, using the familiar materials of settler dwellings. These were "boards and shingles, lime and bricks," for, as he writes in *Walden*, "With a little more wit we might use these materials so as to become richer than the richest now are, and make our civilization a blessing."[45]

Would Thoreau have put his practical philosophy of shelter into action without the prompting of his friend Ellery Channing? As we have seen, the two had traveled together to the Catskill Mountains the previous summer, where their experience of Ira Scribner's unplastered, rustic house—"high placed, airy, and perfumed, fit to entertain a travelling God"—and the high tarn, South Lake, likely prompted thoughts about an experiment at Walden Pond.[46] Replying from New York to a letter from Thoreau on March 5, 1845, Channing wrote:

> The hand-writing of your letter is so miserable, that I am not sure I have made it out. If I have it seems to me you are the same old sixpence you used to be, rather rusty, but a genuine piece.
>
> I see nothing for you in this earth but that field which I once christened "Briars" [Emerson's lot at Walden Pond]; go out upon that, build

yourself a hut, & there begin the grand process of devouring your-self alive. I see no alternative, no other hope for you. Eat yourself up; you will eat nobody else, nor anything else.[47]

Whether Channing's recommendation was decisive is impossible to say, but in Thoreau's own account: "Near the end of March, 1845, I borrowed an axe and went down to the woods by Walden Pond, nearest to where I intended to build my house, and began to cut down some tall, arrowy white pines, still in their youth, for timber."[48]

Thoreau's expressed determination to work within a set of building and architectural conventions long employed by settlers in New England meant that whereas his withdrawal to a marginal location may have been, as he wrote, "very selfish, I have heard some of my townsmen say,"[49] the house he built conformed to certain settler cultural norms. Thoreau not only used materials that were "cheaper and more easily obtainable than suitable caves, or whole logs, or bark in sufficient quantities,"[50] but drew on his own recent building experience.

In September 1844 Thoreau's parents, John and Cynthia Thoreau, had bought a building lot on newly laid out Texas Street near the recently opened Concord railroad depot.[51] Having mortgaged the lot to pay for the house itself, father and son moved a plain, square, two-story house from another site and placed it above the cellar, which Henry Thoreau had dug and lined with stone.[52] Moving houses was a common practice at the time and required construction skills. The dwelling was known in the family as the Texas house.[53] John Thoreau bought at auction at least one small building among those referred to as "shanties," in which Irish immigrant laborers had lived during the construction of the Fitchburg Railroad in the Concord area between 1842 and 1844. Father and son used these materials to build a lean-to shed against the Texas house to accommodate John Thoreau's pencil-making business.[54] The family remained at the Texas house for five years before moving to a larger house on Main Street, closer to the village center. Once again, Thoreau made use of his building skills to renovate it.[55]

Beginning in the summer of 1847, even before he left Walden Pond, and continuing into the fall following his return to the village, Thoreau worked on another construction project. He helped Bronson Alcott build a summer house for Emerson near his residence on the Lexington Road. The thoroughly impractical Bronson Alcott designed it whimsically, to Thoreau's consternation. The summer house was illustrated in the 1853 compendium volume, *Homes of American Authors* (see figure 3).[56] Although it stood for many years, and Emerson employed Thoreau to make repairs when necessary, Emerson reportedly never used it.[57]

FIGURE 3. Richardson and Cox after Richards, *Alcott's Summer House*, wood engraving. From *Homes of American Authors: Comprising Anecdotical, Personal, and Descriptive Sketches, by Various Writers* (New York: G. P. Putnam, 1853), collection of the author.

Thoreau's construction of his own house in 1845 at Walden Pond enhanced his reputation in the village for building skills. He recollects the following incident in his journal in 1857: "While I lived in the woods I did various jobs about the town,—some fence-building, painting, gardening, carpentering, etc., etc. One day a man came from the east edge of the town and said that he wanted to get me to brick up a fireplace, etc., etc., for him. I told him that I was not a mason, but he knew that I had built my own house entirely and would not take no for an answer. So I went."[58]

Returning to Thoreau's own house construction in 1845, I now consider his account in *Walden* of his purchase of Irish laborer "James Collins' shanty" in early April 1845,[59] its disassembly, and the reuse of its boards for his own house, in the context of his moving, modifying, and refinishing the Texas house and its accompanying lean-to the previous fall. Thoreau makes a very clear distinction between railroad builders' dwellings, which he consistently calls "shanties" or even "sties," and his own house, once built. He writes:

> It is a mistake to suppose that, in a country where the usual evidences of civilization exist, the condition of a very large body of the inhabitants may not be as degraded as savages. I refer to the degraded poor, not now to the degraded rich. To know this I should not need to look further than to the shanties which everywhere border our railroads, that last improvement in civilization; where I see in my daily walks human beings living in sties, and all winter with an open door, for the sake of light, without any visible, often imaginable, wood-pile, and the forms of both old and young are permanently contracted by the long habit of shrinking from cold and misery, and the development of all their limbs and faculties is checked.[60]

We have seen in the chapter "Migrants" that Thoreau shared, though not so virulently as many, his fellow native-born citizens' prevalent anti-Irish-immigrant sentiments.[61] This prejudice affects his description of the Collins family dwelling, even though he acknowledges that among such structures it "was considered an uncommonly fine one."[62] He purchased it for $4.25 and took possession the following morning. "I took down this dwelling the same morning, drawing the nails, and removed it to the pond-side by small cart-loads, spreading the boards on the grass there to bleach and warp back in the sun."[63]

Thoreau's house was a combination of timbers he had hewn from the young pine trees he had felled with a borrowed axe and boards salvaged from the Collins dwelling. The latter had had as its "cellar" "a sort of dust hole two feet deep," whereas for his own construction Thoreau dug and lined a cellar six feet square and seven feet deep.[64] He included sills and a board floor with a trapdoor to the cellar, framed walls in the New England manner, a fireplace and chimney, rafters, and a pitched roof, and then shingled the whole without and applied lath and plaster within. Having raised the frames and the roof with the help of friends, as was customary, he was able to move in on July 4, 1845. The house measured ten by fifteen feet and had two windows and a door. By early September, an invited visitor, Joseph Hosmer, reported that the "building was not then finished, the chimney had no beginning—the sides were not battened, or the walls plastered."[65] Thoreau completed the lath and plaster in November, and the plaster was dry by December 6.[66] In *Walden*, as well as describing the process, Thoreau pointedly gives an account of the expenses he incurred in building the house, listing materials and transportation costs. The total was $28.12½ (approximately $1,065 in 2022 dollars).[67]

Thoreau's house-building project differs incontrovertibly from those of Collins and his fellow railroad laborers, that difference being partly one of class. As American studies scholar Lisa Goff has noted, "While Thoreau built at a leisurely pace, recording the feelings and emotions engendered by the process, shanty dwellers like Collins built of necessity, hastily, for otherwise they were homeless."[68] Yet an acknowledgment of class difference does not invalidate Thoreau's philosophical experiment in living.

Thoreau's Walden Pond house was, in part, an exercise in extensive recycling, not only of the boards and even nails from the Collins dwelling, but also of bricks for his fireplace and chimney. As such, it was also an exercise in building deliberately. Yet Thoreau still chided himself when considering his house in relation to the fundamental problem of shelter: "It would be worth the while to build still more deliberately than I did, considering, for instance, what foundation a door, a window, a cellar, a garret, have in the nature of man, and perchance never raising any superstructure until we found a better reason for it than our temporal necessities even."[69] On the other hand, he clearly imputed a moral value to the process of construction, writing, "What does architecture amount to in the experience of the mass of men? I never in all my walks came across a man engaged in so simple and natural an occupation as building his house."[70]

That his house was central to his philosophical project is suggested not only by his discussion of shelter that it exemplified as part of his "own experiment"[71] but by its prominent depiction on the title page of *Walden* (1854) (see figure 4). No reader could avoid seeing a wood engraving of Thoreau's house on the title page. Thoreau's younger sister Sophia had made the drawing on which it was based.[72] After his death she would look after his literary estate, editing numbers of his manuscripts for publication.[73] She depicts the house obliquely so as to include the woodshed immediately behind it. Trees, both evergreen and deciduous (oak and pine),[74] stand beside and behind it, conveying the sylvan character of a wilderness setting. However, their relatively modest stature and the presence of three very young pines at lower right imply that this is second-growth woodland; that is, land that settlers had once cleared or "improved" but that had reverted to a wild state. Thoreau, a land surveyor, and his settler contemporaries would have been fully aware of these connotations, sensitive as they were to what was required of them to clear and maintain "improvements" in a landscape where fields were hard won and required constant attention. Thoreau's choice of illustration and its prominent placement on the title page emphasize the immediate local landscape, in landscape architect Anne Whiston Spirn's sense of a continuum of nature and human intervention in which a locally appropriate building form (reflecting, among other factors, "the congruence of

FIGURE 4. Title page of Henry David Thoreau, *Walden; or, Life in the Woods*, stereotyped woodcut by William Jay Baker and John Andrew after Sophia Thoreau, 1854. Wikimedia Commons.

snowfall and roof pitch," as Spirn suggests) sits upon the ground among shrubs and trees.[75]

Thoreau's choice of his sister's drawing for reproduction on the title page of the book into which he poured his soul is more than a matter of representation of a type of place or of family sentiment. He chose to do this having recently read William Gilpin's *Essays*, the principal exposition of the English artist and cleric's theory of the *picturesque*.[76] Gilpin introduced the picturesque as an aesthetic value that combines aspects of the beautiful and the sublime, the two aesthetic values defined by Edmund Burke in *A Philosophical Enquiry into the Origin of Our Ideas of the Sublime and the Beautiful* (1757). In his journal entry for January 8, 1854, Thoreau discusses Gilpin's text at length and takes issue with Gilpin's assignment of relative values to the roughness and smoothness he associates differentially with these aesthetic characteristics.[77] I shall discuss Thoreau's reading of Gilpin further in the chapter "Artistry." Thoreau chose his sister's drawing to serve together with his title page text as an *emblem* that epitomizes his text. The European Renaissance art of the emblem—a combination of a short text and an image that generates and encapsulates an abstract idea—may have declined by Thoreau's day, but it was still vestigially informing such combinations, as it had long done not only in European emblem books but also in the design of book title pages.[78] This choice is an aesthetic statement by the author, engaging, in Gilpin's terms, both the ideal roughness of what the drawing represents and the smoothness of that representation. "The humble or sincere and true is more commonly rough and weather-beaten, so that from association we prefer it," Thoreau claims, and, he suggests, a smooth rendering in a picture—such as his sister's—can preserve and project those qualities.[79] His choice of title page illustration for *Walden* is an aesthetically driven visual statement in which Thoreau proposes his particular interpretation of the picturesque as applying fundamentally to his house, its vicinity, and the philosophical experiment he conducted there.

For any contemporaneous reader conversant with architectural theory, Sophia Thoreau's illustration on the title page of *Walden* would have invited comparison with the engraved frontispiece by Charles Eisen in the second edition of Marc-Antoine Laugier's *Essai sur l'architecture*, published in 1755 (see figure 5).[80] Eisen shows the seated female personification of Architecture beside classical building fragments. In her left hand she holds dividers, and with her right she indicates a structure to a putto beside her, seen from behind. He is winged, and from his head a flame rises: the personification of Genius. The structure comprises four living trees set in a rectangle. Across their lower crowns lie unhewn branches as joists from which rafters rise to form a pitched roof.

FIGURE 5. Jean Jacques Aliamet after Charles Eisen, frontispiece engraving, in Marc-Antoine Laugier, *Essai sur l'architecture*, 2nd ed., 1755. MIT Libraries: Architecture, Urban Planning, and Visual Arts.

Laugier's book prompted what was to become a new field of architectural theory promoting the understanding of building as the fundamental human need to obtain shelter. His conception and Thoreau's share a starting point. Laugier advocated a return to what he saw as basic principles of building based on the assumption articulated by the first-century BCE Roman architect Vitruvius that classical structures and their elements originated in the use of trees to provide uprights, entablatures, and pitched roofs.[81] His work initiated the discussion in architectural theory known as the "Primitive Hut."[82] Even if Laugier's book did not directly inspire Thoreau, he was nonetheless heir to Laugier's Enlightenment thinking about architecture being the provision of shelter as a response to the natural environment, in which it mediates between humans and nature in aesthetic as well as in purely practical terms. This approach stood in contrast to the dominant European conception of architecture as the pursuit of ideal forms in terms of proportion and ornamentation.

Inevitably, those who adopted Laugier's approach rejected architecture that, as Thoreau characterizes it, "began at the cornice, not at the foundation."[83] Thoreau rejects architectural superfluities, insisting that worthy architecture arises from the needs of the inhabitant or indweller as builder. He ties evaluation of architecture to the moral quality of indwellers, whose "unconscious beauty of life" alone is a necessary condition of any aesthetic qualities a building may have.[84] Thoreau perceived moral failings in those who hanker after what he considered to be superfluities of consumption— "tea, and coffee, and butter, and milk, and beef"[85]—and who ruin their lives working to pay for them. In *Walden* this leads Thoreau to reproach an Irish immigrant, John Field, and his family when he shelters from a rainstorm with them in their hut. He advises John and Mary Field to adopt his own life strategy to lift them out of laboring poverty, but Field, as Thoreau reports, "rated it as a gain in coming to America, that here you could get tea, and coffee, and meat every day."[86] For Thoreau, avoiding such luxuries was not only a matter of moral self-improvement through self-denial that lessened his reliance on earned money, it was also a means of avoiding contributing to sustaining "the slavery and war and other superfluous expenses which directly or indirectly result from the use of such things."[87] It is as well to fathom Thoreau's strategic purpose in presenting his readers with an example of moral shortcomings that most of them—us—share. As Laura Dassow Walls has argued, Thoreau presents his failure to convince the Fields as the moral crisis of *Walden*, exemplifying the limitations of reason to persuade his readers in the first nine chapters, so that in the second part of the book he turns to "Higher Laws" in reason's stead.[88] Stanley Cavell proposes that in thus turning from reason to inspiration Thoreau renders his description of his life in his house in *Walden* in a purposefully scriptural manner. Referring to the most revered of Hindu sacred texts, which Thoreau valued highly, Cavell notes that *Walden* is a scripture in eighteen parts, exactly like the *Bhagavad Gita*.[89] He says of Thoreau, "This writer is writing a sacred text."[90]

In appealing to higher laws and inspiration in *Walden*, Thoreau first turns his attention to the fine details of how his life in and around his house intersects with those of his "brute neighbors"—mice, squirrels, rabbits, birds, ants, and wasps—to reveal what would soon come to be termed an entire *ecology* of which humans are but one constituent, subject to an environmental aesthetics of "living poetry."[91] That ecology is of the earth as a living whole. He writes, "The earth is not a mere fragment of dead history, stratum upon stratum like the leaves of a book, to be studied by geologists and antiquaries chiefly, but living poetry like the leaves of a tree, which precede flowers and fruit,—and not a fossil earth, but a living earth; compared with whose great central life all animal and vegetable life is merely parasitic."[92]

Second, he follows his architectural imagination, which hitherto he had limited to the practical and reasonable demonstration of the virtues of parsimony, into realms of early medieval fantasy. He writes an epic account of his vision of ideal domesticity in just two breathless sentences, the first of which is 320, and the second 76, words long. He begins, "I sometimes dream of a larger and more populous house, standing in a golden age, of enduring materials, and without gingerbread work, which shall still consist of only one room, a vast, rude, substantial, primitive hall, without ceiling or plastering, with bare rafters and purlins supporting a sort of lower heaven over one's head."[93] His description of this vast one-room house—an exponential inflation of his own at Walden Pond—recalls King Edwin of Northumbria's mead-hall, through which a sparrow flies in Bede's famous parable accounting for the king's conversion to Christianity in 627, as well as King Hrothgar's mead-hall, Heorot, in the Anglo-Saxon poem *Beowulf*, available in modern English translations published in 1837 and 1849.[94] William Wordsworth, whose verse Thoreau greatly admired, retells the parable of the sparrow in the mead hall in his sonnet "Persuasion."[95] Thoreau's account of his ideal of grandiose shelter, rendered in bardic, visionary terms, is an expression of a social ideal entailing an implicit repudiation of the received tradition of classical architecture.

Early New England settler houses were far from classically inspired, being derived from English examples of the hall and parlor type. They perpetuated aspects of medieval halls, notably communal spaces rather than separate apartments. Thoreau's enthusiasm for understanding settler houses, demonstrated by his analysis of the Hunt house, was an instance of an emerging aesthetic preference among historically inclined New Englanders for plain New England vernacular buildings. Ellery Channing expresses this preference in an account of a conversation about architecture with Emerson and Thoreau in 1860 during one of their many walks together. Thoreau and Channing's mutual friend, Franklin Sanborn, rendered it in reported speech. Sanborn's Emerson complains of the lack of picturesque sophistication of Massachusetts buildings, saying, "But look at the clapboard farmhouse we are passing! Is there not a needless degree of stiffness and too little ornamentation?" Alluding to the English originator of the term *picturesque*, Sanborn's Channing replies, "Moderate your criticism, my dear Gilpin: utility lies at the bottom of our village architecture; the structure springs out of that." Citing farmers' practical concerns, he goes on to ascribe the adaptation of clapboard and shingle-faced houses to the New England climate and soil. Sanborn's Channing goes so far as to credit the character of such dwellings with solving the problem of establishing and sustaining democracy, part of a historical mythology of the origins and outcome in Massachusetts of the foundation of the republic. Sanborn's Thoreau corrects Channing, characterizing his purely utilitarian account of a farmhouse as "a mere machine for gravitating to pork and potatoes." Sanborn's Thoreau insists that "beauty must have an equal place with utility, if not a precedent," but he shows no sympathy for Emerson's concept of what architectural beauty might consist in, that is, ornamentation.[96] On Sanborn's account, Thoreau's conception of architectural beauty is entangled with utility, either as its equal or possibly even taking precedence. With the subsequent rise of interest in the material past of New England—specifically its early domestic buildings—marked by the endeavors of, among others, Wallace Nutting and William Sumner Appleton, a concern with beauty emergent from utility in architecture, here proposed by Thoreau, became culturally dominant in the region by the turn of the twentieth century.[97]

On September 6, 1847, Thoreau left his house at Walden Pond. His stated reason in *Walden*—"Perhaps it seemed to me that I had several more lives to live, and could not spare any more time for that one"—is, as literary scholar Robert Ray has argued, disingenuous.[98] His true reason for leaving was that Emerson, to whom Thoreau was beholden for the very site of his house, was about to leave for a lengthy tour, sailing for London on October 5. Rather than board elsewhere during her husband's absence, Lidian Emerson asked Thoreau to live at the Emerson house with her and the three young Emerson children.[99] Thoreau was to keep Emerson's complex affairs in order; undertake practical tasks; and help the often sick and chronically fatigued Lidian, whom Thoreau called "a very dear sister to me."[100]

The fate of Thoreau's house after he left it is worth a digression, as it is an example of the recycling and adaptive use of built structures with which Thoreau was familiar, as we have seen in the case of the family's Texas house and its accompanying sheds. That fate only differs from other instances of adaptation in nineteenth-century New England insofar as ultimately it was a source of mementos.

Emerson bought Thoreau's Walden house from him as part of the arrangements made to cover his absence abroad. As we have seen in the chapter "Migrants," Emerson sold it in turn to his gardener, Hugh Whelan.[101] Thoreau, who was unsentimental about the house he had built and lived in for twenty-six months, recounted its immediate fate in letters to Emerson in December 1847 and January 1848.[102] Whelan planned to move the house to the nearby site of Thoreau's bean field, intending to build an extension to more than double its size so that it might serve as a dwelling for himself and his family.[103] Describing Whelan's progress to date somewhat parodically in a letter to Emerson of December 15, 1847, Thoreau facetiously twice refers to the intended transformation of his former house as a "palace."[104] Whelan's project came to nothing. In January 1848 Thoreau reported to Emerson that Whelan had moved the existing house and had purchased stone for the new cellar for the extension, all at a cost of $16, which Thoreau reports having paid (from Emerson's funds). Channing surmised that Whelan also dismantled Thoreau's chimney foundation for his own use at the new site.[105] Thoreau mentions that he had warned Whelan not to dig the cellar for the extension too close to the existing house for fear of subsidence. But this is just what the hapless Whelan did, "& it has caved and let one end of the house down."[106] What is more, Thoreau reported in the same letter that Whelan, who had a drinking problem, had quarreled with his wife and had absconded alone. Thoreau recommended that Emerson might either rent out the "shanty," as he calls the house in this context, and the surrounding land, "or you can very easily & simply let Nature keep them still without great loss."[107]

The house remained abandoned for over eighteen months until the Concord farmer James Clark bought it. Aided by his brother, Daniel Brooks Clark, who recorded the event in his diary, he moved it with an ox team on September 3, 1849, to the Clark farm near the beginning of the Old Carlisle Road (now Estabrook Road), north of the village.[108] Daniel Brooks Clark records digging a cellar hole two days later, which suggests that James Clark's original intention for the structure may have differed from the use to which he actually put it. That is, he initially likely intended to use it in a manner similar to what Thoreau had done, as a retreat, for his grand-niece reported that he was an admirer of Thoreau and his experiment at Walden Pond.[109]

However, nothing came of this, if indeed there was anything of the kind in James Clark's mind in the first place. James Clark, a bachelor, died in 1854, and Daniel Brooks Clark likely inherited the property.[110]

In a letter to Thoreau's friend Daniel Ricketson, dated December 15, 1863, Sophia Thoreau mentions, "I walked up to the north part of the town lately, where his little house now stands, and ate my dinner under its roof, with the mice for company."[111] Yet Ellery Channing is our guide to the later history of the house. He visited it on the Old Carlisle Road farm at least five times between 1863 and 1868. Initially Clark used it to store grain. In September 1863 Channing took a Thoreau admirer from Rochester, Michigan, Calvin Greene, to see the house, and Greene reportedly pried off a shingle as a souvenir.[112] Channing mentions that at this time the house was "still perfect," but he also notes that "the windows were gone in '63, and the plaster mostly cracked off, from the moving to old Clarke's [sic]."[113] In August 1865 Bronson Alcott wrote in his journal about the visit of a Thoreau admirer from Plymouth, Massachusetts, James Spooner, who floated the idea of acquiring the house and reconstructing it on its original site at the pond to serve as a memorial to Thoreau. Nothing came of this quixotic suggestion.[114]

The house decayed further until early June 1868, when its new owner, Daniel Sullivan, disassembled it. Channing saw the remains of the house on June 4, mentioning the rafters.[115] He added, "The house stood in perfect condition so far as the frame and covering, to June 4, '68, a period of 23 years, and would have lasted a century."[116] By that time the farm, and Thoreau's house, had changed hands twice. The Clarks had sold the property to Lewis Flint in 1863, who in turn had sold it to Daniel Sullivan in 1867.[117] Sullivan reportedly used the roof of Thoreau's disassembled house to cover a pig pen and boards and timbers from the house to repair various outbuildings, including a barn.[118] Channing took Anna and Walton Ricketson, the son and daughter of Thoreau's friend Daniel Ricketson, to the site on Sullivan's property in October 1868. They took away several fragments and nails.[119]

Depredations by a growing number of Thoreau admirers who visited Concord may well have hastened the demise of the house and the structures to which constituent parts had been added. For example, the Concord Museum holds five fragments of wood purportedly from the Walden house and three nails bound with string once owned by Walton Ricketson and his sister, Anna.[120] As Barksdale Maynard put it, "These scattered and indistinguishable relics have tantalized generations of Thoreauvians with the promise of pieces of the True Cross."[121] The purported fragments of Thoreau's Walden Pond house became symbolically loaded soon after Thoreau's death in 1862, but the process of investing the house with symbolic significance was clearly begun by Thoreau himself through his choice of it and its location as the site of his experiment in practical philosophy, and, most of all, by his account thereof in his 1854 book. The choice of Sophia Thoreau's depiction of the house for the title page of *Walden* introduces and reinforces the symbolic import that Thoreau accorded the dwelling. The house exemplifies Thoreau's promulgation of modest living as both pragmatically and morally advantageous. Further, even in its translated, transformed, and finally disassembled condition, the house, and even its surviving purported fragments, have served as mindprints, material traces, if not of Thoreau's "oldest men," then of Thoreau himself.[122] And these mindprints of Thoreau's house can function, in part, within the terms of an aesthetics of everyday life and of the environment.

I now turn to shelter as a matter of both individual and social or communal responsibility, which also has an aesthetic as well as an ethical aspect. Shelter in the sense of modest living advocated by Thoreau as being ethically, practically, and aesthetically compelling is a matter of individual responsibility, or at most, that of an immediate family. Thoreau clearly subscribes to the emergent characteristically and peculiarly American ideology of individualism. He writes in "Resistance to Civil Government" (1849; better known as "Civil Disobedience"): "The progress from an absolute to a limited monarchy, from a limited monarchy to a democracy, is a progress toward a true respect for the individual."[123] However, he also looks beyond the individual to consider shelter as a communal responsibility. This is never more apparent than in Thoreau's antislavery speeches and writings.

The crisis brought about by the passage of the federal Fugitive Slave Act in 1850 was a cause of great despondency in Thoreau. He railed against the acquiescence in the provisions of the law by the Massachusetts judiciary and executive when apprehended escapees were returned to their alleged owners. When in 1854 a case was being heard in Boston to decide whether Anthony Burns, an escaped reputedly enslaved man, should be returned to his putative owner in Virginia, Thoreau addressed an antislavery convention in Framingham.[124] His remarks, published in the *Liberator* as "Slavery in Massachusetts," show him to have been in the depths of despair about the conduct of so many of his fellow Massachusetts citizens. "I dwelt before, perhaps, in the illusion that my life passed somewhere only *between* heaven and hell, but now I cannot persuade myself that I do not dwell *wholly within* hell."[125] Even nature could offer no salve: "I walk toward one of our ponds, but what signifies the beauty of nature when men are base?"[126] Slavery caused him to doubt the efficacy of beauty in ameliorating the human lot. As he did in *Walden*, published that same year, Thoreau appeals to a higher law: "What is wanted is men, not of policy, but of probity,—who recognize a higher law than the Constitution, or the decision of the majority."[127]

Thoreau's sense of outrage predated his public response to the Fugitive Slave Act and the Burns case. Laura Dassow Walls plausibly claims that Thoreau's philosophical experiment in living at Walden Pond had been "a declaration of freedom in full view of an America enslaved" and as such, the place not for an escape from the question of how to deal with the chains that bound the enslaved and, in their obedience to unjust laws, himself and his fellow Concord citizens, but "where one confronted it head-on."[128] In *Walden*, Thoreau is constrained to be discreet about his participation in conducting escaped enslaved people from the southern states to Canada, but he pointedly evokes the memory of the "former occupants of these woods" who had been enslaved in Concord and elsewhere prior to the gradual erosion of slavery in Massachusetts when the institution was not recognized in the 1780 Commonwealth constitution. Cases decided by the Supreme Judicial Court in 1783 undermined its viability, even if the court decisions did not decisively extinguish the institution immediately.[129] As we have seen in the chapter "Migrants," Thoreau pointedly describes a community of formerly enslaved people who had lived on marginal land near his own at Walden Pond, the last of them dying in 1822.[130] We have seen him aiding fugitives from the southern states as they made their way beyond the reach of an unjust law to Canada.[131] By invoking these former occupants in *Walden*, he further indicts his fellow inhabitants of Concord for refusing shelter to those to whom, in Thoreau's opinion, the village had obligations.

In Thoreau's account, then, the Walden Pond house became not only a practical demonstration of what shelter might be, but a symbol of shelter in a far broader sense, including communal moral obligations to shelter the fugitive and the oppressed. It is scarcely surprising, then, that various Walden Pond house reproductions and derivations serve as symbols of resistance to discrimination and oppression. Some seeking to protect the environmental integrity of sites have protested threatened encroachments by building a replica of Thoreau's house. An example is the house frame built by Will Elwell and others in 2016 as the Thoreau Cabin Pipeline Barricade in opposition to a proposed gas pipeline through Ashfield, Massachusetts.[132] Artists as well as protestors have replicated Thoreau's house, arguably also to draw attention to the perils of unnecessary development. In the summer of 2002 German artist Tobias Hauser installed a replica of Thoreau's house in the then still largely derelict Leipziger Platz in Berlin. Adjacent to the Potsdamer Platz, once the busiest intersection in Berlin but during the period of the German Democratic Republic (East Germany) bisected by the Berlin Wall and rendered a wasteland, by the early twenty-first century the area was undergoing massive commercial development. Hauser's replica was the same size as the original. It was dwarfed by new commercial buildings and served as a reproachful commentary on urban planning and the contemporaneous social situation in the reunited city.[133] Hauser's Walden Pond house in central Berlin was an installation artwork: an ironic architectural reconstruction indicting the commercial greed exemplified by real estate development. It functioned in part in an aesthetically constituted world. Other artists have harnessed aesthetics by creating works that, while not exact replicas of Thoreau's house, evoke a similar comparison between simplicity and integrity on the one hand and, on the other, the culture of untrammeled capitalism under which the obligation to ensure shelter for all—shelter as a human right—will never be recognized. Anyone who visits Rachel Whiteread's *Cabin* (2015) on the side of Discovery Hill on Governors Island in New York Harbor is likely struck by the contrast between her concrete cast of the negative spaces of a wooden cabin and the view beyond it of the hypercapitalist skyscrapers of Jersey City and lower Manhattan.[134]

Clearly Thoreau is not the only philosopher to have considered shelter as a human need. At least some of Martin Heidegger's late work is sometimes mentioned as unexpectedly related to *Walden*. Writing of *Walden* and Martin Heidegger's essay "Building Dwelling Thinking," Stanley Cavell states that he was "sufficiently startled by the similarities to find the differences of interest and to start wondering about an account of both."[135] Yet I wonder whether in that essay, at least, Heidegger really traveled in Thoreau's wake. He may have claimed that "building as dwelling unfolds into the building that cultivates growing things and the building that erects buildings,"[136] but his approach is not that of Thoreau toward plants and animals, omnipresent in *Walden*. Thoreau maintains that "I go and come with a strange liberty in Nature, a part of herself."[137] In his account, living creatures are constantly inside, under, around, and atop his house. In contrast, they make just one fleeting appearance in Heidegger's essay: "Earth is the serving bearer, blossoming and fruiting, spreading out in rock and water, rising up into plant and animal."[138] Heidegger's "serving bearer" is subservient to, not generatively entangled with, gods and mortals. Heidegger's words are too solipsistically anthropocentric to bear any viable relation to Thoreau's. Thoreau is the philosopher of shelter as part of a larger ecology of living things, of which humans are but one element.

While evoking Thoreau's conditional value of philosophy as a practical matter requiring a particular kind of place for its successful practice, symbolic reiterations of Thoreau's Walden Pond house also evoke his specific reflections on the fundamental human requirement for shelter, which together with food, clothing, and fuel constitutes what we have seen Thoreau call the four "necessaries of life for man in this climate."[139] In fulfilling both of these requirements—practical and symbolic—those structures evoke the interdependence of humans as cultural and natural creatures with the rest of nature. Thanks to the insights of America's premier nineteenth-century philosopher, humble dwelling and exalted theory meet in an unlikely conjunction that undermines many widely held assumptions about the value and status of architecture. From Thoreau's house at Walden Pond—and its epigones elsewhere—we learn that shelter is not only a human need but a human right, and that architecture that ignores the interdependence between humans and the rest of nature, lending privilege to other, often destructive factors, is no fit shelter for humanity.

[CHAPTER FIVE]

Artistry

The basic claim of this study is that aesthetics can provide a useful lens through which to examine aspects of Thoreau's actions and beliefs as revealed by his responses to the large variety of mindprints he encountered, or indeed, in the case of his house, created. Aesthetics clearly emerged in the discussion in the previous chapter as an important factor in Thoreau's ideas about shelter, and I argued that both everyday aesthetics and environmental aesthetics play roles. Here I explore Thoreau's reliance on aesthetics in his examination of worlds by looking at various phenomena subject to aesthetic attention on a spectrum from fine art at one end to everyday, human-made items at the other. I also take natural occurrences—beyond this spectrum—into consideration. I gather all the human contrivances on this spectrum of the human-made under the term *artistry*. By artistry I seek to capture the material products of human ingenuity.

What were some of the implications of the term *aesthetics* in Thoreau's circle? For them, the term aesthetics was something of a novelty that, broadly speaking, they associated with German philosophy.[1] Education reformer, publisher, and sometime business manager of the *Dial* Elizabeth Peabody notes in her 1849 edited volume, *Æsthetic Papers*, that "Germany is the discoverer of the æsthetic, because the German mind, more than any other, embodies the unpersonal principle that underlies the æsthetic view." On the same page she writes, "The unpersonal, which sinks and subordinates the viewer to the object,—which, by putting my personality aside, enables me to see the object in a pure uncolored light,—is the æsthetic."[2] The extent to which Thoreau and his circle engaged directly with German philosophical aesthetic theories, such as those of Baumgarten, Kant, Schlegel, Schelling, and Hegel, is not entirely clear.

Thoreau mentions none of these authors in his journal, although he read John (Johann) B. Stallo's *General Principles of the Philosophy of Nature* (1848) soon after its publication; part II comprises chapters discussing the views of Kant, Fichte, Schelling, Oken, and Hegel.[3] In the writings of these philosophers, aesthetics may have spanned media, but it is clear that Thoreau, like most others in his circle, was far more at ease with literature than with the visual arts. This profoundly affected his attitude toward discussion in aesthetic terms. Thoreau's education at Harvard shaped his preference for literature. Furthermore, he left Harvard an aspiring poet and published a number of poems with the support of Emerson, himself a poet. But after having included eight of Thoreau's poems in the October 1842 issue of the *Dial*, Emerson severely criticized Thoreau's verse in person and effectively brought his career as a poet to an end.[4]

The only members of the circle gathered about Emerson who were truly at ease with visual art, though to varying extents, were Elizabeth Peabody, Margaret Fuller, and Samuel Gray Ward. Elizabeth Peabody and Margaret Fuller both published reviews of the 1839 exhibition in Boston of paintings by one of the most celebrated American artists of the day, Washington Allston.[5] Peabody admired Allston. Originally from South Carolina, Allston spent seventeen years in London, Paris, and Rome before settling in Cambridge, just across the Charles River from Boston, in 1818. He remained there until his death in 1843. Allston regarded Boston as the cultural center of the United States, a status in part conferred by the founding in 1807 of the Boston Athenaeum as a scholarly library. In 1827 the Athenaeum added an art gallery that held annual exhibitions of American and European paintings and sculpture. Before the creation of the Athenaeum gallery, John Doggett's Repository of Arts was the only large-scale venue in Boston to hold regular exhibitions of European and American paintings. In a letter to her mother, Eliza Peabody, Elizabeth Peabody gives an account of viewing artworks at Doggett's Repository soon after her arrival in Boston in 1822.[6] These exhibitions ended in 1825 when Doggett's Repository was converted into a store selling mirrors, frames, and carpets.[7] Two years later, in the founding year of its gallery, the Boston Athenaeum hosted the first American exhibition of Allston's paintings, twelve in number.[8] In 1839 a far larger exhibition of Allston's paintings was held, largely drawn from local private collections. The exhibition catalog lists forty-five works comprising biblical, Shakespearean, and other literary subjects; Italian and American landscapes; and portraits.[9] It was held not at the Athenaeum but at Harding's Gallery, named for the portrait painter Chester Harding, whose studio was in the same building.[10] Harding's Gallery held art exhibitions, some associated with auctions, between 1833 and 1847.[11]

The Allston exhibition at Harding's Gallery found an enthusiastic viewer in Margaret Fuller. She reviewed it in the first issue of the *Dial* and followed up her article with a review of the art exhibition at the Boston Athenaeum in the second issue.[12] The latter included both original works of painting and sculpture and copies of European paintings. In her opinion, "It is never so pleasant to see works of art in a collection, as when they are ornaments of a home," yet "that the public should be sufficiently interested in such objects, to make it worthwhile to collect them yearly for exhibition, is none the less an important event."[13]

If Margaret Fuller was confident writing about visual art, Ralph Waldo Emerson was not. Nonetheless, in the 1830s he delivered three lectures on visual art and published an article on the topic in the *Dial* in 1841.[14] He had visited Malta, various parts of Italy, France, and Great Britain in 1833. Although his journal entries written while traveling in Europe exhibit a certain sensitivity to visual art, that sensitivity did not transfer to his published writings. He distanced himself from a mode of making that had struck him forcefully in Europe but that he associated with Europe rather than a youthful America, defined, in his opinion, by the written word and mechanical ingenuity. "Art was born in Europe and will not cross the ocean, I fear," he wrote in his journal.[15]

In a letter to Margaret Fuller dated April 8, 1840, Emerson commented on draft articles for the first issue of the *Dial* that she had sent to him. Of her review of the Allston exhibition the previous summer, he wrote, "The Allston-Essay I read & admire farther off; not doubting since you say so, that the things are so; still, as the poor curate said, 'it is Athanasius's creed & not mine.'"[16] Although Emerson had been the éminence grise of the *Dial* since its inception, after he formally took over the editorship following Fuller's departure in 1842, he had to address the visual arts himself. Yet when discussing Washington Allston in print, Emerson writes not of his paintings, but of his verse. He begins his 1841 essay "Self-Reliance" with the words, "I read the other day some verses written by an eminent painter which were original and not conventional."[17] As literary scholar C. P. Seabrook Wilkinson has aptly pointed out, Emerson rejected as appropriate sources of inspiration memories of Italy such as those on which Allston relied, caricaturing the painter-poet as an "Italy man."[18] Emerson dismissed the "old arts," painting and sculpture, as a pattern for creativity in the new nation, declaring in his 1841 essay, "Art": "It is in vain that we look for genius to reiterate its miracles in the old arts; it is its instinct to find beauty and holiness in new and necessary facts, in the field and roadside, in the shop and mill."[19] This is an attitude—valuing the aesthetics of everyday life—that Thoreau would later adopt and develop.

For advice on visual art, Emerson relied on Samuel Gray Ward, a poet and aspiring artist who turned banker but retained a serious interest in visual art. Ward was to become one of the founders of the Metropolitan Museum of Art in New York in 1869. In 1838 Emerson had written to Ward that he was "especially curious of information on art & artists, of which however, I warn you, I know nothing."[20] For the first issue of the *Dial* under his editorship (October 1842), Emerson invited Ward to contribute an article on visual art criticism.[21] Ward obliged. His piece took the form of a dialogue between Pictor and Amico. Ward, through the character of Pictor, notes that the article was written at the instigation of "W—," that is, Waldo, the name by which Emerson was familiarly known. While the painter Pictor fears the degeneracy of art in the present, Amico, the critic, exhorts him to have faith that contemporary artists "have the power" found in Raphael, and "what we want is to call it out."[22] Emerson added an editorial note at the beginning of Ward's article, stating, "We will draw one paper out of our portfolio . . . that our Journal may not go quite without homage to the laws of Fine Art; for 'Art,' as Dr. Waagen writes, 'is an expression of the mind, whose peculiar character cannot be supplied by anything else.'"[23] For Emerson, this claim would seem to have been a philosophical premise rather than a conviction. Ward went on to contribute "Notes on Art and Architecture" to the July 1843 issue of the *Dial*.[24]

The opportunities for Thoreau, Emerson, and their friends to see paintings and sculpture in Boston and Cambridge were limited. The catalog of the 1839 Allston loan exhibition reminds us that there were private opportunities to see some original works as well as copies of European paintings in the role of "ornaments of a home." Some such ornaments were original, and some were painted copies of famous works. For instance, Samuel Gray Ward's painted copy of a work in the Galleria Palatina of the Palazzo Pitti in Florence, representing three half-length female figures of the *Three Fates*, hung prominently over the fireplace in Emerson's study.[25] The original painting on panel by Francesco Salviati, dated 1550, was then thought to be by Michelangelo. Those with access to Harvard College could see portraits of past presidents, donors, and other worthies. Several venues, including Doggett's Repository (1821–25), the Boston Athenaeum (1827 onward), and Harding's Gallery (1833–47), mounted exhibitions. When living on Staten Island in 1843 as a tutor to Emerson's nephew, Thoreau, in a letter to his sister Sophia, reports visiting the picture gallery of the National Academy of Design in New York. He gives no details, but he presumably saw Emanuel Leutze's *Return of Columbus in Chains to Cadiz* (1842) and landscapes by Asher Durand.[26] Such an opportunity was a relative exception for Thoreau, although he records in 1851 having seen two panorama paintings when they were exhibited in Boston; he also mentions visiting the Athenaeum gallery when unexpectedly delayed in Boston with Ellery Channing on their way to Provincetown by schooner in July 1855.[27] Literary scholar Richard Schneider identified the traveling exhibitions of panoramas as being of *The*

River Rhine, by Benjamin Champney, and probably the *Mississippi River* by Samuel B. Stockwell.[28] Both were shown in Boston in 1849. The poster advertising Champney's *River Rhine* at Horticultural Hall claims, "There is an artistic finish and a naturalness of manner, which renders the painting entirely illusive, and the spectator is at once transported to the Banks of this River of romance and beauty."[29] The usually unsuggestible Thoreau reports in his journal being absorbed by the sheer spectacle of Champney's *River Rhine*: "I floated along through the moonlight of history under the spell of enchantment. It was as if I remembered a glorious dream as if I had been transported to a heroic age & breathed an atmosphere of chivalry Those times appeared far more poetic & heroic than these."[30]

Schneider also mentions the availability of books and magazines containing reproductions of artworks.[31] However, in terms of high-quality images, translation engravings—prints reproducing artworks, usually paintings—provided the majority of fine art images in Boston, Cambridge, and nearby villages such as Concord. Owners could frame and display them or keep them in portfolios for perusal. Despite his relative lack of engagement with visual art, Emerson celebrated this practice in his poem "Ode to Beauty":

> I turn the proud portfolios,
> Which hold the grand designs
> Of Salvator, of Guercino,
> And Piranesi's lines.[32]

Emerson and his second wife, Lidian, owned numbers of such prints. One was a wedding gift to her in 1835 from Jane Carlyle, wife of Emerson's Scottish friend, the writer Thomas Carlyle.[33] This is a large translation engraving after the celebrated ceiling fresco by Guido Reni, finished in 1614, in the casino (garden pavilion) of the Palazzo Pallavicini-Rospigliosi in Rome (see figure 6).[34] It is still in the Emerson house at the time of writing.[35] Art historian Amy Golahny has pointed out the high esteem in which many American writers and artists held the paintings of Guido Reni at the time, usually referring to him by his first name alone.[36] Thoreau must have been struck by the print, for he wrote a poem about it, "The Aurora of Guido: A Fragment."[37] Sophia Peabody must also have been impressed by this impression or another, for among the maple furniture she decorated with painted scenes derived from Italian paintings for her new husband, Nathaniel Hawthorne, and herself when they moved into the Old Manse in Concord in 1842 was the headboard of their new bed, which she embellished with a scene derived from Guido Reni's composition.[38]

FIGURE 6. Raphael Morghen after Guido Reni, *Aurora*, 1787, engraving. Yale University Art Gallery, gift of Paul DiDomenico, MD, and Ilke Nalbantoglu, MD.

The poem by the young Thoreau is especially indicative of his form of attention to a visual artwork. What he chooses to describe and what to ignore in the scene is revealing of his aesthetic focus. The fresco is a classically derived allegory of the sunrise, in which the god Apollo in his horse-drawn quadriga represents the sun led across the sky by the personification of Dawn (Aurora), and the putto Phosphorus carries a torch to represent Venus, the morning star. Apollo's chariot is flanked by female personifications of the Hours. That the scene in the casino evokes a triumphal procession is strengthened by its proximity to two contemporaneous frescoes of the *Triumph of Fame* (a Roman general) and the *Triumph of Love* (a Dionysian procession) by Antonio Tempesta. With the exception of the first line of the poem, "The god of day his car rolls up the slopes," Thoreau, seemingly willfully, ignores the entire personificatory and allegorical apparatus that dominates and defines Reni's picture. Thereafter, his attention is focused exclusively on natural phenomena, some of which are not even depicted but are imagined by him: "The lingering moon through western shadows gropes, / The early breeze ruffles the poplar leaves, / The curling waves reflect the unseen light, / The seabirds dip their bills in Ocean's foam." (There are no seabirds in the print.) Other than Apollo, who is unnamed, the only figures he mentions are so small and incidental as to be scarcely discernible, or even imaginary: "The fisherman unfurls his sails again; / And the recruited warrior bides the strife." The poem is a deeply perverse account of the picture, as though daring its reader to protest that its author has quite missed its point. Yet that attention to the representation of natural phenomena at the expense of the major figures and the allegory would seem to be Thoreau's very purpose, despite his respect for classical learning deriving from his Harvard literary education. Thoreau would have been familiar with the classical genre of *ekphrasis*, a rhetorical or poetic text originating in Greek philosophy and verse, revived in Renaissance Europe, that describes a picture. As in other circumstances, when addressing a work of fine art Thoreau is presumably not visually oblivious to what he, like us, most obviously sees, but he is ever the contrarian.

Thoreau's focus on the landscape elements of Guido Reni's *Aurora* is a foretaste of his later discussions of visual art. His notes on visual art principally concern landscape painting, specifically in relation to depiction. In his many remarks on visual art in his journals, Thoreau is consistently implicitly troubled by Emerson's claim in an essay published in 1841, "Art," that "in our fine arts, not imitation, but creation is the aim. In landscapes, the painter should give the suggestion of a fairer creation than we know."[39] But Thoreau knows no landscape representation that might fit this description, for in his opinion a landscape in nature invariably exceeds in beauty any human representation of it. That perception, for Thoreau, is a consequence of what the percipient brings to the experience, ideally health, high spirits, and serenity. In 1859 he writes, "There is no beauty in the sky, but in the eye that sees it. Health, high spirits, serenity, these are the great landscape-painters. Turners, Claudes, Rembrandts are nothing to them." Yet he continues, "Men love to walk in those picture-galleries still, because they have not quite forgotten their early dreams."[40]

If depiction—or description—there must be, Thoreau is in favor of the "poetic or lively" and the "unmeasured and eloquent." He compares scientific with poetic description in his journal in 1860:

> The scientific differs from the poetic or lively description somewhat as the photographs, which we so weary of viewing, from paintings and sketches, though this comparison is too favorable to science. All science is only a makeshift, a means to an end which is never attained. After all, the truest description, and that by which another living man can most readily recognize a flower, is the unmeasured and eloquent one which the sight of it inspires. No scientific description will supply the want of this, though you should count and measure and analyze every atom that seems to compose it.[41]

Thoreau leaves open whether that description can adequately take a visual rather than a literary form, although "paintings and sketches" are explicitly on his mind.

One of the major criteria of Thoreau's relative dissatisfaction with painted or printed depictions of items in nature is their want of subtlety of variety in his eyes. In his late essay "Autumnal Tints," Thoreau compares "our paint-box" with the "natural colors" and "autumn colors" of the "leaves of a single tree." The "paint-box" and the "dye-house" cannot compete with the colors available in nature, and "If you want a different shade or tint of a particular color, you have only to look farther within or without the tree or the wood." He asks, "What School of Design can vie with this? Think how much the eyes of painters of all kinds, and of manufacturers of cloth and paper, and paper-stainers, and countless others, are to be educated by these autumnal colors."[42]

Furthermore, Thoreau has moral reservations about the motivations of artists. In his journal for 1851, Thoreau discusses a book by the self-taught Scottish geologist Hugh Miller. He quotes Miller's discussion, centered on an "artist who sculptured the cherry stone" and who "consigned it to a cabinet, and placed a microscope beside it."[43] But he takes Miller to task for speaking "of his [the artist's] work becoming all in all to the worker his rising above the dread of criticism & the appetite of praise as if these were the very rare exceptions in a great artists life—& not the very definition of it."[44] Thoreau's doubts about the motivations of artists therefore appear to carry over to his apprehension of their works. He had earlier expressed the opinion in his journal: "Not how is the idea expressed in stone or on canvas, is the question, but how far it has obtained form and expression in the life of the artist."[45] In his revised version of this argument intended for publication, Thoreau omits this passage, but not the claim that "true art" is "such a masterpiece as you may imagine a dweller on the table-lands of Central Asia might produce, with threescore and ten years for canvas, and the faculties of a man for tools,—a human life."[46] That human life is, for Thoreau, fully entangled with the natural environment, and nature must inevitably be superior to any artwork an artist might produce. In short, as he states in *A Week on the Concord and Merrimack Rivers*, "Art can never match the luxury and superfluity of Nature."[47] To support this claim he states, "In the former all is seen; it cannot afford concealed wealth, and is niggardly in comparison; but Nature, even when she is scant and thin outwardly, satisfies us still by the assurance of a certain generosity at the roots."[48]

Thoreau frequently denigrates visual art by comparing pictures unfavorably with scenes in nature. In a journal entry in June 1853 he writes, "Men will go further & pay more to see a tawdry picture on Canvass a poor painted scene—than to behold the fairest or grandest scene that nature ever displays in their immediate vicinity—though they may have never seen it in their lives."[49] For Thoreau, even the "best works of art" are inadequate.

In a journal entry in 1845, just ten days after moving to his house at Walden Pond, he writes, "Now the best works of art serve comparatively but to dissipate the mind, for they themselves represent transitionary and paroxysmal, not free and absolute, thoughts."[50] However, his reservations about the inadequacies of human-contrived depictions did not prevent him from imagining them, at least in some measure, as ideals, even if in his opinion neither his ideal visual artworks, nor the conditions for their appreciation, exist. In *Walden*, he considers what "the best works of art" might be.

> We have built for this world a family mansion, and for the next a family tomb. The best works of art are the expression of man's struggle to free himself from this condition, but the effect of our art is merely to make this low state comfortable and that higher state to be forgotten. There is actually no place in this village for a work of *fine* art, if any had come down to us, to stand, for our lives, our houses and streets, furnish no proper pedestal for it. There is not a nail to hang a picture on, nor a shelf to receive the bust of a hero or a saint.[51]

But, he adds, perhaps it might yet be possible to create conditions for the adequate use of visual artworks: "Before we can adorn our houses with beautiful objects the walls must be stripped, and our lives must be stripped, and beautiful housekeeping and beautiful living be laid for a foundation: now, a taste for the beautiful is most cultivated out of doors, where there is no house and no housekeeper."[52]

For Thoreau, the primacy of nature does not mean that art and nature cannot be intertwined. In a journal entry written just over a month after his move to Walden Pond, Thoreau claims, "All nature is classic and akin to art. The sumach and pine and hickory which surround my house remind me of the most graceful sculpture." Pursuing this train of thought, Thoreau sees nature subsuming the perfect work of art: "The perfect work of art is received again into the bosom of nature whence its material proceeded—and that criticism which can only detect its unnaturalness has no longer any office to fulfill."[53]

Underlying Thoreau's disdain for visual art is his assumption that paintings and sculpture are imitations, an idea in European thought that goes back to Plato's discussion of pictures in the *Sophist* and his strictures on visual art in the *Republic*.[54] These ideas informed the transcendentalist conception of nature as a collection of symbols representing the Universal Being, an idea articulated most influentially by Emerson in his 1836 book *Nature*.[55] Thoreau metaphorically regards those occurrences in nature that seem artful to appear to him "as if in a peculiar sense I stood in the laboratory of the Artist who made the world and me."⁵⁶ That is, they are primary creations. He writes this of the patterns resembling foliage created by movements of earth and water warmed by the winter sun on the banks of the railroad cutting—called by Thoreau the "deep cut"—between Walden Pond and the village, which he first notes in a journal entry in December 1851 and elaborates on at length in *Walden*.⁵⁷ In his journal, he writes of what appeared to him to be the "fancy sketches & designs of the artist.... As if for ages sand and clay might have thus flowed into the forms of foliage—before plants were produced to clothe the earth."⁵⁸ In *Walden* he writes that "the Artist who made the world and me" is as though "still at work, sporting on this bank, and with excess of energy strewing his fresh designs about."⁵⁹ In his journal, that metaphorical Artist has, in Thoreau's mind, created not an imitative replica but a living entity, leading him to claim, "The earth I tread on is not a dead, inert mass. It is a body—has a spirit—is organic—and fluid to the influence of its spirit—and to whatever particle of that spirit is in me. She is not dead but sleepeth."⁶⁰ This leads him to state in the elaborative passage in *Walden*, "I feel as if I were nearer to the vitals of the globe, for this sandy overflow is something such a foliaceous mass as the vitals of the animal body."⁶¹

For Thoreau, in contradistinction to the natural art of the artist, the art that mortals make is imitative. He articulates his conception of visual art as imitation clearly when expressing his aesthetic response to the pine cladding of buildings, in a journal entry in September 1851: "I love to see the yellow knots & their lengthened stain on the dry, unpainted Pitch-pine boards on barns & other buildings The Dugan house, for instance—The indestructible yellow fat—it fats my eyes to see it—worthy for art to imitate.—telling of branches in the forest once."⁶² Thoreau holds that even if art can imitate the yellow stains on a knotty pine board, nonetheless it is far better to contemplate the boards themselves, for those boards are constituents of an actual world subject to the aesthetics of everyday life.⁶³ Nonetheless, the art that successfully imitates the boards may, in some equivocal sense, be worthy. The artist can make a choice of what he or she seeks to imitate. Thus, Thoreau observes in a journal entry in September 1854, "The conventional acorn of art is of course of particular species, but the artist might find it worth his while to study Nature's varieties again."⁶⁴ The pine boards that Thoreau admires aesthetically fall within a third category between the wholly natural and imitative visual art: artifacts of modest, purposive human craft. This is where Thoreau consistently finds one species of aesthetic fulfillment. It is akin to Emerson's "new and necessary facts, in the field and roadside, in the shop and mill," and I shall return to it.

For all his skepticism about visual art, Thoreau sees a role for it in his community. Despite what he views as its inherent limitations insofar as it is imitative, in a journal entry in September 1851, he states, "There are certain refining & civilizing influences as works of art—journals—& books & scientific instruments—which this community is amply rich enough to purchase which would educate this village—elevate its tone of thought, & if it alone improved these opportunities easily make it the centre of civilization in the known world—put us on a level as to opportunities at once with London & Arcadia—and secure us a culture at once superior to both."[65] He makes this point in objection to the town's expenditure of "16000 dollars on a Town House a hall for our political meetings mainly—and nothing to educate ourselves who are grown up." Works of art—"pictures & statues"—are among the "civilizing influences" that could lift the inhabitants of Concord out of their state of being "contented to be countrified—to be provincial."[66] Thoreau returns to this point almost a year later, complaining once again in his journal of the lack of continuing education for adults, other than that provided by the "half starved Lyceum in the winter," where Thoreau and other local thinkers regularly lectured, and where he had served as both secretary and elected curator, contributing to choosing and inviting speakers, making travel arrangements, and securing payments.[67] He elaborates the points expressed in this journal entry in *Walden*: "It is time that villages were universities, and their elder inhabitants the fellows of universities, with leisure—if they are, indeed, so well off—to pursue liberal studies the rest of their lives." He continues, "In this country, the village should in some respects take the place of the nobleman of Europe. It should be the patron of the fine arts. It is rich enough. It wants only the magnanimity and refinement."[68]

A double standard would seem to be inevitable in Thoreau's thinking on this topic. He could conduct his philosophical experiment at Walden Pond largely in solitude—at least, without dependence in many respects on his family and friends—but could only arrive at and sustain that experiment with the cultural resources of Concord (however inadequate in his estimation), Cambridge, and Boston, both beforehand in preparation and afterward in reflecting on and writing about his experiment. He holds visual art—however inferior to nature owing to its imitative character—to be a desirable if not a necessary component of those resources.

If Plato's philosophy of art is implicit in Thoreau's discussion of the relationship of art to nature, that of the writings of the Church of England cleric and artist William Gilpin is explicit, at least from 1852 onward.[69] In an April journal entry that year, Thoreau writes, "Gilpin says well that the object of a light mist is a '*nearer distance*'"; in October he writes, "Gilpin speaks of 'floats of timber' on the river Wey, in 1775. as picturesque objects."[70]

Thereafter, he regularly uses the term *picturesque*, previously not found in his journal, and he quotes and refers to Gilpin frequently. Thoreau read borrowed copies of Gilpin's works but was interested enough that when passing through Boston in October 1855, he made inquiries about their cost at prominent booksellers and publishers. He copied a list of Gilpin's British publications and their prices while visiting Little, Brown, and Co.[71]

Although Gilpin did not coin the term picturesque—it derives from the Italian *pittoresco*—he had used it in his book *An Essay upon Prints: Containing Remarks upon the Principles of Picturesque Beauty; The Different Kinds of Prints; And the Characters of the most noted Masters* (1768). There he defines picturesque as "a term expressive of that peculiar kind of beauty, which is agreeable in a picture."[72] However, in 1782, in his *Observations on the River Wye, and Several Parts of South Wales, etc. Relative Chiefly to Picturesque Beauty; Made in the Summer of the Year 1770*, Gilpin proposed the picturesque not as a "peculiar kind of beauty," but promoted it to equality with the *beautiful* and the *sublime*, already established by Edmund Burke as distinct aesthetic categories.[73] Gilpin's key work, though, in establishing the picturesque as an aesthetic category, is his *Three Essays: On Picturesque Beauty; on Picturesque Travel; and on Sketching Landscape* (1792).[74] At the outset of a lengthy discussion in his journal of Gilpin's usage of the picturesque in January 1854, Thoreau states, "Gilpin's 'Essay on Picturesque Beauty' is the key to all his writings."[75]

Gilpin proposed an interplay between the properties of a scene in nature and a representation of it such that the viewer of the natural landscape sees properties of composition in it akin to those in a picture, and the viewer of a picture sees those natural properties reflected as though back in that picture itself. The natural landscape and the pictorial representation are thereby mutually reinforcing in certain of their perceptible shared properties, specifically their aesthetic properties. For Thoreau, however, the value of the term lies not so much in conceiving of pictures of landscapes as valuable because of the "picturesque" qualities they might exhibit as in conceiving of natural scenes as though informed by certain characteristics proper to pictures. His aesthetic attention is almost invariably to the natural scene alone. For example, in a journal entry in November 1852, writing about the view of the woods and hills beyond Fairhaven Bay in a misty rain, he states, "I saw these between the converging boughs of two white pines a rod or two from me on the edge of the rock, and I thought that there was no frame to a landscape equal to this—to see between two near pine boughs whose lichens are distinct a distant forest & lake—the one frame the other picture."[76]

This, though, is far from the entirety of Thoreau's critical assessment of Gilpin's text. His critique makes it clear that he is indeed interested in the qualities of paintings and sculptures. Thus, he doubts Gilpin's assertion that a stylistically rough manner in the artist's execution of both is preferable to a smooth manner. He agrees: "True, there are many reasons why the painter should select the rough. It is easier to execute; he can do it more justice. In the case of the patriarchal head, those lines and wrinkles which man's life has produced his hand can better represent than the fullness and promise of infancy; and then, on the whole, perhaps, we have more sympathy with performance than promise." Further: "The humble or sincere and true is more commonly rough and weather-beaten, so that from association we prefer it." Yet referring to the smooth forms of two of the most celebrated statues of classical antiquity, the *Venus de' Medici* in the Uffizi in Florence and the *Apollo Belvedere* in the Vatican, Thoreau asks, "But will Mr Gilpin assert that the Venus and Apollo are not fit objects for painting?"[77] Thoreau goes on to argue that Gilpin's attention to surfaces, rough or smooth, is "superficial" (Thoreau's term): "He goes not below the surface to account for the effect of form & color—&c. . . . He fails to show why roughness is essential to the picturesque because he does not go beneath the surface."[78] Thoreau points to the character of the item represented, not its depiction, as the key focus of aesthetic attention: "I should say that no arrangement of light & shade without reference to the object, actual or suggested, so lit & shaded can interest us powerfully—anymore than the paint itself can charm us."[79] Once again, Thoreau's principal focus of attention is on what the artist perceives and strives to depict, not on the resulting depiction, even though he acknowledges in principle that paintings of subjects either superficially rough or smooth can have value. Thoreau's insistence on focusing on the subject matter of a depiction ties sensual apprehension to moral assessment, an association that Gilpin emphatically denies. Thoreau quotes Gilpin's denial, expressing surprise that it should come from a cleric: "He says 'We might begin in moral style; and consider the objects of nature in a higher light, than merely as amusement. We might observe that a search after beauty should naturally lead the mind to the great origin of all beauty; &c—But though in theory this seems a natural climax, we insist the less upon it, as in fact we have scarce ground to hope, that every admirer of *picturesque beauty*, is an admirer also of the *beauty of virtue*;—' And he a clergyman, 'vicar of Boldre—!'"[80] Thoreau's association of the picturesque with moral qualities finds clear expression in *Walden*, where he writes, "The most interesting dwellings in this country, as the painter knows, are the most unpretending, humble log huts and cottages of the poor commonly; it is the life of the inhabitants whose shells they are, and not any peculiarity in their surfaces merely, which makes them *picturesque*."[81] Rarely can Thoreau dissociate aesthetic from ethical concerns.

Thoreau concludes his critique of Gilpin with the following assessment: "The elegant Gilpin. I like his style & manners better than anything he says."[82] Yet Thoreau had clearly been stimulated by his reading of Gilpin to follow discussions of the picturesque further. In a journal entry in February 1854 he quotes Uvedale Price's *An Essay on the Picturesque*, first published in 1794 and in an expanded edition in 1796. He selects passages from this book that give privilege to the effects that Price has observed in nature, not in pictures, noting that he himself has made similar observations:

> Price on the Picturesque—says "The midsummer shoot is the first thing that gives relief to the eye, after the sameness of color which immediately precedes it; in many trees, and in none more than the oak, the effect is singularly beautiful; the old foliage forms a dark background, on which the new appears, relieved & detached in all its freshness & brilliancy: it is spring engrafted upon summer."—Is not this the effect which I noticed by Fair Haven side last summer or autumn toward night—that watered & variously shaded foliage? As for Autumn, he speaks of "the warm haze, which, on a fine day in that season, spreads the last varnish over every part of the picture."[83]

Price, though, in a passage between the two that Thoreau quotes, but which he omits, relates his observations in nature to his observations of paintings, using the former to add value to the latter. Price writes, "It has often struck me, that the whole system of the Venetian colouring (particularly that of Giorgione and Titian, which has been the object of great imitation) was formed upon the tints of autumn; and that their pictures have thence that golden hue, which gives them (as Sir Joshua Reynolds observes) such a superiority over all others."[84]

Thoreau does not emulate Price's focus of attention. He remains adamantly fixed on the natural landscape alone, even if he frequently uses metaphors of depiction in visual art to describe scenes in nature, and even if his apprehension of a natural scene as picturesque implicitly validates the aesthetic qualities of the imagined picture qua picture that the natural scene evokes and reflects. As literary scholar Lawrence Buell has remarked, for Thoreau, "this interest in landscape aesthetics was a project in itself."[85]

These responses suggest that Thoreau's aesthetics of both natural and depicted landscapes cannot be wholly detached from his ethics. Thoreau grapples with the consequences of this focus on the landscape in nature itself in a journal entry in January 1852. Giving far more detail than I quote here (indicated by the ellipsis), he writes:

> As I stood on the partially cleared bank at the E end of the pond I looked S over the side of the hill into a deep dell still wooded, and I saw not more than 30 rods off a chopper at his work—I was half a dozen rods distant from the standing wood—and I saw him through a vista between two trees (it was now mainly an oak wood, the pine having been cut) and he appeared to me apparently half a mile distant yet charmingly distinct as in a picture of which the two trees were the frame.... It was perhaps one of those coincidences and effects which have made men painters. I could not behold him as an actual man—he was more ideal than in any picture I have seen. He refused to be seen as actual. Far in the hollow yet somewhat enlightened aisles of this wooded dell. Some scenes will thus present themselves as picture. Those scenes which are picture—subjects for the pencil—are distinctly marked—they do not require the aid of genius to idealize them. They must be seen as ideal.[86]

Thoreau here ironically reverses the standard claim in art theory texts that the artist must refine and idealize imperfect nature to create an ideal representation. Instead, he proposes the contingent natural scene when viewed in particular conditions—with key elements at a distance—as itself the ideal.

There is an unresolved tension in Thoreau's musings on visual art between a consistent intuition that it can be of value, notably in promoting the cultural armature that can support philosophical experiments in living such as his own, and his conviction that nature itself must eclipse art as an object of aesthetic and moral contemplation.

Thoreau's reading of Gilpin and Price far from exhausts his explorations of the literature of European art. In April 1852 he relates one of Giorgio Vasari's instances of the *paragone* (literally *comparison*), the competition in the fifteenth and sixteenth centuries between Italian advocates of sculpture and painting respectively regarding which was superior. It concerns an account reported by Titian's friend, Giorgio Barbarelli. Barbarelli asks which is superior in terms of comprehensiveness of visual information, a sculpture seen from but one viewpoint or a painting also seen from one viewpoint. In these terms, one might assume them equal. But the painting Barbarelli specifies includes reflections on armor hanging beside the figure of a man, a mirroring pool before him and a looking glass on the other side of him. Together, these give a greater sense of all-round representation from a single viewpoint than can a sculpture.[87] Thoreau uses this example for his own epistemological and ethical ends: "So I would fain represent some truths as roundly and solidly as a statue—or as completely & in all their relations as Barbarelli his warrior. So that you may see round them."[88]

Thoreau's exploration of the literature of art was not confined to discussions of the picturesque and Vasari's *Lives*. In the fall of 1857 Thoreau read volume 2 of the first English translation, published as the *History of Ancient Art* in 1856, of the single most significant eighteenth-century work of art history, Johann Joachim Winckelmann's *Geschichte der Kunst des Alterthums*, published in German in 1764.[89] Winckelmann's role in the development of both archaeology and the history of art as methodical disciplines cannot be overstated. He distinguished, defined, and applied stylistic criteria to the art of classical antiquity and was the first to propose progressive categorical differences among periods of Greek, Hellenistic, and Roman art.[90] Although Thoreau's engagement with classical antiquity was consistent and intense—he published several commentaries on ancient texts in the *Dial*—unlike Emerson, he had never had the opportunity to view firsthand surviving architectural remains and sculpture in Europe, and his interest in this world focused on the written word. His recorded comments on his reading of Winckelmann in Giles Henry Lodge's English translation are confined to recounting a couple of ideas about beauty in the abstract, specifically in the context of aging as a percipient. In March 1857 he writes, "Winckelmann . . . says of Beauty, 'I have meditated long upon it, but my meditations commenced too late, and in the brightest glow of mature life its essential has remained dark to me; I can speak of it, therefore, only feebly and spiritlessly.'"[91]

Probably more important for the development of Thoreau's own thinking on visual art was his considerable investment of time in reading significant works by the English art critic and theorist John Ruskin, published before the fall of 1857, when Thoreau conducted his reading campaign.[92] He read all four volumes of Ruskin's *Modern Painters* that had been published to that date (1843–56; a fifth was to appear in 1860), as well as *The Seven Lamps of Architecture* (1849).[93] *Modern Painters* begins as a defense of the paintings of J. M. W. Turner, reinforcing Turner's claim that contemporary landscape painting in the spirit of the picturesque is superior to landscape painting that preceded it. Ruskin argues that Turner's art offers profound insights into forces in nature, including the character of the atmosphere. He goes on to explore how, in his opinion, such renderings of nature revealed the deep symbolism that nature offers humanity. After reading the first volume, Thoreau notes in his journal: "I am disappointed in not finding it a more out-of-door book, for I have heard that such was its character, but its title might have warned me. He does not describe Nature as Nature, but as Turner painted her, and though the work betrays that he has given a close attention to Nature, it appears to have been with an artist's and critic's design."[94] He clearly preferred the subsequent volumes. In a letter to one of his long-term correspondents, Harrison Blake, a former Unitarian minister in Worcester, Massachusetts, Thoreau asks, "Have you ever read Ruskin's books? If not, I would recommend you to try the second and third volumes (not parts) of his 'Modern Painters.' I am now reading the fourth, and have read most of his other books lately. They are singularly good and encouraging, though not without crudeness and bigotry. The themes in the volumes referred to are Infinity, Beauty, Imagination, Love of Nature, etc.,—all treated in a very living manner. I am rather surprised by them."[95] Thoreau reveals his proclivities in the sentence that follows: "It is remarkable that these things should be said with reference to painting chiefly, rather than literature."

Despite his reservations, reading Ruskin helped Thoreau to sharpen his specifically visual acuity when contemplating natural phenomena. Robert Richardson points out that the book by Ruskin that helped Thoreau most in this regard is *The Elements of Drawing* (1857).[96] This is an instructional book for beginning painters. The fundamental principle that Ruskin advances in it is that artists should draw what they see, not what they know to be before them. He writes, "The whole technical power of painting depends on our recovery of what may be called the *innocence of the eye*; that is to say, a sort of childish perception of these flat stains of colour, merely as such, without consciousness of what they signify, as a blind man would see them if suddenly gifted with sight."[97] Thoreau clearly read *The Elements of Drawing* attentively. In a journal entry in November 1857 he takes issue with Ruskin over the latter's "law of reflection": "Suppose all the objects above the water *actually* reversed (not in appearance, but in fact) beneath the water, and precisely the same form and in relative position, only all topsy-turvy. Then, whatever you can see, from the place in which you stand, of the solid objects so reversed under the water, you will see in the reflection, always in the true perspective of the solid objects so reversed."[98] Thoreau, disagreeing that "the reflection is merely the substance 'reversed' or 'topsy-turvy,'" does not explain the reason for his disagreement.[99] An entry in his journal made some six weeks earlier makes his objection clear: "Looking now toward the north side of the pond, I perceive that the reflection of the hillside seen from an opposite hill is not so broad as the hillside itself appears, owing to the different angle at which it is seen. The reflection exhibits such an aspect of the hill, *apparently*, as you would get if your eye were placed at that part of the surface of the pond where the reflection seems to be. In this instance, too, then, Nature avoids repeating herself. Not even reflections in still water are like their substances as seen by us."[100]

As Schneider observed, "Thoreau found instead that reflections often intensify color, sometimes distort or exaggerate forms, and sometimes even reveal forms or colors that are not in the objects themselves."[101] In spite of certain reservations about Ruskin's claims derived from his own observations, Thoreau's subsequent journal entries are frequently Ruskinian in their attention to ocular experience. This development reaches its apogee in Thoreau's elegiac piece first prepared as a lecture in 1859, then published in the *Atlantic Monthly* in October 1862, "Autumnal Tints." However, Thoreau's emphasis on the precise observations of the fall colors of the New England woodlands and their presentation not as decay but as a ripening, all following a rule that they "acquire brighter colors just before their fall," is entirely his own.[102]

However engaged Thoreau might have been with the writings of several theorists on visual art, he invariably lauds the sharpening of the sensibilities that, in his opinion, only the actualities of nature can provide. Even while immersed in Ruskin, he writes in a journal entry in October 1857, "It is a great amusement, and more profitable than I could have invented, to go and spend an afternoon hour picking cranberries. By these various pursuits your experience becomes singularly complete and rounded. The novelty and significance of such pursuits are remarkable. Such is the path by which we climb to the heights of our being; and compare the poetry which such simple pursuits have inspired with the unreadable volumes which have been written about art."[103]

Thoreau, as poet-turned-essayist and experimental philosopher, was himself an artist in his improvised life. In some respects he conformed to a certain stereotype of the artist, whether knowingly or not, in his appearance and behavior. The Cambridge landscape painter, poet, and magazine editor Christopher Pearse Cranch might have been describing Thoreau rather than a deceased ideal artist when he wrote in his poem "The Artist," published in the *Dial* in 1842:

>With us he lived a common life,
>And wore a plain familiar name,
>And meekly dared the vulgar strife
>That to inferior spirits came,
>Yet bore a pulse within, the world could never tame.
>. . .
>They could not guess or reason why
>He chose the ways of poverty;
>They read no secret in his eye,
>But scorned the holy mystery,
>That brooded o'er his thoughts and gave him power to see.[104]

Even though Thoreau exhibited some of the traits of an artist, his attitude toward visual art was equivocal. He acknowledged its role in creating an armature within which informed thought could occur, but not in superseding nature as a means of accessing the ineffable, with the single exception of an ideal instance he composed in emulation of a Hindu tale for the final chapter of *Walden*, discussed below. In contrast, his attitude to practical artistry, as distinct from fine art, was wholly positive. I now turn to Thoreau's thoughts on practical artistry. Thoreau discerned aesthetic, ethical, and metaphysical value not only in nature itself but in aspects of human beings' fundamental craft skills employed to meet the basic human needs, as he saw them, of the "several heads of Food, Shelter, Clothing, and Fuel."[105]

Emerson had described craft skills as the "useful arts." He began his 1841 essay, "Art" with this claim: "Because the soul is progressive, it never quite repeats itself, but in every act attempts the production of a new and fairer whole. This appears in works both of the useful and the fine arts, if we employ the popular distinction of works according to their aim, either at use or beauty."[106] In a proclamation that Thoreau would reject as impossible, Emerson states this then standard opinion: "In landscapes, the painter should give the suggestion of a fairer creation than we know."[107] The skill of the artist in whatever medium, Emerson asserts, is to draw attention to the peculiarities of a single object of attention, "to make that for the time the deputy of the world. . . . For the time, it is the only thing worth naming."[108] But Emerson then confounds his contemporaneous reader's expectations by stating that the purpose of a painting is purely preparatory. It teaches the viewer to become attuned to the visual qualities of what the percipient can better view in the "eternal picture which nature paints in the street with moving men and children, beggars, and fine ladies."[109] One of Emerson's principal accusations against art is that it "makes the same effort which a sensual prosperity makes, namely, to detach the beautiful from the useful, to do up the work as unavoidable, and hating it, pass on to enjoyment."[110] Implicitly denying Immanuel Kant's condition for the definition of fine art, Emerson proclaims, "These solaces and compensations, this division of beauty from use, the laws of nature do not permit."[111] Instead, Emerson wishes to find the beautiful—and other aesthetic qualities—in the everyday, "in new and necessary facts, in the field and roadside, in the shop and mill."[112] "Beauty," Emerson declares, "must come back to the useful arts, and the distinction between the fine and useful arts be forgotten."[113] In Emerson's view, when purged of "mercenary impulses" and when "its errands are noble and adequate," new technologies—"the galvanic battery, the electric jar, the prism, and the chemist's retort, . . . mills, railways, and machinery"—will fulfill this role as the "supplements and continuations of the material creation."[114]

Thoreau concurred with Emerson in many respects about these claims. He adopted and developed Emerson's ideas. However, Thoreau had what can appear to be conflicted ideas about craft pursuits. Emerson's key qualifier is that human endeavors should be purged of what he terms "mercenary impulses," and that the "errands" motivating humans to innovate and make should be "noble and adequate." Thoreau is censorious when, in his uncompromising opinion, people fail to meet these stringent yet vague conditions. Thoreau's general accusation is that "men have become the tools of their tools."[115] For Thoreau, humans are in a "higher state" when they avoid this demeaning condition, and art at its best can play a role in expunging it. In *Walden*, as we have seen, he writes, "The best works of art are the expression of man's struggle to free himself from this condition, but the effect of our art is merely to make this low state comfortable and that higher state to be forgotten."[116]

Thoreau did, however, imagine what it might be for an artist to free himself through uncompromising devotion to the pursuit of artistic perfection. He tells such a story in the concluding chapter of *Walden*, inspired by his earlier reading of Hindu scripture, notably, as Hindu scholar Richard Davis has pointed out, the *Viṣnu Purāna*.[117] The object of the artist's pursuit was a perfect wooden staff, and describing his concentration and determination, he writes: "Time kept out of his way, and only sighed at a distance because he could not overcome him."[118] While the artist determinedly sought a suitable stick and eventually fashioned it, his city of Kouroo disappeared, its ruling dynasty died out, and the polestar—which Davis notes lasts a day of Brahma, or 4,320,000,000 years—was replaced by a new polestar. On completing the staff, in Thoreau's words, "it suddenly expanded before the eyes of the astonished artist into the fairest of all the creations of Brahma. He had made a new system in making a staff, a world with full and fair proportions."[119] Thoreau concludes the parable: "The material was pure, and his art was pure; how could the result be other than wonderful?"[120] Thoreau's tale of uncompromising artistic creation toward the end of his scriptural book, *Walden*, encapsulates an unrealizable ideal of artistry, but it is an artistry that takes a practical item, a wooden staff, as its means of world renewal.

In actuality, Thoreau himself could not wholly avoid Emerson's "mercenary impulses" in his own life. He worked successfully on the improvement of the products of his family's pencil manufactory, and after his father's death in 1859 he and his sister Sophia assumed responsibility for the family plumbago refining business.[121] He was also a land surveyor, conducting metes-and-bounds surveys of frequently irregular property boundaries for land deeds, defining rectangular subdivisions of woodland for timber felling, and doing infrastructure surveying for roads and other civil engineering projects for the Town of Concord, his most lucrative single client.[122] Although the high practical and aesthetic quality of his drawn and annotated land surveys suggests a certain pride in their execution, nonetheless he described his own business as a land surveyor in derogatory terms. In a journal entry in December 1851 he writes:

> I have been surveying for 20 or 30 days—living coarsely—even as respects my diet—for I find that that will always alter to suit my employment—Indeed, leading a quite trivial life—& tonight for the first time had made a fire in my chamber & endeavored to return to myself. I wished to ally myself to the powers that rule the universe—I wished to dive into some deep stream of thoughtful & devoted life—which meandered through retired & fertile meadows far from towns. I wished to do again—or for once, things quite congenial to my highest inmost and most sacred nature—To lurk in crystalline thought like the trout under verdurous banks—where stray mankind should only see my bubble come to the surface.
>
> I wished to live ah! as far away as a man can think. I wished for leisure & quiet to let my life flow in its proper channels—with its proper currents. When I might not waste the days—might establish daily prayer & thanksgiving in my family. Might do my own work and not the work of Concord & Carlisle—which would yield me better than money.[123]

Nonetheless, he acknowledges elsewhere that what he regards as "a quite trivial life" is essential for most people, including himself. This need be no impediment to a certain fulfillment, for, as he puts it in a journal entry in September 1851, "Every artizan learns positively something by his trade."[124] In the same entry, he discusses at length the skills required of a stonemason who prepares "Westford granite for fence-posts," making comparisons with the equally demanding skills of carpenters who prepare raw lumber. Even though he states in the middle of his description, "One would say that mankind had much less moral than physical energy—that every day you see men following the trade of splitting rocks, who yet shrink from undertaking apparently less arduous moral labors—the solving of moral problems," he acknowledges the skill required for fulfilling the task well.[125]

In a journal entry in November 1855 Thoreau offers a surprisingly sympathetic account of the life of a modest Sudbury farmer, Reuben Rice. He begins, "It is interesting to me to talk with Rice, he lives so thoroughly and satisfactorily to himself. He has learned that rare art of living, the very elements of which most professors do not know. His life has been not a failure but a success," adding later in his account of their conversation, "not such a failure as most men's." They discuss tools, which Thoreau had complained of lacking. Rice says he "ought to have a chest of tools," to which Thoreau replies, "it was not worth the while. I should not use them enough to pay for them." Rice's rejoinder is direct: "'You would use them more, if you had them,' said he." Thoreau describes Rice as successful in terms of the property he has acquired, but that he "practices a fair and neat economy, dwells not in untidy luxury. It costs him less to live, and he gets more out of life, than others. . . . He works slowly but surely, enjoying the sweet of it."[126] Thoreau's otherwise unforgiving attitude to ways of life involving crafting with tools, so stringently expressed while pursuing his experiment in practical philosophy at Walden, is here softened to the point of compromise.

Thoreau may not have had all the tools he needed—he did not have the means to spend "as much as $3000 thus on my tools," as Rice told him he had done[127]—but he certainly had those that were vital to his endeavors as a surveyor. His iron surveying chain and his various drafting instruments are in the Concord Museum.[128] Thoreau's chain is a modified engineer's chain, three rods long rather than the standard surveyor's chain of four rods, comprising twelve-inch and six-inch links with brass tabs.[129] There is clearly an artistry in the use of the chain and compass to survey a piece of irregularly shaped land, and further artistry in creating an annotated plan using the measurements made in the field. Thoreau's plans are works of graphic art whose precision and clarity serve a practical purpose.

Thoreau's most extraordinary achievement as a surveyor, and the most remarkable product of his craft, is his survey of Walden Pond, He conducted an angle intersection survey of the pond when it was frozen in January 1846. This entailed establishing about twenty sighting posts along the shoreline and two primary traverse stations before measuring the shoreline four rods at a time with a borrowed chain. He then cut over a hundred holes in the ice through which to lower a plumb line to gauge the depth of the water at each plotted point. Finally, collating the data required considerable mathematical skill.[130] Walls describes Thoreau's achievement, the annotated survey plan, as "a remarkable work of art, a working survey that accurately mapped Walden Pond to the inch: length, breadth, and depth."[131] It most certainly is a work of art, but a work of art that is equally a work of practical utility.

Thoreau may have valued the useful arts as practiced by himself and others for both their practical and aesthetic characteristics, but he also valued what he called in a November 1853 journal entry, "a step beyond pure utility."[132] This was how Thoreau characterized what he thought was a Native American stone pestle that he mentions "J. Hosmer" (probably his friend from childhood, Joseph Hosmer) showing him, his son having found it while plowing.¹³³ He describes it as having "a rude bird's head, a hawk's or eagle's, the beak and eyes (the latter a mere prominence) serving for a knob or handle."

> It is affecting, as a work of art by a people who have left so few traces of themselves—a step beyond the common arrowhead & pestle & axe— Something more fanciful—a step beyond pure utility. As long as I find traces of works of convenience merely however much skill they show—I am not so much affected—as when I discover works which evince the exercise of fancy & taste however rude—It is a great step to find a pestle whose handle is ornamented with a bird's head knob—It brings the maker still nearer to the races which so ornament their umbrella & cane handles. I have then evidence in stone that men lived here who had fancies to be pleased—& in whom the first steps toward a complete culture were taken—It implies so many more thoughts such as I have—The arrow-head too suggests a bird—but a relation to it not in the least godlike—But here an Indian has patiently sat & fashioned a stone into the likeness of a bird— and added some pure beauty to that pure utility—& so far begun to leave behind him war & even hunting—& to redeem himself from the savage state.¹³⁴

Thoreau accompanies his written journal entry with a small schematic sketch of the item. It is highly likely that it served not only as a pestle but also as a musical instrument, a lithophone, which produces a clear note when struck.¹³⁵ A bird's-head pestle or lithophone was in the collection that he bequeathed with the rest of his Native American items to the Boston Society of Natural History and is now in the Peabody Museum of Archaeology and Ethnology at Harvard University (see figure 7).¹³⁶ Whether the item in the museum is the same one that Hosmer showed to Thoreau has proved impossible to establish.

The addition of "some pure beauty to that pure utility" that Thoreau discerned in the bird's-head pestle or lithophone confirms his reluctance to dissociate the two qualities aesthetically. But not only is this item—and many others that combine beauty and utility—a subject of an albeit uncommon form, in this instance, of everyday aesthetics; it is for Thoreau a mindprint. As I explained earlier, this is the term he coins when discussing how a human-made item can evoke the person responsible for its making. In a March 1859 journal entry, in which he first uses the term, he writes, "I would fain know that I am treading in the tracks of human game,—that I am on the trail of mind,—and these little reminders never fail to set me right. When I see these signs I know that the subtle spirits that made them are not

FIGURE 7. Precontact Native American bird's-head pestle, stone, Concord, Massachusetts, collected by H. D. Thoreau. Courtesy of the Peabody Museum of Archaeology and Ethnology, Harvard University, 69-34-10/2382 (photo by Samantha Van Gerbig), © President and Fellows of Harvard College.

far off, into whatever form transmuted."[137] The further implications of this understanding are discussed in the chapter "Collections."

The fact that artifacts apprehensible in terms of everyday aesthetics—those that combine beauty and utility—are human-made differentiates them from purely natural phenomena, although the border between them is more permeable than one might initially assume. Much has been written about Thoreau's perception of beauty and sublimity in nature, the latter notably in the case of his account of his ascent of Mount Katahdin in 1846.[138] Literary scholar Lawrence Buell has placed Thoreau's claims regarding nature within the "decline and revival of the kinship between nonhuman and human" between the mid-nineteenth and late twentieth centuries, when "modern ecologism brought it [kinship] back."[139] But late twentieth- and twenty-first-century advocates of what Buell points to as high modernism have challenged the reputation of Thoreau as a champion of contemporary ecological consciousness. Ill-informed critics have sought to discredit him, for instance by bringing up the incident of the wildfire that he and his friend Edward Hoar inadvertently started in April 1844.[140]

Thoreau's engagement with the natural world before, during, and after his experiment in practical philosophy at Walden Pond was both ethical and aesthetic. For him, "the perception of beauty is a moral test."[141] This conviction is not reductive, for the perception of beauty for Thoreau is also—and, I suggest, equally—an aesthetic test. For him, what is most beautiful is not necessarily what is most obvious. In a journal entry in September 1858 he writes, "I was inclined to think that the truest beauty was that which surrounded us but which we failed to discern, that the forms and colors which adorn our daily life, not seen afar in the horizon, are our fairest jewelry."[142]

Furthermore, for Thoreau beauty is associative. That is, he associates it with inferences he makes about those who people a scene. These human associations are as often as not disappointing. Exploring this idea in a journal entry in October 1859, he writes, "When I see only the roof of a house above the woods and do not know whose it is, I presume that one of the worthies of the world dwells beneath it, and for a season I am exhilarated at the thought. I would fain sketch it that others may share my pleasure. But commonly, if I see or know the occupant, I am affected as by the sight of the almshouse or hospital."[143] This dissipation of aesthetic pleasure in the face of a realization of human actualities is a reminder that for Thoreau, the aesthetics of artistic representation and of nature are intertwined. Here it is worth recalling the August 1845 journal passage quoted earlier: "The perfect work of art is received again into the bosom of nature whence its material proceeded, and that criticism which can only detect its unnaturalness has no longer any office to fulfill."[144]

What, then, is the relationship between an aesthetics of human contrivance—art and items of practical utility—and of nature? The question of general principle that Arnold Berleant asks in his discussion of the aesthetics of art and nature addresses just this point. Berleant asks "whether there is one aesthetic or two, a single aesthetic that encompasses both art and nature, or one that is distinctively artistic and another that identifies the appreciation of natural beauty."[145] Berleant proposes what he terms an "aesthetics of engagement" that "encompasses both art and nature."[146] He continues, "It opens regions of experience that have been closed to aesthetic appreciation by theories that have survived through exclusion. By extending appreciation to nature in all its cultural manifestations, the entire sensible world is included within the purview of aesthetics."[147]

Berleant's is not the only strategy that philosophers have used to address the challenge that Ronald Hepburn set in his groundbreaking article that seeks to incorporate an analysis of the aesthetics of nature into what he termed a "unified aesthetic system."[148] This was a long-neglected topic when Hepburn first published his paper in 1966. Hepburn notes that expression theory was the last widely accepted unified aesthetic system. Thoreau's advocacy of nature as communication from the entity that Hepburn terms the

"Author of Nature" and Thoreau the "Artist who made the world and me" accords with his conception of artifacts—certain of them, at least—as mindprints.[149] Mindprints instantiate the inexpungible present of material items. They are not so much indicators of pasts that one can render into history as exemplars of overarching laws, human, natural, and divine. Mindprints, however difficult of interpretation, are above all communicative, even if ineffably so. Mindprints permit the collapse of the temporal distance between maker and percipient. This is a conception of a relationship between any given present and any given past sanctioned by Emerson's conception of history as he articulated it in his essay "History," first published in 1841. This conception rests on his claim, stated at the outset: "There is one mind common to all individual men. Every man is an inlet to the same and to all of the same."[150] In consequence, within this "mind common to all individual men" the passage of time need be of no account. In the light of this principle, and despite the fact that he developed a respect for particularities in certain respects that subverted simple trust in an Emersonian common mind, Thoreau could intuit a temporal collapse between his own thoughts and those of the person responsible for an item he considered to be a mindprint. In Thoreau's schema of the human past outlined in *A Week on the Concord and Merrimack Rivers*, the lives of sixty generations—of women in Thoreau's telling—"would span the interval from Eve to my own mother."[151] In his account, the passage of time scarcely registers change across these generations. But discerning commonality through such temporal collapse was not inevitable. It required appropriate moral and aesthetic engagement on his part. For Thoreau, some aspect of the mind of either the artist or artificer of an artifact and of the "Artist who made the world and me" can be accessible through that appropriate moral and aesthetic engagement with the item of creation, thereby allowing him to come "nearer to the vitals of the globe."[152] Thoreau's aesthetic system is expressive. This is so despite the distinction that Thoreau draws between the natural art of the Artist and the imitative art that mortals make.

Insofar as utilitarian items, in contradistinction to purposefully purposeless fine artworks, are creative responses to human needs rather than superfluous imitations, Thoreau is usually more sympathetically engaged with practical artifacts than with pictures or sculptures. In consequence, his aesthetics of the human-made gives precedence to the familiar and the everyday, to use Yuriko Saito's terms.[153] There may be but one aesthetics encompassing art, items of practical utility, and nature, but for Thoreau distinctions, even if of degree alone, nonetheless remain open to human discernment on both ethical and aesthetic grounds. Despite these distinctions, for Thoreau artistry, whether human or divine, encompasses them all.

[CHAPTER SIX]

Collections

In the previous chapter the focus was on a wide range of entities subject to aesthetic attention—artworks, utilitarian items, and manifestations of nature—that Thoreau and his circle encountered. Some of these were their own, such as Lidian Emerson's print after Guido Reni's *Aurora*, but most were not. In this chapter I turn to gatherings of items that Thoreau assembled deliberately and retained for study and contemplation. He did so until his death, after which he arranged for all of them, with two exceptions, to enter museums.

By the mid-nineteenth century, museums were still a relatively new type of institution dating from the late seventeenth century onward. They absorbed all kinds of material items, artworks, and natural history specimens, among others. These novel institutions proliferated from the early nineteenth century onward. They were among the major generators of knowledge claims in the European world. They only ceded their scholarly authority in many areas to even more novel institutions, research universities, in the early twentieth century.[1] As historian Steven Conn argues, the formation of collections and then museums in North America occurred predominantly between the 1830s and the 1860s within a paradigm of a search for order and meaning in the material world. This was based on the premise that one could make knowledge claims derived from observations that led to the distinction of particular characteristics. These observations permitted classification within a schema held to represent some truth about the world. This was no easy task, as those who undertook it made clear.

Ralph Waldo Emerson indicated the challenge in his essay "Experience," published in 1844: "I take this evanescence and lubricity of all objects, which lets them slip through our fingers then when we clutch hardest, to be the most unhandsome part of our condition. Nature does not like to be observed, and likes that we should be her fools and playmates."[2] Emerson proposed that meaning was available not only through observation but through the discernment of unifying spiritual causes and eternal laws that on his account governed all things. As I stated in the chapter "Worlds," he specifies this in his 1837 address at Harvard's commencement, claiming "there is no puzzle, but one design unites and animates the farthest pinnacle and the lowest trench."[3]

Throughout the nineteenth century, American society developed an increasing concern with the ordering and reordering of material items so that they should no longer appear what Emerson called "a dull miscellany and lumber-room," but offer meanings, whether in and of themselves or in consequence of their place in an orderly scheme.[4] Museums were the principal institutional means of addressing this project. They did so in the first instance by means of classification: the discernment of similarities and differences among the sensually apprehensible properties exhibited by those material items. The Smithsonian Institution, founded in 1836, became the largest single body in America devoted to this project. The Smithsonian was itself divided into several specialized units, and although these have changed, it remains so. Other museums soon followed.

Henry David Thoreau may well have been Emerson's protégé, indebted to him for intellectual stimulation no less than for material support in his role as gardener and odd job man to the Sage of Concord, but he was quite recalcitrantly his own man. There was a profound difference of ideas between the two thinkers concerning material items and what might be learned from them. Thoreau is far more circumspect than Emerson when considering material items, as his discussion "Brute Neighbors," the twelfth chapter of *Walden*, suggests. In an introductory comic dialogue between a Hermit (representing himself) and his visitor, a Poet (representing the transcendentalist Ellery Channing), Thoreau parodies idealism by abandoning meditation to go fishing, thereby suggesting that what is of value—spirit—is not to be found in the mind alone, but by direct experience of nature: within nature, not—as for Emerson—through it. As literary scholar Richard Schneider points out, "Once one recognizes this dualistic debate between the Transcendentalist and the naturalist in Thoreau's attitude, every natural object that he describes takes on a double meaning, one physical and one symbolic."[5]

The dialogue concluded, Thoreau begins a new section of the chapter in his own authorial voice with the hortatory question: "Why do precisely these objects which we behold make a world?"[6] This is the passage I cited near the beginning of this book, where I suggested that Thoreau's use of the indefinite article is deliberate. The implication of a plurality of worlds derives from an explicit statement in a journal entry written shortly after moving into his house at Walden Pond in July 1845. There he writes that "we seem to lead our human lives amid a concentric system of worlds, of realm on realm, close bordering on each other."[7] I want now to examine this matter of *worlds* with a little care, attending to its precision: a precision that Thoreau's own use of the term *precisely* might suggest is appropriate.

Thoreau writes of "these objects which we behold"—these being the "brute neighbors" that are the subject of this chapter. He begins with the "mice which haunted my house," which "were not the common ones, which are said to have been introduced into the country, but a wild native kind not found in the village." He continues, "I sent one to a distinguished naturalist, and it interested him much." That distinguished naturalist was Louis Agassiz, of whom more below. Thoreau then writes of birds—phoebes, robins, partridges, woodcocks, and turtle doves. Birds were a long-term interest of Thoreau, and he developed a relatively novel way of studying them using a spy glass. There follows a detailed description of a battle between red and black ants and how he took a wood chip on which a black ant was fighting two red ants into his house, where he placed it on a windowsill beneath a tumbler and studied the combat under what he calls a microscope, actually a single lens. He then describes the annual arrival in the fall of the loon, and he concludes this chapter by describing in detail his study of its behavior from his boat. He accomplishes all this with great precision, during which we keep in mind his initial question: "Why do precisely these objects which we behold make a world?"

Thoreau's mentor, Emerson, writes of the constitution of *the* world; but in writing of "*a* world" Thoreau signals a difference of conception that is all the difference in the world. Unlike Emerson, Thoreau does not assume the existence of a totality that exists as such, the spiritual character and meaning of which we might attempt to grasp in its entirety. Thoreau accedes to the principle of contingency, acknowledging multiple possible viewpoints—he sketches those of the Hermit and of the Poet specifically on this occasion in the introductory passage in "Brute Neighbors"—and each of these viewpoints encompasses *a* world. Such thinking may be far from Nelson Goodman's ways of "worldmaking," but Thoreau's worlds, "realm on realm," are prismatic and not necessarily wholly compatible and reconcilable in their aggregate entirety.[8] They are *worlds*. Each world coheres by comprising its own selection of items. Each, I suggest, has an *aesthetic* coherence.

Thoreau engaged in such selection repeatedly, and in various registers: first, by means of observation and description (as in "Brute Neighbors"); and, second, by means of collection. Collection therefore takes on a particular significance as we try to understand Thoreau's engagement with mindprints, among other items, that constitute worlds he apprehended in aesthetic as well as in ethical and metaphysical terms. Thoreau collected in several categories. He formed collections of botanical and mineralogical specimens; birds' eggs, nests, and skins; a few animal pelts and antlers; and ancient North American Indigenous artifacts. Channing noted: "His pockets were large enough to hold and keep not only his implements, but the large multitude of objects which he brought home from his walks; objects of all kinds,—pieces of wood or stone, lichens, seeds, nuts, apples, or whatever he had found for his uses. For he was a vigorous collector, never omitting to get and keep every possible thing in his direction of study."[9]

Thoreau's collecting accelerated in the late 1840s. After the Thoreau family had moved to a house on Main Street in Concord in 1850, Thoreau's private space was the finished attic above the main part of the house. There he constructed shelves from boards gathered from the riverbank, later adding boxes and bins. He arranged and displayed his various collections beneath the sloping attic ceilings, as described by Channing: "He tucked plants away in his soft hat in place of a botany-box. His study (a place in the garret) held its dry miscellany of botanical specimens; its corner of canes, its cases of eggs and lichens, and a weight of Indian arrow-heads and hatchets, besides a store of nuts, of which he was as fond as squirrels."[10] Surrounded by meaningful material items, he could entertain his friends, and read and write in peace.[11]

A superficial assumption would be that Thoreau shared a proclivity widespread in European and European diasporic culture for house dwellers to surround themselves with items with personal associations, whether souvenirs or family relics, singly or in collections of like items, often in profusion.[12] Thoreau, though, had no time for superfluities. He made this clear in his purely functional furnishing of his Walden Pond house. He reports provocatively in *Walden*: "A lady once offered me a mat, but as I had no room to spare within the house, nor time to spare within or without to shake it, I declined it, preferring to wipe my feet on the sod before my door."[13] He limited his attic furniture to his cot from that house, a bureau, and two chairs.[14]

I assume that Thoreau selected and retained each one of his collection items for a purpose. That purpose, broadly speaking, concerns Thoreau's increasing attention to how material items in the natural world relate to one another, not in accordance with Emerson's ideas—as "types and symbols of Eternity," as William Wordsworth put it[15]—but in a proto-ecological manner of regarding nature as an internally, mutually interacting entity not dependent on external forces, much as the great German geographer and naturalist Alexander von Humboldt had proposed. Laura Dassow Walls has shown that Thoreau immersed himself in Humboldt's works as soon as English translations became available, from 1849 onward, stating, "Humboldt arrived in Thoreau's hands at the very moment Thoreau both needed him and was prepared to apprehend him."[16] Humboldt helped Thoreau to free himself from Emersonian transcendentalism. Thoreau's carefully recorded attention to material items, both in the field and brought back to his attic, was a mark of his newly consolidated purpose in the last decade of his life. As historian Andrea Wulf has noted, "What Humboldt observed across the globe, Thoreau did at home."[17] Thoreau's collection of material items was an integral part of his philosophical inquiry into the entanglements of humans with the natural world, whether "raw" in the form of plants and minerals or "cooked" in the form of human-made artifacts.[18]

In taking a more detailed look at Thoreau's collection activity, I begin with the world of flora. Thoreau's fascination with plants began while he was an undergraduate at Harvard between 1833 and 1837. He studied natural history with the only person then in the college teaching the subject, the college librarian, Thaddeus William Harris.[19] In 1837 Harris and a number of undergraduates whom he had encouraged, including Thoreau, formed the college's Natural History Society. Harris led the members on field trips to find and identify plants, birds, and the insects that were his special study. Harris introduced Thoreau to a practice—collection and observation walks—that he would continue for the rest of his life. The two men remained friends until Harris's death in 1856.[20]

Several of Thoreau's companions on walks described his extraordinary knowledge of local flora, where they were to be found, and when they should bloom. In his "Biographical Sketch" of Thoreau, Emerson draws particular attention to Thoreau's facility in this regard. Emerson notes that "he knew the country like a fox or a bird, and passed through it as freely by paths of his own." Emerson notes that, on one of their walks together, having searched successfully for a plant he knew should be in flower, Thoreau "drew out of his breast-pocket his diary, and read the names of all the plants that should bloom on this day whereof he kept an account as a banker when his notes fall due. The Cypripedium not due until to-morrow. He thought, that, if waked up from a trance, in this swamp, he could tell by the plants what time of the year it was within two days."[21] Emerson observed: "Under his arm he carried an old music-book to press plants."[22]

From 1850 onward Thoreau assembled about nine hundred pressed botanical specimens on sheets of paper, most of which include a Latin plant name but only about half of which are annotated with a collection site.[23] He was likely stimulated by the publication in 1848 of a work by a botanist whom the Harvard corporation had appointed to the faculty in preference to Harris, Asa Gray, *A Manual of the Botany of the Northern United States*.[24]

Of equal importance to the development of Thoreau's interest in plants and his eventual use of Latin names was George Emerson's *Report on Trees and Shrubs Growing Naturally in the Forests of Massachusetts* (1846).[25]

During Thoreau's lifetime, increasingly professionalizing academic scientists were developing their procedures and assumptions. The ascent of such figures at Harvard as Louis Agassiz and Asa Gray marked a shift that contemporaries noted in favor of emergent academic science, with its procedures of methodical observation, experimentation, and claims of unemotional objectivity. Even Emerson, who valued poetic understanding highly, would write of Thoreau: "He resumed his endless walks and miscellaneous studies making every day some new acquaintance with Nature, though as yet never speaking of zoölogy or botany, since, though very studious of natural facts, he was incurious of technical and textual science."[26] In the mid-nineteenth century "technical and textual science" was displacing "miscellaneous studies" and mere "acquaintance with Nature." Thoreau is direct about his preference, although he refuses to make a clear-cut distinction between science and poetic—or aesthetic—apprehension. In January 1852 he writes in his journal, "Botanies instead of being the poetry are the prose of flowers. I do not mean to underrate Linnaeu's [Linnaeus's] admirable nomenclature much of which is itself poetry."[27] The following month, following a description of the method of bee hunting used by Concord farmer Reuben Rice, which showed a considerable knowledge of bees and their habits, he writes, "I love best the unscientific man's knowledge there is so much more humanity in it."[28]

The ultimate expression of pretended objectivity in scientific writing is the relentless use of the passive voice to expunge from any account individual human peculiarity and even the acknowledgment of agency. Philosophers are almost invariably suspicious of the passive voice, for good reason, as it often evades or conceals, though poorly, agency and responsibility. Thoreau was aware of this flaw and warns of it at the outset of *Walden*. Stating that he will retain the use of the first person singular—*I*—he notes, "We commonly do not remember that it is, after all, always the first person that is speaking."[29] Recent commentators who adhere to notions of unproblematic scientific objectivity—and by using this phrase I am not endorsing the nonsensical claim that scientific facts are no more than opinions—tend to see no middle ground between a spurious objectivity voiced passively and a flow of poetic and purely subjective utterance. The zoologist John Anderson suggests that "the florid nature of his [Thoreau's] language could not but encourage serious scientists to dismiss more and more of natural history as being too vague and too philosophical to be worthy of attention."[30] There may well be some scientists for whom Thoreau's language is too philosophical to be readily comprehensible, in which case it is best left to philosophers to point out its value.

Certain of Thoreau's fundamental assumptions are foreign to scientific procedure. One example is the claim that phenomena can best be understood through personal intuition as expressions of laws independently rather than inductively ascertained. Yet I believe that Thoreau's fundamental assumptions often have values of their own, including within the context of the examination of phenomena that scientists often claim as their exclusive preserve. Thoreau himself had developed the beginnings of such an attitude by November 1857. In a key passage in his journal, he writes:

> I think that the man of science makes this mistake, and the mass of mankind along with him: that you should coolly give your chief attention to the phenomenon which excites you as something independent on you, and not as it is related to you. The important fact is its effect on me. He thinks that I have no business to see anything else but just what he defines the rainbow to be, but I care not whether my vision of truth is a waking thought or dream remembered, whether it is seen in the light or in the dark. It is the subject of the vision, the truth alone, that concerns me. The philosopher for whom rainbows, etc., can be explained away never saw them. With regard to such objects, I find that it is not they themselves (with which the men of science deal) that concern me; the point of interest is somewhere between me and them (i.e. the objects).[31]

Thoreau does not develop precisely how "the point of interest is somewhere between me and them," but his acknowledgment that perceived and percipient are in what one might term a relationship of entanglement not precluding mutual influence aligns Thoreau's emergent epistemology with certain contemporary ideas. To avoid anachronism, I think it worth suggesting that the epistemological sketch that Thoreau offers in this passage is a fundamentally *aesthetic* idea. Again and again in Thoreau's accounts, the effect on him of an item he perceives is dependent on an explanation of that perception as one of feeling involving the emotions; that is, it is a matter of *sensibility*. Arnold Berleant is unusual among contemporary philosophers in having developed such a conception of aesthetics as, "at its base, a theory of sensibility."[32] For Thoreau, this sensibility is "the truth alone." We shall see its most highly developed expression in Thoreau's discussion of Native American arrowheads, but first I turn to the other collection categories that concerned him.

As well as plants, Thoreau gathered minerals and geological specimens, for the most part from Concord and its vicinity; "a large number of the nests and eggs of the birds of New England"; and "Indian antiquities."[33] In spite of the disappearance of most of Thoreau's ornithological collection, it is worth mentioning that he was a consistent observer of the world of birds. Initially, like most people of his generation, he examined birds as dead specimens, whether trapped or shot. His acceptance as a corresponding member of the Boston Society of Natural History in 1850 followed his donation the previous year of the remains of a goshawk that the Concord inhabitant Jacob Farmer had shot and given to Thoreau. The society's curator of birds, Samuel Cabot, was able to establish that it represented a peculiarly American species (the northern goshawk, *Accipiter gentilis*) that differed from the European goshawk, a distinction that John James Audubon had denied.[34] Acknowledging Thoreau's gift, Cabot wrote that "his skin is already off and stuffed,—his remains dissected, measured, and deposited in alcohol."[35]

Like many of his contemporaries, Thoreau also collected eggs and nests. He records fighting a fire in a farm field in the summer of 1850: "The fire stopped within a few inches of a partridge's nest today June 4th—whom we took off in our hands and found 13 cream colored eggs."[36] However, Thoreau's relationship to birds changed after he acquired a telescope or spyglass in 1854. With it he was able to observe birds closely as living creatures in their habitat, a relatively new practice for naturalists. This accords with Thoreau's aesthetic attitude to the vitality of the natural world. Channing drew a distinction between Thoreau's procedures and the violent collecting that was then the norm: "Hawks, ducks, sparrows, thrushes, and migrating warblers, in all their variety, he carefully perused with his fieldglass,—an instrument purchased with toilsome discretion, and carried in its own strong case and pocket. Thoreau named all the birds without a gun, a weapon he never used in mature years. He neither killed nor imprisoned any animal, unless driven by acute needs."[37] The standard way of identifying birds at this time was to shoot them so that the naturalist could closely examine each dead body and classify it. Identification manuals were published to aid the ornithologist. Alexander Wilson's *American Ornithology* was first published in nine volumes between 1808 and 1814.[38] Its descriptions are based on the examination of dead birds, not the observation of living ones. Thoreau owned the 1852 single-volume edition.[39] In a journal entry in March 1853, Thoreau muses on the advantages of the spyglass over the gun: "Would it not be well to carry a spy glass in order to watch these shy birds—such as ducks & hawks—? In some respects methinks it would be better than a gun. The latter brings them nearer dead, but the former alive. You can identify the species better by killing the bird—because it was a dead specimen that was so minutely described—but you can study the habits & appearance best in the living specimen."[40] He tried out a spyglass in June, and ten months later, in April, 1854, bought his own in Boston for eight dollars.[41] He carried it with him constantly. The spyglass survives in the Concord Museum.[42] Yet just four months later, Thoreau records his collection of a turtle, which involved killing it. This prompted self-disgust: "I have just been through the process of killing the cistudo for the sake of science—but I cannot excuse myself for this murder—& see that such actions are inconsistent with the poetic perception—however they may serve science—& will affect the quality of my observations. I pray that I may walk more innocently & serenely through nature—No reasoning whatever reconciles one to this act—It affects my day injuriously—I have lost some self respect—I have a murderer's experience in a degree."[43] In addition to the ethical reflection, the important point here is Thoreau's definition of the cognitive frameworks within which he conceives of his experiences of natural phenomena. One "may serve science," while the other is "poetic perception"; on his account, the two are irreconcilable.[44] I take "poetic perception" to be *aesthetic perception*, and it is aesthetic perception that principally governs Thoreau's cognitive processes in respect to the material worlds of which the turtle, in this instance, is a constituent.

Thoreau's extant mineral collection contains just twelve types, each represented by one, two, or three specimens.[45] This may or may not be its original extent. Robert Thorson, a geoscientist, has attempted to give Thoreau's mineral collection due weight. He notes that Thoreau's interest in the world of rocks may have been stimulated by the example of Lemuel Shattuck, who in his *History of Concord* (1835) included "a section on geology that was typical of the era, being long on classification and short on explanation."[46] Shattuck's pages on geology form part of his chapter on natural history.[47] Thorson surmises that Thoreau may have taken the list of minerals given by Shattuck, or a better one provided by the Amherst College professor of chemistry and natural history Edward Hitchcock in his *Final Report on the Geology of Massachusetts* (1841), as the starting point for building his own collection.[48] Thorson calls Thoreau's assemblage "an odd collection. Thoreau mixed mundane specimens of local rock with gem-like crystals of quartz, gleaming masses of metal, and several curios like sulfur and tufa, all of which can apparently be found within places where Thoreau traveled."[49] Several specimens have brittle, discolored, handwritten labels attached.

Thoreau had a very specific reason to take an interest in minerals. His father, John, and his uncle, Charles Dunbar, founded and ran a pencil manufactory in Concord. In the late 1830s, Henry Thoreau developed an innovative means of improving the core that minimized the effect of inclusions in the graphite (also called plumbago) that resulted in an uneven, faint, or smeared line. He came up with the idea of milling the New England graphite more finely than had been done before in a mill of his own and his father's design, then mixing it with fine clay as a binder to produce a core that wrote evenly and reliably.[50] The result was a pencil as fine as those produced in France since the 1790s by a similar process of combining milled graphite and clay, introduced by Nicolas-Jacques Conté. This kind of pencil, produced in America for the first time by the Thoreau workshop, could be manufactured in different gradations of hardness for different purposes, giving the Thoreau enterprise a considerable competitive advantage.[51] To have come up with this solution, Henry Thoreau showed no small degree of mineralogical knowledge.

The Thoreaus obtained recognition for their achievement, including awards and testimonials. In 1844 Emerson's brother-in-law, the physician and geologist Charles T. Jackson, wrote, "I would especially recommend to Engineers your fine hard pencils as capable of giving a very fine line, the points being remarkably even and firm."[52] Emerson presumably remembered this endorsement, as well as Thoreau's continuing mineralogical and geological interest and knowledge, when in 1847 he recommended Thoreau to Jackson, who in that year was appointed to lead a government team to survey an area rich in copper as the United States geologist for the Lake Superior land district in Michigan. Assistantships were sought-after political patronage appointments, and Thoreau's candidacy got nowhere.[53]

In his "Biographical Sketch," Emerson claimed that after the success of Thoreau's pencil-making innovations, "His friends congratulated him that he had now opened his way to fortune. But he replied, that he would never make another pencil. 'Why should I? I would not do again what I have done once.'"[54] This is misleading. As engineer Henry Petrovski has shown, Thoreau's involvement in pencil making continued, even if not entirely consistently. He put considerable effort into trying to improve the insertion of the core into the wood casing. He sought to pay for the publication of *A Week on the Concord and Merrimack Rivers* in 1849 with the proceeds of the sale of pencils in New York, though he had to sell them at a loss owing to the prevalence of imported pencils.[55] He was indebted to his publisher and used the proceeds of his surveying practice to pay off the debt over the following four years.[56]

By 1853 a new use for finely milled graphite led the Thoreaus to abandon pencil making. Instead, they supplied large quantities of their milled graphite to a Boston printing firm that had developed a process of electrotyping or stereotyping. This entailed producing a mold from a typeset bed from which printers could derive plates so that they could print the same page on several presses simultaneously. This proved profitable for the Thoreaus, who later sold their proprietary finely milled graphite to other printing firms in Boston and New York.[57] After his father died in 1859, Henry Thoreau officially took over the business, although, as Kathy Fedorko has pointed out, his sister Sophia is likely to have done much of the work.[58]

Thoreau seems never to have relinquished his interest in practical mineralogy. In *Walden* he states that if he wanted a boy to learn about the arts and sciences, he would not send him to listen to a lecture but would have him make "his own jackknife from the ore which he had dug and smelted."[59] Thoreau's mineral collection intersected not only with his passionate interest in the character of the environs in which he lived but also with the ever-pressing demands of his family business. He was only ever to relinquish those demands temporarily when pursuing his projects in practical philosophy.

Clearly Thoreau was far from alone in his interest in geology and minerals. Collecting minerals was a widely shared activity in the eighteenth and nineteenth centuries. Furniture makers produced specialized compartmentalized cabinets for the preservation of specimens. An especially impressive surviving example is a group of walnut cabinets custom built for the physician, antiquarian, and natural historian John Woodward. Upon his death in 1728, Woodward bequeathed his collection of nearly ten thousand geological specimens, minerals, fossils, and shells to the University of Cambridge with an endowment for a lectureship. The original cabinets and their contents are on display in the university's Sedgwick Museum of Earth Sciences.[60] Thoreau's collection was obviously far more modest, but he ensured that it was housed appropriately. Using his woodworking skills, he built compartmentalized stacking boxes for it. One set of boxes made of mahogany and pine—a stack of three, each with eighteen compartments and a sliding lid—survives in the Concord Museum.[61] However, Thoreau made this set not for himself but for a fellow mineralogy enthusiast. He brought it with him as a gift when visiting Joseph and Ellen Osgood in Cohasset in 1849, while on his way with Ellery Channing to Cape Cod for a walking tour. Though it was long assumed to have been a gift from Thoreau to Joseph Osgood, historian Reed Gochberg has recently established that Thoreau intended the set of boxes for Ellen Osgood, née Sewall.[62]

Ellen Sewall, the daughter of a Unitarian minister in Scituate, had stayed with her aunt, a boarder of the Thoreaus, for two weeks in the summer of 1839. Both young Thoreau brothers, John and Henry, were smitten, and both courted her. In 1840 Ellen accepted John's marriage proposal, but Sewall parental pressure ended the engagement. Thereupon Henry proposed by mail, but Ellen's father, who abhorred the transcendentalism of the apostate Emerson, obliged his daughter to refuse him. Four years later she married the Unitarian minister Joseph Osgood.[63] Thoreau remained friends with Ellen Osgood and developed a friendship with her husband. Of the two, it was Ellen Osgood who was the geology enthusiast, a fact well known to John Thoreau, who as a Christmas gift in 1839 gave her South American opals for her mineral collection.[64] One pink opal is among the Thoreau and Sewall Family Papers in the Huntington Library, San Marino, California.[65] Gochberg shows that Ellen Sewall likely developed her enthusiasm for geology when studying from the age of thirteen at the Roxbury Female Academy, just south of Boston. Minerals provided a long-term affective link between Thoreau and his one known love, whom as a young man he had courted and lost.

The third collection that Thoreau formed was what the Boston Society of Natural History described as his "collection of Indian antiquities, consisting of stone implements and weapons (chiefly) found by himself in Concord."[66] How did Thoreau come to form this extensive and impressive collection indicative of a world of human habitation prior to contact with settlers? Thoreau was constantly aware of the past presence in particular localities of Indigenous peoples. He knew from experience that fall plowing and winter frost heaves turned up Indigenous implements. Having found three arrowheads on November 16, 1850, he notes that "the season for them began some time ago, as soon as farmers had sown their winter rye—but the spring after the melting of the snow is still better."[67] Nathaniel Hawthorne, describing his own proclivity for gathering Native artifacts on the land surrounding the Old Manse in Concord, admitted that Thoreau had first set him on the search, and that Thoreau had, in Hawthorne's words, "a strange faculty of finding what the Indians have left behind them."[68] Emerson reports an anecdote regarding Thoreau's "strange facility": "One day, walking with a stranger, who inquired where Indian arrow-heads could be found, he replied, 'Everywhere,' and, stooping forward, picked one on the instant from the ground."[69]

Thoreau's companions were constantly aware of his sharpness of sensory perception. As Yuriko Saito suggests, "Aesthetics as a philosophical inquiry should start with wondering at what we take for granted."[70] Thoreau was a master of attending to what others take for granted, with a sensory acuity that doubtless heightened his capacity for aesthetic responses to a wide range of phenomena. Among those items in which Thoreau took a long-term interest are the many material remains of earlier inhabitants that he found over the decades, recording his observations and reflections in his journal. For instance, in his entry for August 22, 1860, he describes finding thirty-one pottery shards, some decorated, in a recently washed out section of Clamshell Bluff on the bank of the Sudbury or Musketaquid River, plus, in another area of the site, "a delicate stone tool . . . of a soft slate stone,"

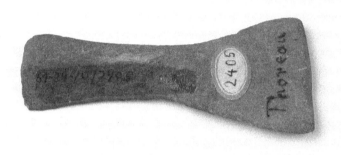

FIGURE 8. Precontact Native American clam-shell opener, stone, Concord, Massachusetts, collected by H. D. Thoreau. Courtesy of the Peabody Museum of Archaeology and Ethnology, Harvard University, 69-34-10/2405, © President and Fellows of Harvard College.

which he sketched.[71] The implement remained in his collection and is now in the Peabody Museum of Archaeology and Ethnology at Harvard University. It is a single stone, delicately fashioned to form what appears to be a gently flaring handle and a wider flat, flared blade. Thoreau suspected that it was used for opening clams, and it is currently described in the online collections database of the Peabody Museum as a "clam-shell opener" (see figure 8).[72]

Stimulated by his aesthetic responses to apparently ordinary and casually distributed projectile points and other stone implements, Thoreau expressed a profound respect for their Indigenous makers: "It is a matter of astonishment how the Indians ever made them with no iron or steel tools to work with—And I doubt whether one of our mechanics with all the aids of Yankee ingenuity could soon learn to copy one of the thousands under our feet."[73]

Even though adherence to prejudices regarding the relative status of the "savage" and the "civilized," prevalent in contemporaneous American society, colors numbers of Thoreau's statements about Native peoples, as discussed in "Migrants," Indigenous arrowheads gave rise to one of Thoreau's most protracted, complex and significant articulations of his ideas about the power of material items to constitute a world. This takes the form of an extended meditation on Indigenous arrowheads in his journal entry for March 28, 1859. Thoreau's attention to them is neither historical nor ethical, but rather aesthetic. As we have seen, he articulates an intuition about them as mindprints. Thoreau does not discuss their beauty or their sublimity, but rather their evocative intensity. He writes, "Each one yields me a thought. I come nearer to the maker of it than if I found his bones."[74] For Thoreau, the arrowhead "was originally winged for but a short flight, but it still, to my mind's eye, wings its way through the ages, bearing a message from the hand that shot it."[75] Although geoscientist Robert Thorson notes that Thoreau's "archaeological interpretations were quite keen for a discipline that had not yet coalesced,"[76] the significance of arrowheads for him is not that they evoke particular, identifiable times in the past. Rather, for Thoreau they are an abiding presence that is also an eternal present. Arrowheads, not only those made by American settlers' predecessors in New England but from a vast array of peoples and times, exist in a perpetual sequence: making, use, awaiting discovery, loss, rediscovery, and reuse. In his vision: "Myriads of arrow-points lie sleeping in the skin of the revolving earth, while meteors revolve in space."[77] Yet they do not all remain perpetually in the dust. For Thoreau, they cycle through the earth and through human hands, surviving all the destruction that humans wreak. He writes, "When some Vandal chieftain has razed to the earth the British Museum, and, perchance, the winged bulls from Nineveh shall have lost most if not all of their features, the arrowheads which the museum contains will, perhaps, find themselves at home again in familiar dust, and resume their shining in new springs upon the bared surface of the earth then, to be picked up for the thousandth time by the shepherd or savage that may be wandering there, and once more suggest their story to him."[78] Furthermore, in his conception: "They cannot be said to be lost nor found."[79] Rather, arrowheads outlast the succession of individual humans in a mutually constitutive relationship between humans more generally and such stone items. He ends his meditation with an extraordinary soliloquy in the person of an arrowhead:

> When you pick up an arrowhead and put it in your pocket, it may say: "Eh, you think you have got me, do you? But I shall wear a hole in your pocket at last, or if you put me in your cabinet, your heir or great-grandson will forget me or throw me out the window directly, or when the house falls I shall drop into the cellar, and there I shall lie quite at home again. Ready to be found again, eh? Perhaps some new red man that is to come will fit me to a shaft and make me do his bidding for a bow-shot. What reck I?"[80]

This is not a historical approach in the common sense of the term. Neither is Thoreau's attitude that of the many "Euro-American collectors, who held them [arrowheads] up as signifiers of supposed Indigenous primitivity or radical difference and enjoyed arranging them into geometric or floral shapes," as historian Christine DeLucia has put it.[81] Thoreau may have been highly attentive to the particular features of Indigenous lithic items and surmised that their distribution and concentration indicate successive waves of human habitation.[82] However, he makes no attempt to construct a history of Native presence in terms of changes over time. His aesthetics as applied to arrowheads advances a form of *historical understanding* as I define it in contradistinction to *historical retrieval*. That is, "historical understanding encompasses a great sequence and even reticulation of the pasts of tangible things as they relate to the present, the very here and now."[83] I claim that Thoreau's approach to arrowheads is *a form* of historical understanding because it proposes the circumstances of existence of an arrowhead in terms that are speculative and generalizing rather than specifically inferable from the particular characteristics and successive circumstances of any given example. I define the latter, specific, form of historical understanding as offering an "account for the present effects of a tangible thing in the inevasible light of an entire pattern of past use, acknowledging that successive uses unavoidably affect subsequent understandings of earlier uses."[84] Thoreau proposes not particularities but a principle, yet that principle has historical efficacy because its aesthetic basis can prompt the very curiosity that leads the inquirer to grasp particularities in its light.

Thoreau's fascination with the evocative—the aesthetic—power of arrowheads was of long standing. In one of his earliest journal entries, for October 26, 1837, the young Thoreau recounts how he and his brother, John, were searching for Indigenous arrowheads beside the Sudbury or Musketaquid River near Clamshell Bluffs. Thoreau reports describing the features of the land as though from an Indigenous point of view as they stood together on what he took to be an "eligible lookout post." He states that he "broke forth into an extravagant eulogy on those savage times," imagining the presence in ages past of Native peoples on the very site where they stood. He recounts:

> "Here," I exclaimed, "stood Tahatawan; and there, (to complete the period,) is Tahatawan's arrowhead[.]"
> We instantly proceeded to sit down on the spot I had pointed to, and I, to carry out the joke, to lay bare an ordinary stone which my whim had selected, when lo! the first I laid hands on, the grubbing stone that was to be, proved a most perfect arrowhead, as sharp as if just from the hands of the Indian fabricator!!!"[85]

Commentators often trace Thoreau's serious concern with Native American items—and Native Americans themselves—to this incident in his youth. Historian Duncan Caldwell sees this as a transformative moment in Thoreau's intellectual and emotional development, claiming that such arrowheads prompted Thoreau to acknowledge that whoever had made them were persons as real as himself, and therefore, even though unidentifiable, "Thoreau's correspondents across time."[86] They peopled the landscape. Caldwell also claims that Thoreau's continuing search for Native American stone artifacts as traces of those who peopled the landscape was a means of capturing the particular spectral presence of his brother, John, whose death from tetanus in 1842 haunted Henry for the rest of his life.[87] Whether or not prompted by continuing grief over his brother's death, by the time he wrote of arrowheads as mindprints twenty-two years later, Thoreau had developed this youthful fancy and its accompanying apparently fortuitous discovery into a mature intuition of historical understanding. That historical understanding depended on his conception of relationships between humans and items in material worlds, whether human-made, human-modified, or beyond immediate human intervention.

Contradictory though it may appear, I contend that Thoreau complemented his speculative and generalizing form of aesthetic historical understanding with another that depends on what Channing epitomized as the "particular and definite." "The particular and definite were much to Thoreau," Channing wrote in his 1873 memoir of the philosopher.[88] He made this remark in the course of an instructive episode in their friendship that occurred on November 9, 1851, during one of their regular walks. Describing it, Channing quotes Thoreau's manuscript journal entry, self-interestedly but understandably omitting Thoreau's more critical remarks about Channing himself. I quote the original passage from Thoreau's journal:

> In our walks C takes out his note-book some times & tries to write as I do—but all in vain. He soon puts it up again—or contents himself with scrawling some sketch of the landscape. Observing me still scribbling he will say that *he* confines himself to the ideal—purely ideal remarks—he leaves the facts to me. Sometimes too he will say a little petulantly—"*I* am universal. I have nothing to do with the particular and definite." He is the moodiest person perhaps that I ever saw. . . . I too would fain set down something beside facts. Facts should only be as the frame to my pictures—They should be material to the mythology which I am writing. Not facts to assist men to make money—farmers to farm profitably in any common sense. Facts to tell who I am—and where I have been—or what I have thought. . . . My facts shall all be falsehoods to the common

sense. I would so state facts that they shall be significant shall be myths or mythologic. Facts which the mind perceived—thoughts which the body thought with these I deal—I too cherish vague and misty forms—vaguest when the cloud at which I gaze is dissipated quite & nought but the skyey depths are seen."[89]

The particular and definite, as they constitute a world—whether of botany, ornithology, geology, or the history of Indigenous peoples—are, in Thoreau's estimate, significant only insofar as they are what he terms "mythologic." They overturn received opinion; they are "falsehoods to the common sense." Yet the pictures he would make had to be framed by facts. Channing reported: "His habit was to go abroad a portion of each day, to fields or woods or the Concord River. 'I go out,' he said, 'to see what I have caught in my traps which I set for facts.'" Channing perceptively summarized Thoreau's purpose: "He looked to fabricate an epitome of creation, and give us a homœopathy of Nature."[90]

In contrast to Thoreau, the outsider naturalist and philosopher, the Swiss natural historian Louis Agassiz was the consummate scientist insider.[91] Agassiz arrived in Boston from Neuchâtel, Switzerland, in the fall of 1846. He had been invited to lecture by the Lowell Institute and would soon be appointed to head the new Lawrence Scientific School at Harvard. He began teaching in the spring of 1848. By 1846 Louis Agassiz had achieved renown in two areas: paleoichthyology and glaciology. He had published his monumental five-volume *Recherches sur les poissons fossiles* between 1833 and 1843 and his *Études sur les glaciers* in 1840.[92] However, Agassiz is best known today as the leading apologist for human polygenism, the theory of independent human ethnicities and separate creations, the various human races being endowed with unequal capacities. This is not the element in Agassiz's thinking—rebarbative as it is—that I shall discuss here.

Agassiz shared with Thoreau an emphasis on acute observation, the techniques and advantages of which he had learned from his professor of anatomy and physiology at the University of Munich, Ignaz Döllinger. In his autobiographical sketch, Agassiz wrote, "With Döllinger I learned to value the accuracy of observation. As I was living in his house he gave me personal instruction in the use of the microscope.... Döllinger was a careful, minute, persevering observer, as well as a deep thinker."[93] In 1831 Agassiz moved to Paris, where he became the protégé of Georges Cuvier at the Muséum national d'histoire naturelle. From Cuvier he learned the forensic skills on which he based his subsequent research, notably the method of applying the principle of the correlation of parts to reconstruct fragmentary fossil remnants. This allowed him to infer the complete animal from just one surviving part of its body and then to place the reconstructed creature within the natural order of species.[94] Although Alexander von Humboldt had returned to Berlin from Paris in 1827, he visited the French capital, and Agassiz came under his influence, especially in matters of making detailed observations in the field. Humboldt's interest secured a chair for Agassiz at the Prussian-dominated University of Neuchâtel in 1832, and Humboldt secured the funds for Agassiz's journey to the United States in 1846.[95] Thoreau responded enthusiastically to Humboldt's work, so the two men, Agassiz and Thoreau, shared a high regard for the great German.[96]

Agassiz accepted Cuvier's assertion that there was no evidence of species having developed from other species. Agassiz followed Cuvier in holding that species were immutable, an opinion that his work on glaciers and the effects of ice reinforced. In 1837 he introduced the concept of an ice age— later, ice ages—to account for geological phenomena caused by glaciation.[97] His proposal that a vast sheet of ice had advanced southward during the Pleistocene epoch to the borders of the Mediterranean and Caspian Seas allowed him to develop a new theory of catastrophism to account for species loss, replacing that of the biblical Flood. This theory accommodated his claims of new and discrete, postglacial creations, each confined to its particular and appropriate part of the world.

Agassiz's conception of what would now be called intelligent design accorded well with ideas regarding the divinity of a complex creation familiar to many New Englanders from the transcendentalist lectures and publications of Emerson and his associates. Yet in contradistinction to the transcendentalists, Thoreau and Agassiz shared an emphasis on the detailed observation of specific elements of the natural—and in Thoreau's case, also Indigenous human—worlds. For both Agassiz and Thoreau, the collection and extremely detailed examination of material entities was essential and inevasible.

Agassiz had relied on collections, both private and institutional, throughout Europe to be able to write *Poissons fossiles*. Among the most important collections of both fossils and extant creatures was his own. He set about acquiring specimens as soon as he arrived in Boston in the fall of 1846, relying on a network of intellectually sympathetic new acquaintances organized on his behalf by Smithsonian curator Spencer Fullerton Baird and, locally, the man who was to become Agassiz's assistant and secretary, James Elliot Cabot. Cabot presumably recruited Thoreau, then living in his house at Walden Pond.[98]

This was the start of a difficult relationship between Thoreau and Agassiz.[99] In the spring of 1847, as their exchange of correspondence makes clear, Thoreau sent several shipments comprising numerous specimens to Cabot for Agassiz's collection. They comprised various fish—some alive—turtles, a snake, a mouse, and a small live fox, which literary scholar Patrick Vincent suggests was Thoreau's "playful warning to the man of science not to objectify nature or view it as a closed system."[100] He also gave an account of species known to him in the Concord River, including some jocular remarks, probably aimed at teasing Agassiz, such as, "The little pickerel, which I sent last, jumped into the boat in its fright."[101]

Yet Thoreau's initial enthusiasm for providing Agassiz with specimens soon petered out. There are several possible reasons. Thoreau may have come to dislike the principle of accumulating large numbers of creatures either dead or fated to die. Stimulated by Agassiz's example, he may have preferred to concentrate on his own, rather different, collecting and observing practices. He may have felt piqued at having failed to attract Agassiz's personal attention, even following a personal introduction at one of Agassiz's Lowell Lectures in Boston.[102] In a letter dated December 29, 1847, to Emerson, then in England, Thoreau reports a serious social slight to Lidian Emerson and, as he presumably experienced it, to himself as Emerson's deputed caretaker of the Emerson household in the great man's absence: "We have made up a dinner—we have made up a bed—we have made up a party—& our own minds & mouths three several times for your Professor, and he came not—Three several turkeys have died the death—which I myself carved, just as if he had been there, and the company too, convened and demeaned themselves accordingly—Everything was done up in good style, I assure you with only the part of the Professor omitted."[103] Perhaps the socially calculating Agassiz stood up Lidian Emerson an unpardonable three times (in Thoreau's account) because only Boston's elite, of which Emerson was an unquestioned member, could satisfy his appetite for aggrandizement.[104] Nonetheless, less than two years later, likely prompted by his cousin, Rebecca Billings's husband George Thatcher, Thoreau wrote to Agassiz to ask him if he might lecture at the Bangor Lyceum in Maine. He reminds Agassiz: "You may recognize in your correspondent the individual who forwarded to you through Mr Cabot many firkins of fishes and turtles a few years since and who also had the pleasure of an introduction to you at Marlboro' Chapel."[105] Agassiz politely turned down the invitation, but concluded his letter: "This will satisfy you, that whenever you come this way, I shall be delighted to see you, since I have also heard something of your mode of living," as though in Agassiz's imagination Thoreau might have been akin to a potentially interesting specimen.[106]

In the Saturday episode of *A Week on the Concord and Merrimack Rivers* (1849), Thoreau reports Agassiz as having claimed that a species of bream and several species of minnow in the Concord or Musketaquid River were "undescribed."[107] Thoreau may have regarded this pronouncement as arrogant in the light of both Indigenous knowledge, and his own, of such fish. He may also have been irritated by the two mentions of his name in the first volume of Agassiz's monumental *Contributions to the Natural History of the United States of America*, which appeared in 1857. He is one of no fewer than nine New Englanders whom Agassiz mentions as having supplied him with specimens—"Mr. D. Henry Thoreau, of Concord"—and he credits "Mr. D. H. Thoreau" as one of three Massachusetts residents who had found the turtle species he discusses as *Emys meleagris* Ag, crediting himself with its identification as a species ("Ag") even though it had earlier been designated *Emydoidea blandingii* (Holbrook, 1838) or, colloquially, Blanding's Turtle.[108] Thoreau describes an example he found in a ditch at Concord's Great Meadows. He identifies it as "a small *Cistudo Blandingii* swimming off rapidly" and describes it and its habits in great detail, contrasting it with "my large one," that is, most likely the example he had sent to Cabot for Agassiz ten years previously, and which remains in the Museum of Comparative Zoology (founded by Agassiz) at Harvard (see figure 9).[109] This very turtle came up as a subject of disagreement in the sparring that Thoreau describes between Agassiz and himself when they finally sat in a room together. This occurred on March 20, 1857, at the Emerson family dinner table. Thoreau's description of the occasion and his remarks in entries over the following days suggest that the encounter had rankled him, but also prompted self-reproach.[110]

Thoreau's final disillusionment with Agassiz followed his reading of Charles Darwin's *On the Origin of Species* (1859). Darwin proposed the instability of species, natural selection, responsiveness to local environment, and evolution. These were ideas with which Agassiz, true to Cuvier's principles, profoundly disagreed. He would continue to do so for the rest of his life. Agassiz consistently denied that species could evolve and thereby produce new species. The proliferation of independent, immutable species, each distinct within its own locality, was Agassiz's specialty.

Walter Harding describes how Harvard professor of botany Asa Gray had given his brother-in-law, Charles Brace, a copy of Darwin's book, which had been published just five weeks earlier, that he had brought with him on New Year's Day to Concord.[111] As Franklin Sanborn reported in a letter to Theodore Parker, Brace, Thoreau, and Bronson Alcott dined with Sanborn and discussed the new book and theories of evolution.[112] Thoreau got hold of a copy of Darwin's book (likely borrowing it) and took six pages of notes on it. In another letter to Parker, dated March 11–12, 1860, Sanborn mentions that the retired educator and autodidact scholar Sarah Alden Bradford Ripley, resident in Concord, had been reading Darwin. "She likes it as does

FIGURE 9. Blanding's Turtle (*Emydoidea blandingii*), collected by H. D. Thoreau. Herpetology Collection, Museum of Comparative Zoology, Harvard University, Herp:R-1501 (photo by Samantha Van Gerbig), © President and Fellows of Harvard College.

Thoreau," he reported.¹¹³ In May, Emerson wrote in his journal: "Agassiz says, 'There are no varieties in nature. All are species.' Thoreau says, 'If Agassiz sees two thrushes so alike that they bother the ornithologist to discriminate them, he insists they are two species; but if he sees Humboldt and Fred Cogswell, he insists that they come from one ancestor.'" (The editors note that Cogswell was "a kindly, underwitted inmate of Concord Almshouse.")¹¹⁴ Thoreau had clearly lost patience with Agassiz's entire concept of speciation.

Agassiz, though, despite increasing scholarly isolation resulting from his rejection of Darwin's ideas, nonetheless created a remarkable museum at Harvard. Once he had decided to accept a chair at Harvard in 1847, the college treasurer purchased an unused bathhouse to accommodate his ever-growing collections. His assistants from Europe were kept busy preparing specimens and drawing them for lithographic reproduction under Agassiz's own supervision.¹¹⁵ The results for his various ambitious publications are some of the most spectacular book illustrations ever produced.¹¹⁶

Agassiz's specimens were also vital for teaching, for which a museum was essential. Agassiz was able to found such a museum in 1859 within the university. He named it the Museum of Comparative Zoology. On November 13, 1860, Emerson was among the worthies who attended the dedication ceremony.¹¹⁷ It became and has remained one of the principal American engines of research and scholarship on vertebrate and invertebrate creatures, currently housing over twenty-one million specimens, including many type specimens that serve as ultimate references for the definition of a given species.

Thoreau's lifetime saw the beginning of the rise of museums in the United States.¹¹⁸ Three major museums were founded in Boston and Cambridge in the decade between 1859 and 1869: the Museum of Comparative Zoology (MCZ), the New England Museum of Natural History of the Boston Society of Natural History (now the Museum of Science), and the Peabody Museum of Archaeology and Ethnology.¹¹⁹ All three in their different ways fostered forms of scholarship that held in various degrees of tension principles derived from both idealism and an urge to observe the world—or worlds—closely, by gathering materials for further methodical, empirical study that might reveal underlying principles of organization. The ripples of these forms of inquiry radiated from Cambridge before fading in the early twentieth century, although all three museums—the MCZ, the Museum of Science, and the Peabody—still exist.

In a journal entry written before or around the time of his collecting activity on behalf of Agassiz, Thoreau wrote uncompromisingly:

I hate museums, there is nothing so weighs upon the spirits. They are the catacombs of Nature. One green bud of Spring one willow catkin, one faint trill from a migrating sparrow, might set the world on its legs again.

I know not whether I muse most at the bodies stuffed with cotton and sawdust—or those stuffed with bowels and fleshly fibre.

The life that is in a single green weed is of more worth than all this death.[120]

A few days later, he added the following:

Men have a strange taste for death who prefer to go to museums to behold the cast off garments of life—rather than handle the life itself. Where is the proper herbarium—the cabinet of shells—the museum of skeletons but in the meadow—where the flower bloomed—by the sea-side where the tide cast up the fish—or on the hills where the beast laid down his life. Where the skeleton of the traveller reposes on the grass there may it profitably be studied. What right has mortal man to parade any skeleton on its legs when once the gods have unloosed its sinews—what right to imitate heaven with his wires—or to stuff the body with sawdust—which nature has decreed shall return to dust again?[121]

This splenetic outburst is in large part an aesthetic response to such museums as the young Thoreau had seen. He was entirely convinced at this stage in the development of his ideas of the superiority of observing any naturally occurring phenomena—plants, animals of all kinds, and rocks—in their vital settings as items with which humans could interact. This did not inhibit him from collecting certain categories of materials and proposing their classification, as was the particular purpose of museums.

By the time of his visit to Plymouth in July 1851, Thoreau had mellowed enough in his attitude that he could write dispassionately and purely descriptively of what he saw in Pilgrim Hall, the museum of the Pilgrim Society that had opened in 1824. He notes relics of the early English settlement among the Native inhabitants, accompanying his words with two small sketches of the Native items: "Saw 2 old arm chairs that came over in the Mayflower.—the large picture by Sargent.—Standish's sword.—gunbarrel with which Philip was killed—mug & pocket-book of Clark the mate—Iron pot of Standish.—Old pipe-tongs Ind relics a flayer a pot or mortar of a kind of fire proof stone very hard—only 7 or 8 inches long. A Commission from Cromwell to Winslow (?)—his signature torn off."[122] He takes the trouble to list some at least of the items he saw but makes no comments on their aesthetic qualities, historical usefulness, or any other purpose they might then have served.

Three years later, in November 1854, on his way back from lecturing in Philadelphia, Thoreau visited the Exhibition of the Industry of All Nations in New York, which closed that month. It was known after its 1851 predecessor in London as the New York Crystal Palace. The first world's fair held in the United States, the exhibition had opened in 1853. It was housed in a large domed cruciform structure of cast iron and glass on the site of what is now Bryant Park. It presented an enormous range of manufactured consumer goods, technological marvels, and works of fine and decorative art.[123] Thoreau was taken in tow by the celebrity editor of the *New York Tribune* and Margaret Fuller's last employer, Horace Greeley. They had known one another since Thoreau's Staten Island sojourn in 1843. Greeley was a reliable promoter and placer of various of Thoreau's articles.[124] He led Thoreau into a social whirl of exhibit visits and an opera performance, Vincenzo Bellini's *I puritani*.[125] Thoreau notes: "Saw sculptures and paintings innumerable."[126] Indeed, the exhibition of paintings and sculpture was the largest yet assembled in the United States. The master showman P. T. Barnum had taken over as president of the exhibition the previous spring. He cannily introduced a new display of wonders named Barnum's Museum, at which Thoreau mentions having seen two "camelopards" (giraffes). Reflecting his own collecting interest, Thoreau also mentions "at Museum some large flakes of cutting arrowhead stone made into a sort of wide cleavers, also a hollow stone tube, probably from mounds."[127]

A month later, during a visit to Nantucket, Thoreau states in his journal, "Visited the museum at the Athenaeum. Various South Sea implements, etc., etc., brought home by whalers."[128] These are the kinds of things, including various numinously invested wooden clubs and paddles, that had captured the imagination of a fair part of the population of coastal and island Massachusetts. The largest such collection was in the East India Marine Society in Salem. The reputation of Oceanian things brought back by mariners, supercargoes, and whalers reached a wide reading audience through the description of the interior of the fictional Spouter-Inn in New Bedford in Herman Melville's *Moby-Dick; or, The Whale* (1851).[129] Thoreau, however, showed no sustained interest in such things, although he read the published journals of British mariner James Cook and quotes them in *A Week on the Concord and Merrimack Rivers* and *Cape Cod*.[130]

Late in his relatively short life, Thoreau became more tolerant of museums, perceiving them as at least to some extent worthwhile. In September 1858 he went to Salem, where he visited both the Essex Institute and the East India Marine Society. In his journal he describes Native American items in both institutions, as well as the birds' eggs and the herbarium in the former, making comparisons with items in his own collections.[131] In February 1860 he was still expressing serious reservations about museums: "I feel, of course, very ignorant in a museum. I know nothing about the things which they have there,—no more than I should know my friends in the tomb. I walk amid those jars of bloated creatures which they label frogs, a total stranger, without the least froggy thought being suggested. Not one of them can croak. They leave behind all life they that enter there, both frogs and men."[132]

Seven months later, in September, he clearly saw value in the antiquarian project initiated by Cummings Davis in Concord. Davis had moved to Concord in 1850 and opened a store near the railroad depot, which he later moved to the center of the village, selling food, drink, and newspapers. He formed a collection of items representative of the history of the Musketaquid-Concord area. This collection became the basis of the Concord Antiquarian Society, founded in 1886, which in turn became the present-day Concord Museum.[133] Davis noted that Thoreau had visited him in 1856, when the latter had given Davis a cartridge box carried by British troops during the assault on Concord on April 19, 1775, the first day of hostilities in the Revolutionary War.[134] Thoreau later gave Davis the stuffed skin of a Canada lynx, killed in the northern part of Concord, and a ball of vegetable fibers from the shore of Flint's Pond, neither of which survives in the Concord Museum.[135] On September 15, 1860, just two days after having reexamined the hastily taxidermied Canada lynx, then still in the possession of the Carlisle inhabitant who had killed it, Thoreau writes that he had visited "Mr. Davis's museum." He mentions some items given by Lydia Hosmer, including a small pocket sundial inscribed 1626 that she claimed had been brought by a settler ancestor. He was particularly interested in "some stone weights in an ancient linen bag, said to have been brought from England." They appealed to him because "I love to see anything that implies a simpler mode of life and greater nearness to the earth." His observation that "they were oval stones or pebbles from the shore,—or might have been picked up at Walden" may have enhanced their appeal for him.[136] A year later Thoreau visited Davis once again with his sister, Sophia, and his New Bedford friend and fellow early settler house enthusiast, Daniel Ricketson.[137] Davis's collection was antiquarian rather than of natural history specimens, and as Thoreau's engagement with the earliest settler houses in Concord described in the chapter "Shelter" suggests, he was interested in the material traces of the human past of his town.

By the time of his death in 1862, Thoreau's tolerance for museums had clearly grown, given how he had decided on the disposition of his collections. The subsequent history of Thoreau's collections, and the part they played in museum formation and even in contemporary museum scholarship, is the subject to which I now turn. Former New England Botanical Club herbarium curator Ray Angelo gives details of the history of Thoreau's herbarium.[138] In the year in which Thoreau died, 1862, the Boston Society for Natural History, of which he had been a member, began building its new museum.[139] After Thoreau's death his mother, Cynthia, and his sister, Sophia, following Thoreau's wishes, ensured that his "pressed plants, numbering more than one thousand species, arranged by himself, together with those western plants collected in his journey of 1861" (as described by Charles Jackson in the *Proceedings of the Boston Society of Natural History*) were conveyed to that society, of which he had been a corresponding member since 1850.[140] The number is likely an overestimate and was probably closer to eight hundred specimens. The approximately one hundred remaining specimens, comprising Thoreau's collection of grasses and sedges, went at his stipulation to his friend Edward Hoar, with whom Thoreau had journeyed in backwoods Maine in 1857, and who was one of two other Concord inhabitants who had a serious collecting interest in botany. The Boston Society of Natural History gave the bulk of the herbarium sheets to the Concord Free Public Library in 1880, which in 1959 gave them to the Gray Herbarium of the Harvard University Herbaria. Edward Hoar's daughter, Mrs. M. L. B. Bradford, gave the grasses and sedges she had inherited to the New England Botanical Club herbarium in 1912. The club subsequently deposited these sheets in the Harvard University Herbaria, though without donating them.[141] As part of its project to digitize and make freely available images of its 5.5 million dried specimens, in 2017 the Harvard University Herbaria published on Flickr 648 sheets of specimens from the group bequeathed by Thoreau to the Boston Society of Natural History.[142]

Thoreau could scarcely have conceived of the current major uses of his herbarium. One is the extraction of minute samples of DNA for research purposes; the other is to trace changes in botanical incidence and distribution since Thoreau's day, largely owing to global warming.[143] The authors of one of the resulting scientific studies state that the fact that Thoreau "kept meticulous notes on plant species occurrences and flowering times" makes his botanical material invaluable for this urgent purpose.[144]

There is an apparent irony in the manner in which Thoreau's observations and collections, notably of flora, have assumed a new importance. Contemporary skeptical science studies scholars, prompted by the work of Michel Foucault, Paul Feyerabend, Bruno Latour, and Karen Barad, call into question claims of selfless objectivity in science. Aspects of Thoreau's working methods have contemporary resonance in ways that the unquestioned objectivity of a discrete Cartesian human subject observing phenomena quite beyond itself does not. The factors in question include Thoreau's aesthetic grounds for giving attention to natural phenomena; his insistence that "I would so state facts that they shall be significant shall be myths or mythologic"; and his emphasis on humans and material items being mutually constitutive in terms of the generation of significance ("the point of interest is somewhere between me and them").[145]

Concerning Thoreau's collection of birds' eggs and nests, but for one item I have so far been unable to trace this material. Historians Karen Rader and Victoria Cain note that in order to focus on public education rather than research, the New England Museum of Natural History (subsequently renamed the Museum of Science) divested itself of various collections, transferring them to the Museum of Comparative Zoology at Harvard in the 1920s.[146] Katie Barrett, assistant curator at the Museum of Science, notes that the museum also transferred items to other institutions throughout its history. The only item from Thoreau's ornithological collection still in the museum's collection that she can identify is a nest of a yellow warbler (*Setophaga petechia*), with eggs, on display in the exhibit *The Museum Then and Now*.[147] As Cain observes, the Boston Museum of Science "is a determinedly local institution and bestows pride of place on exhibits that explore the surrounding landscape and hometown scientific research."[148] Vulnerable and decayed items in the collection may simply have been jettisoned when the museum was undergoing collection purges and a change of focus in the 1920s and 1930s. As Barrett remarks, "Some records were likely thrown away over time, lost, or the collection transfers weren't formally documented when they occurred."[149]

Thoreau's mineral and geological specimens are a different matter. Rather than going with the rest of his methodical collections to the Boston Society of Natural History, Thoreau's minerals went to one of his close friends, Franklin Sanborn, who had moved to Concord in 1855 after graduating from Harvard. Sanborn published a biography of Thoreau in 1882 but mentions the collection neither there nor in his known correspondence.[150] Thoreau's minerals that had gone to Sanborn passed to Clara Endicott Sears, a wealthy devotee of transcendentalism. In 1910 Sears purchased the site in Harvard, some fifteen miles west of Concord, of Fruitlands, Bronson Alcott and Charles Lane's failed self-sufficient utopian community formed in 1843. In 1914 she opened the grounds to the public, having founded a museum in the 1820s farmhouse where the "consociate family" that constituted Fruitlands had lived. Among the items she had acquired for this project was material from Sanborn, including Thoreau's mineral collection. The collection was exhibited in the farmhouse for many years but was relatively recently placed in storage.[151]

What part did Thoreau's collection of Native American antiquities play in museum formation? In 1866 the London-based banker George Peabody donated funds to Harvard for a museum and a professorship in American archaeology and ethnology. This led to the construction in 1869 of the Peabody Museum of Archaeology and Ethnology as an extension to the building housing Louis Agassiz's Museum of Comparative Zoology.[152] The first curator of the Peabody Museum was Jeffries Wyman, Hersey Professor of Anatomy at Harvard since 1847, and, since 1854, president of the Boston Society for Natural History.[153] In 1866 Wyman chose the position at the new Harvard museum over the directorship of the newly built New England Museum of Natural History, founded by the Boston Society of Natural History. The society took advantage of the founding of the Peabody Museum to divest itself of its archaeological materials, sending them with Wyman to the new Harvard museum. Among the materials from the Boston Society of Natural History that Wyman received into the new Peabody Museum was the group of Indigenous items left by Thoreau. The museum received the collection on the completion of its new building in 1869 and announced its receipt in its third annual report, where it is described as comprising about nine hundred objects: "over one hundred specimens of axes, pestles, gouges, mortars, chisels, spear points, ornaments, etc[.], and a larger number of arrow points of very varied patterns and materials."[154] In his description of the galleries published in 1898, the curator, Frederic Ward Putnam, notes that in the north room of the third floor, "the wall cases on each side of the fire-place contain several lots of stone implements from Massachusetts; among them are those picked up by Thoreau in his rambles along the Concord river."[155] Duncan Caldwell provides an analytical overview of the stone items in Thoreau's collection, which range in date from a late paleolithic lanceolate point from approximately 10,000 to 10,500 years before the present, through an especially rich gathering of material from the archaic period (9,000 to 3,000 years before the present), to the woodland period (3,000 years before the present to the time of European settlement).[156]

In the twentieth and twenty-first centuries, items from the Native stone implements collection have found only occasional use within the museum, whether for research or display. This is largely because, from an archaeological point of view, they are orphans. Thoreau gathered them casually, coming across them by chance during his regular hikes around the Concord countryside, so not many can be definitely associated with a particular site. Only in a few instances can a mention of a find in the journal be associated with a particular item in the collection. The aforementioned "clam-shell opener," found by Thoreau at Clamshell Bluff on the Sudbury River and described in his journal entry for August 22, 1860, is a rare example of the identification of an implement with a site. No one has comprehensively studied the collection to establish the character of each piece beyond its basic classification. The principal scholarly interest of the items is therefore their association with Thoreau. Indeed, his name is inscribed on several of them, though presumably Thoreau himself did not do this. For instance, the collection includes an atlatl weight, or bannerstone, made of drilled stone, used as part of a spear-thrower (see figure 10).[157] Some bannerstones, up to six thousand years old, are among the most sophisticatedly fashioned stone implements from ancient North America. Several can be found in the Metropolitan Museum of Art in New York, valued there for their striking aesthetic qualities reminiscent of twentieth-century modernist sculpture.[158] The example that once belonged to Thoreau is not so immediately evocative of modernist forms as the New York bannerstones, but its gray stone is streaked with darker parallel bands perpendicular to the drilled hole, so its maker presumably chose it for its visual qualities and aligned the hole

FIGURE 10. Precontact Native American winged atlatl weight, stone, Concord, Massachusetts, collected by H. D. Thoreau. Courtesy of the Peabody Museum of Archaeology and Ethnology, Harvard University, 69-34-10/2412, © President and Fellows of Harvard College.

deliberately to accentuate them. It is an item with a deliberately contrived aesthetic appeal. Thoreau's name inscribed in black on this bannerstone literally seems to overlay any other significance it may hold, although its aesthetic character alerts us to the aesthetic appeal of all such items to Thoreau and to the aesthetic basis of the discursive use to which he put them, notably in his journal.

Items from Thoreau's collection of Native stone implements have only rarely been exhibited in recent years. A stone pestle or lithophone with a carved bird's head was included in an exhibition at Harvard about the categorization of material things in museums and elsewhere, *Tangible Things*, in 2011.[159] It was among the very varied items gathered to exemplify the category "archaeology and anthropology" and is discussed briefly and illustrated in the subsequent publication.[160] Three stone projectile points from Thoreau's collection fashioned from rhyolite, a volcanic stone prized by Native Americans, were included in the Peabody Museum exhibition *The Legacy of Penobscot Canoes: A View from the River* (2014–16), which examined the intercultural significance of birchbark canoes from Maine.[161] Thoreau describes the Panawáhpskewi (Penobscot) and their canoes in his accounts of his second and third visits to the Maine backcountry in 1853 and 1857, once again offering aesthetic as well as practical assessments.[162]

In 1990 the US Congress passed the Native American Graves Protection and Repatriation Act. This strong legislation mandates the repatriation on demand by institutions in receipt of federal funds to federally recognized tribal nations of ancestors (previously called "human remains" by settler descendants) and certain kinds of cultural materials. The items in Thoreau's collection of Indigenous items would seem not to be subject to repatriation under its terms. As far as can be ascertained, they are not grave goods, nor would they be used in the practice of Native religion, nor are they objects of cultural patrimony within the meaning of the act. Further, it is doubtful whether a viable federally recognized direct successor community could be identified after a lapse of up to ten thousand years for things found in Musketaquid-Concord. This does not mean that their guardians can treat them casually, and they are not likely to, as the scholars at the Peabody Museum have a track record of respect for Indigenous sensibilities. Thoreau's collection of Native American items entered the Peabody Museum at a time when, as Steven Conn has shown, white American immigrants and their descendants were writing Indigenous peoples out of history and relocating them to anthropology as part of the natural world.[163] Even Thoreau was not entirely free from the taint of such ethnological prejudice, though he assumed an increasingly sympathetic stance toward Native peoples as he gained personal familiarity with Native individuals, an important matter discussed in the chapter "Sounds."[164] Anthropological scholarship in museums has changed greatly since those days, the emphasis now being on long-term collaborations between museum scholars and Native communities and their leading thinkers, in which the latter can take the initiative.[165] This is part of an unfinished process of decolonization or indigenization.

Numbers of Thoreau's personal possessions that were not part of his deliberately formed collections have also been placed in museums, notably the Concord Museum.[166] Although some of these items appear in other chapters of this volume, they are not a focus of attention here. They are not part of the movement of items from a methodical private collection that reflected Thoreau's preoccupations to methodical museum collections for long-term research and occasional public exhibition. A common thread that runs through Thoreau's collecting is aesthetic, for it concerns the items' imbrication with human feelings involving the emotions. Insofar as a philosophy underlies Thoreau's collection of material items, it is a philosophy of facts that lie "somewhere between me and them" in an entanglement that contemporary scholars have subsequently sought to define. (I previously mentioned Foucault, Feyerabend, Latour, and Barad, but there are many others.) Those facts are "myths or mythologic" in that they concern material items that reach beyond matter to immaterial realms, for any material items that make *a* world so as to be mindprints comprise both material and immaterial constituents insofar as they are subject to human cognition. The material worlds that Thoreau sought to represent by means of his collections, "realm on realm," the Native American artifacts in particular, comprising mindprints, were aesthetically constituted in conformity with the dominant aesthetics discussed in the preceding chapters, those of the natural environment and of everyday life.

Although the sense of sight would seem to dominate the apprehension of all the items in collections discussed in this chapter, it is important to recognize that their aesthetic qualities also frequently appeal to the sense of touch. The collector's manipulation of knapped stone items can evoke a feeling of connection between their own hands and those of an item's maker, contributing to a sense that they transcend temporal boundaries.[167] Furthermore, the identification of the Indigenous figured stone cylinder as a possible lithophone—a musical instrument—alerts us to the significance in aesthetic apprehension of sound, the subject of the next chapter.

[CHAPTER SEVEN]

Sounds

Thoreau's collections aided him in trying to answer big questions about the worlds he apprehended. Those collections were, in part, aesthetically constituted. Thoreau brought his keen visual acuity to bear on their formation and examination. Even as some scholars now question the current dominance of sight, it is a truism that European thinking going back to antiquity lends privilege to sight among the senses as defined by Aristotle, and, although not discounting them, relatively undervalues the other senses as sources of empirical knowledge claims.[1] Cultural systems beyond Europe and its diaspora pay greater attention than do Europeans to the evidence of other senses. I have been especially motivated to explore Thoreau's sensitivity to sound by the emphasis on hearing in many Indigenous American epistemologies, in which hearing can be as important as—or even more important than—looking.[2] Thoreau's carefully recorded encounters with Native Americans likely reinforced any predisposition he may have had to take sound and hearing seriously as evidence for knowledge claims about the worlds he pondered. For a questing person, listening entails being aurally sensitive to a wide range of phenomena: to other humans and to oneself; to birds, animals, and plants; to ancestors and spirits; and to the earth herself.

Just three days after moving into his Walden Pond house, Thoreau noted in his journal, "Sound was made not so much for convenience, that we might hear when called, as to regale the sense—and fill one of the avenues of life."[3] He incorporated sounds on equal terms with sights and smells when discussing the big questions he asked. In an April 1852 journal entry, he asks, "Why should just these sights & sounds accompany our life? Why should I hear the chattering of blackbirds—why smell the skunk each year? I would fain explore the mysterious relation between myself & these things."[4] These were among the questions he was addressing while writing and revising *Walden*. Thoreau proposes an understanding of sensory apprehension that is akin to ideas familiar in the present through entanglement and material engagement theory.⁵ In an 1857 journal entry he writes, "If I were to discover that a certain kind of stone by the pond-shore was affected, say partially disintegrated, by a particular natural sound, as of a bird or insect, I see that one could not be completely described without describing the other." Acknowledging a human role in such a reciprocal relationship, he continues immediately, "I am that rock by the pond-side."⁶ I am not suggesting an anachronistic understanding of Thoreau's notions of sensory reciprocity and a fit between "a bird and the ear that appreciates its melody" as what he termed "a natural fact."⁷ Rather, I propose that in formulating some of his numerous reflections on sound and hearing and their roles in constituting material worlds, Thoreau had learned a great deal from Native American interlocutors.

In late November 1850 a group of Panawáhpskewi (Penobscot) visiting from Maine camped beside the Musketaquid (Concord) River in Concord.⁸ Thoreau records in his journal visiting them after the first snowfall of the season. He made notes on what he learned from them. Those notes concern clothing, spears, a sled, canoes, cradle boards, birch bark vessels for holding water and for cooking with hot stones, cooking spits, a ritual device for dispersing clouds ("ar-tu-e-se a stick—string & bunch of leaves, which they toss & catch on the point of the stick"), snowshoes, and hunting traps. He carefully includes his own transcriptions of the visitors' words for most of these items and, for the first time in his journal, drawings.⁹ In order to record the words, he had to listen deliberately and carefully, and his decision in this respect indicates his conviction that the human sound associated with an item is as important as its visual appearance. Further, he makes no distinction between the items that any European settler might deem practical and a thing with a ritual use (the *ar-tu-e-se*), simply including it in the sequence, noting, "Make great use of it. Count with it—Make the clouds go off the sun with it."¹⁰ Conspicuously, he does not comment on whether or not it is efficacious.

Thoreau also remarks on a birchbark horn that his hosts at the camp demonstrated. They used this to imitate what Thoreau describes as the bellowing of a moose, audible, he reports, for eight or ten miles. He had the opportunity to witness such a horn lure in use three years later when he journeyed in the Maine backcountry with his cousin's husband, George Thatcher, for the second time. They traveled with a Panawáhpskewi guide, Joseph Aitteon, in Aitteon's birchbark canoe. Aitteon used his birchbark horn at night in an attempt to lure moose.¹¹ Thoreau describes how, dozing, he "would be aroused and brought back to a sense of my actual position by the sound of Joe's birch horn in the midst of all this silence calling the moose, *ugh, ugh, oo-oo-oo-oo-oo-oo*, and I prepared to hear a furious moose come rushing and crashing through the forest, and see him burst out on to the little strip of meadow by our side."[12] Hearing a great horned owl, Thoreau "told Joe that he [the owl] would call out the moose for him, for he made a sound considerably like the horn; but Joe answered, that the moose had heard that sound a thousand times, and knew better."[13] Thoreau was learning to distinguish nighttime forest sounds from his Panawáhpskewi companion. He acknowledged that he had much to learn, describing a nighttime occurrence during a perfectly calm night: "Once, when Joe had called, again, and we were listening for moose, we heard, come faintly echoing, or creeping from far through the moss-clad aisles, a dull, dry, rushing sound with a solid core to it, yet as if half smothered under the grasp of the luxuriant and fungus-like forest, like the shutting of a door in some distant entry of the damp and shaggy wilderness. If we had not been there, no mortal had heard it. When we asked Joe in a whisper what it was, he answered, 'Tree fall.'"[14] Thoreau was learning not only about what a sound might signify, but about a Native economy of speech exemplified by Aitteon's two-word explanation, "Tree fall."

Thoreau's encounter later on this trip with three more Native Americans was a key ear-opening experience for him that decisively gave him a new understanding of the Indigenous people who had inhabited what settlers call New England since the deep past. He moved toward an equivalent in sound of what in stone artifacts we have seen him call mindprints. When the group set up camp for the night at the carry at the head of Moosehead Lake, Maine, he shared a tent at their invitation with Joseph Aitteon and three other Native men. That night he heard a conversation in a Native tongue for the first time. In interpreting his response, I wish to peel away the contemporaneous settler tropes of the "wild," "primitive," and "deterioration" in which Thoreau couched his description in order to recover his sense of wonder and respect:

> While lying there listening to the Indians, I amused myself with trying to guess at their subject by their gestures, or some proper name introduced. There can be no more startling evidence of their being a distinct and comparatively aboriginal race than to hear this unaltered Indian language, which the white man cannot speak nor understand. We may suspect change and deterioration in almost every other particular but the language which is so wholly unintelligible to us. It took me by surprise, though I had found so many arrowheads, and convinced me that the Indian was not the invention of historians and poets. It was a purely wild and primitive American sound, as much as the barking of a *chickaree*, and I could not understand a syllable of it; but Paugus, had he been there,

would have understood it. These Abenakis gossiped, laughed, and jested, in the language in which Eliot's Indian Bible is written, the language which has been spoken in New England who shall say how long? These were the sounds that issued from the wigwams of this country before Columbus was born; they have not yet died away; and, with remarkably few exceptions, the language of their forefathers is still copious enough for them. I felt that I stood, or rather lay, as near to the primitive man of America, that night, as any of its discoverers ever did.[15]

This revelation seems to have occurred while one or perhaps two of the four men in the group were out hunting moose, so the conversation Thoreau overheard was between Joseph Aitteon and the man Thoreau refers to as the "St. Francis Indian." Thanks to the Maine folklorist Fannie Hardy Eckstorm and her father, fur trader Manly Hardy, the identities of Thoreau's Indigenous interlocutors are known. Hardy, who was a close friend of George Thatcher, traveled the same route as Thoreau, Thatcher, and Aitteon shortly after them and picked up news of them from the people he met. He used this information to annotate his copy of *The Maine Woods*, published in 1864. His daughter used this marginalia to identify Thoreau and Aitteon's companions in letters edited and published posthumously in 1955.[16] Thoreau's "St. Francis Indian," whom he notes was a "foreigner," was from Canada. Thoreau states that this man wrote his name for him, which he records as "Tahmunt Swasen."[17] Hardy identified him as Swasin Tahmont (also called Joachim Tahmont), an Alsig8ntegkw Aln8bak (Saint-François River Abenaki) from near the confluence of the Saint-François and St. Lawrence Rivers in Quebec. Of the other two men, one was Sebattis Dana (called "Sabattis" by Thoreau). Dana was then living in Old Town, site of the Panawáhpskewi (Penobscot) reservation, though Hardy records that he was originally from Quoddy, on the easternmost part of the Maine coast, and a Wəlastəkwewiyik (Maliseet). The second man remains unidentified. All were Aln8bak (Abenaki) people who would have spoken related but distinct Algonquian languages that were largely mutually intelligible. Aitteon and Dana would have spoken versions of Alənapatəwéwakan (Eastern Abenaki), whereas Tahmunt's language would have been Aln8ba8dwaw-8gan (Western Abenaki). Understandably, Thoreau assumes that they "gossiped, laughed, and jested, in the language in which Eliot's Indian Bible is written." However, he was mistaken, for John Eliot wrote his Bible translation (the New Testament published in Cambridge, Massachusetts, in 1661, and the Old and New Testaments in 1663) in the Natick dialect of the Muhsachuweesut (Massachusett or Massachuset) language. Being an Algonquian language, Muhsachuweesut may well have been broadly intelligible to Aitteon, Dana, and Tahmunt, but it was not what any of them would have spoken.[18]

Thoreau had already pondered the possible significance of utterances unintelligible to him in *A Week on the Concord and Merrimack Rivers* (1849): "Give me a sentence which no intelligence can understand," he writes in the "Monday" episode. "There must be a kind of life and palpitation to it, and under its words a kind of blood must circulate forever. It is wonderful that this sound should have come down to us from so far, when the voice of man can be heard so little way, and we are not now within earshot of any contemporary."[19] Thoreau may have been aware of speculations by some transcendentalists—notably Elizabeth Palmer Peabody—that Indigenous languages might be close to the very origins of language.[20] Aitteon's, Dana's, and Tahmont's voices—gossiping, laughing, and jesting—were, for Thoreau, sounds that had "come down to us from so far" as the sonic equivalents of the stone artifacts that he regarded as mindprints.

When Thoreau wrote that passage, developing it from the manuscript he prepared while living at Walden Pond between 1845 and 1847, he was thinking not of Native peoples but of Homer, certain strains of music, and the Hindu *Vedas*. In the passage beginning "What are ears? what is Time?" he associates music and the Greek and Indian writings he mentions with "the idea of infinite remoteness, as well as of beauty and serenity, for to the senses that is farthest from us which addresses the greatest depth within us. It teaches us again and again to trust the remotest and finest as the divinest instinct, and makes a dream our only real experience."[21] His experience in the backwoods of Maine in 1853 led him to reconceive the notion he had formed in response to ancient Greece and India as a transcendence he could thenceforth associate yet more vividly with the Native inhabitants of North America. This was to be a theme—prompted by *sound*—that he would pursue for the rest of his short life.

By the time Thoreau made his second, ear-opening visit to the Maine backwoods in 1853, he had long entertained the idea that human voices play a crucial part in shaping human society. In 1838 he wrote, "In obedience to an instinct of their nature men have pitched their cabins and planted corn and potatoes within speaking distance of one another, and so formed towns and villages." He may have continued with the following reservation—"but they have not associated, they have only assembled, and society has signified only a convention of men"—but his principal recognition was that being within speaking distance of one another plays a role at least in rudimentary or foundational modes of human assembly.[22]

However fugitive the words "laugh and gossip" may be, Thoreau suggests that their recollection can evoke a sense of sound traversing time through the imagination. On his account, this lends temporal depth to a place, even if it has been abandoned by its onetime inhabitants. He suggests as much when discussing those marginalized former enslaved Concordians of African descent who were his ghostly neighbors at Walden Pond. He writes, "Within the memory of many of my townsmen the road near which my house stands resounded with the laugh and gossip of inhabitants, and the woods which border it were notched and dotted here and there with their little gardens and dwellings, though it was then much more shut in by the forest than now."[23]

These are the sounds of human communication, and Thoreau has much to say about this phenomenon, both positive and negative. He relished what he called *gossip*, by which he meant what a later generation would term *the news*, noting in *Walden*: "Every day or two I strolled to the village to hear some of the gossip which is incessantly going on there, circulating either from mouth to mouth, or from newspaper to newspaper, and which, taken in homœopathic doses, was really as refreshing in its way as the rustle of leaves and the peeping of frogs."[24] He acknowledges, though, that communication through speech is uncertain, writing, "The bullet of your thought must have overcome its lateral and ricochet motion and fallen into its last and steady course before it reaches the ear of the hearer, else it may plow out again through the side of his head."[25]

The sound of the human voice that Thoreau valued as much as any was song. In a journal entry in September 1850 he states, "To hear a neighbor singing! All other speech sounds thereafter like profanity. A man cannot sing falsehood or cowardice He must sing truth & heroism. to attune his voice to some instruments. It would be noblest to sing with the wind."[26] A year later he records, "I hear the sound of singers on the river young men and women—which is unusual here—returning from their row. Man's voice thus uttered fits well the spaces—It fills Nature. And after all the singing of men is something far grander than any natural sound."[27]

These were sounds of song heard in the distance, and Thoreau constantly and consistently notes distant sounds, whether human voices or other consequences of human actions, such as church bells, railroad locomotives, and musicians playing instruments in the evening. Most of all, Thoreau notes sounds in nature, whether distant or not, ranging from the rustle of leaves to bird and animal calls and the cracking of the earth in extreme winter cold. In his sensitivity to such sounds, Thoreau enjoys what musicologist Jeff Todd Titon has perceptively described as "prolonged and intense engagement with sound-worlds," developing a "relational epistemology and alternative economy based in sound."[28]

Various thinkers have discussed the distinctions and continuities that Thoreau makes between music and other sounds.[29] As Branka Arsić points out, the composer "John Cage was perhaps the first interpreter of Thoreau who didn't separate the latter's thinking on sound and listening from his thinking on music."[30] Cage, celebrated for inviting attention to the irrepressibility of everyday sounds in, for instance, his "silent" piece, *4′33″* (1952), was an admirer of Thoreau and created his 1975 piece, *Lecture on the Weather*, for "twelve speaker-vocalists (or -instrumentalists)" by (in his words) "subjecting Thoreau's writings to I Ching chance operations to obtain collage texts."[31] Cage noted that for Thoreau sound and music form a continuum, writing, "Music, he [Thoreau] said, is continuous; only listening is intermittent."[32]

Others have picked up on Cage's insight. Jeff Todd Titon points out that Thoreau "regarded human music as a manifestation of the more inclusive and significant category, sound."[33] Thoreau gives an early indication of his evaluative taxonomy and his preferences in a journal entry in August 1838, in which he writes, "Some sounds seem to reverberate along the plain, and then settle to earth again like dust; such are Noise—Discord—Jargon. But such only as spring heavenward, and I may catch from steeples and hilltops in their upward course, which are the more refined parts of the former—are the true sphere music—pure, unmixed music—in which no wail mingles."[34]

In a journal entry in 1852 Thoreau expresses a longing for the capacity to apprehend sound that he ascribes to children, writing, "A child loves to strike on a tin pan or other ringing vessel with a stick, because, its ears being fresh, sound, attentive, & percipient, it detects the finest music in the sound, at which all nature assists."[35] For him, "unprejudiced ears hear the sweetest & most soul-stirring melody in tinkling cowbells & the like (dogs baying the moon), not to be referred to association—but intrinsic in the sound itself."[36] Although there are plenty of passages in Thoreau's writings in which he expresses his enjoyment of human-made music—and he made music himself—he also expresses a preference rhetorically for what he deems to be music in natural or inadvertent sounds.[37] Furthermore, in considering human-made music, although he enjoyed a good tune—Charles Dibdin's elegiac sea song "Tom Bowling" (c. 1788) was a favorite that he often sang—he holds that "the music is not in the tune—it is in the sound."[38] Yet this thought did not prevent Thoreau from understanding human-made music as expressive or from performing expressively himself. Edward Emerson, Ralph Waldo Emerson's son who as a child knew Thoreau well, wrote, "No one who has heard 'Tom Bowling' from Thoreau could ask if he were capable of human feeling."[39]

Thoreau's favored sounds-as-music were products of both the natural and human-made worlds, and his understanding of them was aesthetic. Many of the natural sounds to which Thoreau draws attention in his writings again and again are those of birds, toads, frogs, and insects. Wherever he went, sounds constituted his world of that moment: sounds that others might hear—crickets and sparrows—or that would escape all but the most attentive, such as he records hearing on Fairhaven Hill in July 1852: "I hear the scratching sound of a worm at work in this hardwood-pile on which I sit."[40]

After nine years of work and seven drafts, Thoreau distilled his pre-1854 thoughts on sound worlds in *Walden*, notably, though far from exclusively, in its chapter titled "Sounds." There he describes the situation of his house near the pond and reflects on time, stating, "My days were not days of the week, bearing the stamp of any heathen deity, nor were they minced into hours and fretted by the ticking of a clock."[41] He contrasts this world in which sounds reflect a freeform time with the effect of the railroad, only a third of a mile distant, on which the cars travel noisily, altering the world through which they pass by their novel movement of people and commodities. Above all, Thoreau notes that the railroad has changed the inhabitants' sense of time through its sounds. In *Walden* he writes, "They go and come with such regularity and precision, and their whistle can be heard so far, that the farmers set their clocks by them, and thus one well-conducted institution regulates a whole country."[42] He pointedly contrasts locomotives—characterized by turn as a "travelling demigod, this cloud-compeller," an "iron horse . . . with his snort like thunder," and "an *Atropos*, that never turns aside"—with the sounds of the birds he could hear from his pond-side house, beginning with the nocturnal whippoorwills that "chanted their vespers for half an hour, sitting on a stump by my door, or upon the ridge pole of the house. They would begin to sing almost with as much precision as a clock, within five minutes of a particular time, referred to the setting of the sun, every evening."[43] In other words, the sound world of the whippoorwill was as reliable to one who listens for it as was the whistle of the locomotive, yet even though they intersect, those worlds differ from one another profoundly.

One sound that came to obsess Thoreau was that of wind in telegraph wires. In *A Week on the Concord and Merrimack Rivers* (1849), he recounts hearing, just over the New Hampshire state line in Plaistow, "a faint music in the air like an Æolian harp, which I immediately suspected to proceed from the cord of the telegraph vibrating in the just awakening morning wind."[44] He was familiar with the aeolian harp, for he had one himself, designed to be wedged on the sill of a window.[45] He contrasts what he describes as the higher and lower uses of the telegraph, claiming that through "that vibrating cord high in the air over the shores of earth . . . I heard a fairer news than the journals ever print. It told of things worthy to hear, and worthy of the electric fluid to carry the news of, not of the price of cotton and flour, but it hinted at the price of the world itself and of things which are priceless, of absolute truth and beauty."[46]

Once the telegraph wires had been installed along the track of the Fitchburg Railroad, which he habitually followed between Walden Pond and the village, Thoreau went to hear what he called the "telegraph harp" repeatedly. In a September 1851 journal entry he notes, "As I went under the new telegraph-wire, I heard it vibrating like a harp high over head.—[I]t was as the sound of a far off glorious life a supernal life which came down to us.—and vibrated the lattice work of this life of ours."[47] Thoreau soon realized that the full power of the sound came through the wooden poles. Having put his ear to a pole, he writes that "it is as if you had entered some world famous cathedral resounding to some vast organ."[48] The significance of the telegraph harp for Thoreau lay in its powerful aesthetic evocation of "absolute truth and beauty." As such, it was a particularly clear instance of how, as he puts it, "the fibres of all things have their tension and are strained like the strings of a lyre."[49] Moreover, the music he heard in the sound prompted him to suggest that its effect was "as if every fibre was affected and being seasoned or timed, rearranged according to a new & more harmonious law."[50]

In Thoreau's conception, those "fibres of all things" clearly, and by definition, extended well beyond the telegraph harp. Writing about the roots of white pine trees in a journal entry in November 1850 he notes, "The different branches of the roots continually grow into one another—so as to make grotesque figures—sometimes rude harps whose resonant strings of roots give a sort of musical sound when struck—such as the earth spirit might play on."[51] The following summer he extended his notion of what a harp might be from individual items to the phenomenal world as a whole, writing in his journal:

> There is always a kind of fine Æolian harp music to be heard in the air—I hear now as it were the mellow sound of distant horns in the hollow mansions of the upper air—a sound to make all men divinely insane that hear it—far away overhead subsiding into my ear. to ears that are expanded what a harp this world is! The occupied ear thinks that beyond the cricket no sound can be heard—but there is an immortal melody that may be heard morning noon and night by ears that can attend & from time to time this man or that hears it—having ears that were made for music.[52]

Being attuned to the harp of the world is, for Thoreau, not only a matter of cultivating aesthetic attentiveness but a question of being aurally attuned to what others ignore. With this in mind, less than three weeks later he could write of an experience one evening at the old house he admired on the west bank of the Musketaquid or Sudbury River in the southwestern corner of Concord: "Sitting on the doorstep of Conant-house—at 9 o clock I hear a pear drop—how few of all the apples that fall do we hear fall."[53] He heard it with "ears that are expanded," as he had so recently put it.

As is so often the case, this perception of a pear dropping and the reflection it prompted may have been aesthetically couched, but Thoreau's response was not exclusively aesthetic. Rather, it was ethical and metaphysical, pertaining to the laws of the universe. He makes this explicit in the "Higher Laws" chapter of *Walden*: "Though the youth at last grows indifferent, the laws of the universe are not indifferent, but are forever on the side of the most sensitive. Listen to every zephyr for some reproof, for it is surely there, and he is unfortunate who does not hear it. We cannot touch a string or move a stop but the charming moral transfixes us."[54]

For Thoreau, the aesthetic and ethical lessons that sounds perceived as music by "ears that are expanded" have to teach are embedded in an apparent paradox, which he outlines in a February 1854 journal entry: "Nothing is so truly bounded & obedient to law as music, yet nothing so surely breaks all petty & narrow bonds."[55] Yet he holds in *A Week on the Concord and Merrimack Rivers* that "music is the sound of the universal laws promulgated. It is the only assured tone. There are in it such strains as far surpass any man's faith in the loftiness of his destiny. Things are to be learned which it will be worth the while to learn."[56] To hear music in sounds is to break "petty and narrow bonds." These are the bonds that bind humans as they age, maturing and declining from the child who "loves to strike on a tin pan or other ringing vessel with a stick" to whom "there is music in sound alone."[57] In a journal entry in July 1851 Thoreau recalls, "In youth before I lost any of my senses—I can remember that I was all alive—and inhabited my body with inexpressible satisfaction, both its weariness & its refreshment were sweet to me. This earth was the most glorious musical instrument, and I was audience to its strains. To have such sweet impressions made on us—such ecstasies begotten of the breezes! I can remember how I was astonished."[58] Thoreau expresses a determination to recover as far as possible a lost childlike sensitivity to sounds. But how is one to achieve this state of recovered sensibility? How can one expand one's ears?

Describing sounds heard during a nighttime walk to Walden Pond in a June 1851 journal entry, Thoreau complains, questions, and counsels: "We live but a quarter part of our life—why do we not let on the flood—raise the gates—& set all our wheels in motion—He that hath ears to hear, let him hear. Employ your senses."[59] Later that summer he suggests that the physical exertion of a long walk in the heat of summer can create the conditions for attaining a heightened sensibility, writing of his state after such a walk, "Every sound is music now. The grating of some distant boat which a man is launching on the rocky bottom—though here is no man nor inhabited house—nor even cultivated field in sight—this is heard with such distinctness that I listen with pleasure as if it was music."[60] A year later, the sound of a distant piano heard from his garret window at noon—"the music is not in the tune; it is in the sound"[61]—rekindled his aural sensibility. In response, he writes, "By some fortunate coincidence of thought or circumstance I am attuned to the universe—I am fitted to hear—my being moves in a sphere of melody—my fancy and imagination are excited to an inconceivable degree—This is no longer the dull earth on which I stood."[62] But, we might ask, through such recovery, what exactly does one attain?

The ideal attainment is a healthy soul. Ten years previously, in an April 1841 journal entry, Thoreau had drawn attention to what he terms the "healthy ear," writing, "Music is the sound of the circulation in nature's veins.—It is the flux which melts nature—men dance to it—glasses ring and vibrate—and the fields seem to undulate.—The healthy ear always hears it—nearer or more remote."[63] In 1851 he does not appeal to the ear as a synecdoche, as he had done ten years previously in the passage just quoted. Instead, he is direct in stating that the goal for which one must aim is "a soul in health."[64] In *Walden* he quotes the disciple of Confucius known to him as Thseng-tseu (Zeng Shen, now commonly known as Zengzi) on a human being's failure to perceive adequately through the senses: "'The soul not being mistress of herself,' says Thseng-tseu, 'one looks, and one does not see; one listens, and one does not hear; one eats, and one does not know the savor of food.'"[65] In his discussion of "a soul in health," he claims that when the soul is "mistress of herself," courage can "put upon the face of things" a quality that he terms "a perpetual flow of spirit."[66] According to Thoreau, these are the conditions that allow one through aesthetic and ethical appreciation to penetrate beyond metaphor and symbol to the actuality of phenomena, thereby perceiving "sphere music" and the divine. He declares this belief in the "Friday" section of *A Week on the Concord and Merrimack Rivers*:

> We need pray for no higher heaven than the pure senses can furnish, a purely sensuous life. Our present senses are but the rudiments of what they are destined to become. We are comparatively deaf and dumb and blind, and without smell or taste or feeling. Every generation makes the discovery that its divine vigor has been dissipated, and each sense and

faculty misapplied and debauched. The ears were made, not for such trivial uses as men are wont to suppose, but to hear celestial sounds. The eyes were not made for such groveling uses as they are now put to and worn out by, but to behold beauty now invisible. May we not see God? Are we to be put off and amused in this life, as it were with a mere allegory? Is not Nature, rightly read, that of which she is commonly taken to be the symbol merely?[67]

For Thoreau, sphere music is not metaphorical but an actuality present in the tiniest aurally perceptible phenomena, so long as one has recovered the necessary sensibility. As he puts it in a journal entry at the end of 1852, "Unless the humming of a gnat is as the music of the spheres—and the music of the spheres is as the humming of a gnat, they are naught to me."[68] Insofar as Thoreau's recognition of the value of such phenomena is aesthetic, the "humming of a gnat," the "squeaking of the snow under our boots,"[69] and any number of other natural and human-made sounds that constitute Thoreau's sonic worlds engage the aesthetics of the environment and everyday aesthetics. As he puts it in an April 1859 journal entry, "We may say that each gnat is made to vibrate its wings for man's fruition. In short, we hear but little music in the world which charms us more than this sound produced by the vibration of an insect's wing and in some still and sunny nook in spring."[70] As we have seen, while Thoreau values the music to be discerned in a wide range of natural and human-made sounds, he does not wholly discount music as generally understood. It is not, though, an adequate channel to sphere music, unless heard by chance at a distance.

In Thoreau's opinion, when the soul is "in health," and "mistress of herself," the ear being healthy, sound can affect the human body profoundly. He describes this physical as well as psychical effect in a journal entry in July 1851:

> I hear the sound of Heywood's Brook falling into Fair Haven Pond—inexpressibly refreshing to my senses—it seems to flow through my very bones.—I hear it with insatiable thirst—It allays some sandy heat in me—It affects my circulations—methinks my arteries have sympathy with it What is it I hear but the pure waterfalls within me in the circulation of my blood—the streams that fall into my heart?—what mists do I ever see but such as hang over—& rise from my blood—The sound of this gurgling water—running thus by night as by day—falls on all my dashes—fills all my buckets—overflows my float boards—turns all the machinery of my nature makes me a flume—a sluice way, to the springs of nature—Thus I am washed thus I drink—& quench my thirst.[71]

And three days later, he writes, "The creaking of the crickets seems at the very foundation of all sound. At last I cannot tell it from a ringing in my ears. It is a sound from within, not without You cannot dispose of it by listening to it. When I am stilled I hear it. It reminds me that I am a denizen of the earth."[72]

This intermingling of sounds as though from within the body with those from without led Thoreau to conceive of the human body, properly attuned, as itself a musical instrument. This thought came to him in a dream that he recounts in a journal entry in October 1851. He dreamed that he was first sailing, then walking, with Bronson Alcott, quoting verses the while.

> And then again the instant that I awoke methought I was a musical instrument—from which I heard a strain die out—a bugle—or a clarionet—or a flute—my body was the organ and channel of melody, as a flute is of the music that is breathed through it. My flesh sounded & vibrated still to the strain—& my nerves were the chords of the lyre. I awoke therefore to an infinite regret—to find myself, not the thoroughfare of glorious & world-stirring inspirations—but a scuttle full of dirt—such a thoroughfare only as the street & the kennel—where perchance the wind may sometimes draw forth a strain of music from a straw.[73]

Pursuing the need to keep the soul—and body—in health if sounds are to provide "glorious and world-stirring inspirations," Thoreau reports in a September 1853 journal entry:

> It occurred to me when I awoke this morning, feeling regret for intemperance of the day before in eating fruit, which had dulled my sensibilities, that man was to be treated as a musical instrument, and if any viol was to be made of sound timber and kept well tuned always, it was he, so that when the bow of events is drawn across him he may vibrate and resound in perfect harmony. A sensitive soul will be continually trying its strings to see if they are in tune. A man's body must be rasped down exactly to a shaving. It is of far more importance than the wood of a Cremona violin.[74]

If the human body, properly attuned, can function as a musical instrument, sensitive to an intermingling of sounds from within and without, it is as though the faculty often described as the inner ear begins to hear sounds not perceptible to those with what Thoreau regards as corrupted senses. The inner ear is what hears what Thoreau, in the conclusion to *Walden*, famously terms a "different drummer": "If a man does not keep pace with his companions, perhaps it is because he hears a different drummer. Let him step to the music which he hears, however measured or far away."[75] Thoreau's evocation of the "sensitive soul" out of step with others recalls his description of his experience with his brother, John, in the "Monday" section of *A Week on the Concord and Merrimack Rivers*: "Far in the night, as we were falling asleep on the bank of the Merrimack, we heard some tyro beating a drum incessantly, in preparation for a country muster, as we learned." For Thoreau, this "stray sound from a far-off sphere" that "came to our ears from time to time, far, sweet, and significant" was far from being an irritant, for, as he puts it: "These simple sounds related us to the stars. Ay, there was a logic in them so convincing that the combined sense of mankind could never make me doubt their conclusions. I stop my habitual thinking, as if the plow had suddenly run deeper in its furrow through the crust of the world."[76]

The sounds that constitute sonic realms, leading Thoreau's mental plow to run through the "crust of the world," are invariably simple, whether natural or human-made. They encompass, but are far from confined to, the wind in the trees, the cracking of the ground by frost, the cries of birds, the hum of insects, the woodcutter's axe, distant church bells, and musical instruments: drums, clarinets, and flutes. These are all subject to the aesthetics of the environment and of the everyday. Music performed for an audience—a standard subject for aesthetic regard—is of but little account to Thoreau. "One will lose no music by not attending the oratorios and operas," he claims in an August 1851 journal entry. He continues, "The really inspiring melodies are cheap and universal, and are as audible to the poor man's son as to the rich man's"; "no heavenly strain is lost to the ear that is fitted to hear it, for want of money—or opportunity."[77] These humble sounds, when audible to a sensitive, healthy soul that is "mistress of herself," directly afford transcendence.

These humble sounds also serve as substitute mindprints, analogues of the artifacts that Thoreau associates principally, though not exclusively, with the Native peoples of what had become New England. He makes this clear in a journal entry in April 1851, inspired by the song of a robin at Punkatasset Pond, two miles north of Concord village.

> Did he sing thus in Indian days?, I ask myself—for I have always associated this sound with the village & the clearing, but now I do detect the aboriginal wildness in his strain—& can imagine him a woodland bird—and that he sang thus when there was no civilized ear to hear him—a pure forest melody even like the wood thrush. Every genuine thing retains this wild tone—which no true culture displaces—I heard him even as he might have sounded to the Indian, singing at evening upon the elm above his

wigwam—with which was associated in the red-man's mind the events of an Indian's life.—his childhood. Formerly I had heard in it only those strains which tell of the white man's village life—now I heard those strains which remembered the red-man's life—such as fell on the ears of Indian children.—as he sang when these arrow-heads which the rain has made shine so on the lean stubble field—were fastened to their shaft. Thus the birds sing round this piece of water—some on the alders which fringe—some farther off & higher up the hills—It is a centre to them.[78]

Thoreau condenses this thought—the robin's song as capable of compressing time—in the "Spring" chapter of *Walden*, writing, "I heard a robin in the distance, the first I had heard for many a thousand years, methought, whose note I shall not forget for many a thousand more,—the same sweet and powerful song as of yore."[79]

This thought—to bring the mindprints that are arrowheads into propinquity with the song of a robin—depends on the role that Native peoples played in Thoreau's developing philosophy. During his second visit to the Maine backwoods in 1853, his overhearing Joseph Aitteon, Swasin Tahmont, and Sebattis Dana speaking in their own tongues seemed to collapse time and further attune an already sensitized mind to the myriad everyday sounds around him. The effect of his third visit to Maine, in 1857 with Edward Hoar, was more profound yet. As Laura Dassow Walls put it, their guide, Joseph Polis, a Panawáhpskewi (Penobscot) leader, confounded everything Thoreau knew.[80] Polis was a remarkable man. He had not only represented his nation in Augusta, the capital of Maine, and in Washington, DC, but although a Protestant Christian, he was also a shaman, a fact not known to Thoreau.[81] Walls recounts how during their time in the Maine backwoods, Polis, clumsily pressed by Thoreau, carefully and selectively indoctrinated the philosopher into aspects of Native knowledge, so that when Thoreau returned to Concord, his enthusiasm for and astonishment at the breadth and profundity of that knowledge surprised his friends and acquaintances.[82] Thereafter, Thoreau continued to add to his thousands of pages of notes on Native American peoples in what by the time of his death in 1861 would be twelve manuscript volumes.[83]

One of the characteristic musical instruments of the Algonquian peoples of northern New England is the flute. Carved from hardwood, it functions on the whistle principle. Thoreau makes no mention of Native flutes but was presumably aware of them, whether brought by Native groups when visiting Concord or witnessed during his visits to Maine. The flute has a special place in Thoreau's worlds of sound. The flute—of the transverse kind with four brass keys—was the instrument that Thoreau himself played. His own boxwood flute, inscribed with his name and that of his brother, John, is in the Concord Museum.[84] Henry records in his journal playing the flute while in his boat in May on Walden Pond and in August 1841 on the Musketaquid River, so John had most likely given his flute to Henry before his death early in 1842.[85] Playing his flute was clearly an evening meditative activity for Thoreau based on improvisation, which he called "unpremeditated music," regarding it as "the true gauge which measures the current of our thoughts, the very undertow of our life's stream."[86]

The sound of the flute plays a vital role in the development of Thoreau's philosophy. At the end of the "Higher Laws" chapter of *Walden*, Thoreau casts himself as "John Farmer," preoccupied with his labors even after bathing and seating himself at his door. Of Farmer, Thoreau writes, "He had not attended to the train of his thoughts long when he heard some one playing on a flute, and that sound harmonized with his mood. Still he thought of his work . . . But the notes of the flute came home to his ears out of a different sphere from that he worked in, and suggested work for certain faculties which slumbered in him."[87] The sound of a distant flute prompted the adoption of a way of life that might eventually lead to his soul becoming sensitive, healthy, and "mistress of herself," thereby being directly afforded transcendence. Discussing the concluding lines of *Walden*, Laura Dassow Walls notes, "He who, midway through *Walden*, had been arrested on the threshold of life, is now himself the player on the flute, whose notes reach the ears of those who, hearing, might be released to begin their own journey toward the dawn."[88]

As an avid reader of Hindu holy books who had conceived *Walden* in the form of sacred scripture on the pattern of the *Bhagavad Gita*, Thoreau knew, as the *Bhagavata Purana* recounts, that Krishna, eighth avatar of Vishnu and supreme Hindu deity, played the flute.[89] A transverse flute is one of the Lord Krishna's most prominent attributes. Among the twenty-one works in forty-four volumes, mostly of Hindu scriptures, delivered to Thoreau as a gift in November 1855 from his English friend Thomas Cholmondeley, were two translations, one into English and the other into French, that include the *Bhagavata Purana*.[90] Writing to thank Cholmondeley, Thoreau asks, "What was that dim peak that loomed for an instant far behind, representative of a still loftier and more distant range. 'Vishnu Purana,' an azure mountain in itself.—gone again, but surely seen for once."[91] (The *Bhagavata Purana* is among the *Vishnu Purana*.) Thoreau had already read borrowed copies of many of these works, including the *Bhagavata Purana*. *Walden*, published the previous year, contains many references to Hindu scriptures.[92] Reporting Cholmondeley's gift in a letter to Daniel Ricketson on Christmas Day 1855, Thoreau wrote, "I am familiar with many of them &

know how to prize them."[93] Because of Lord Krishna's example, the sound of the flute, among human-made instruments, has a sacred dimension that cannot have escaped Thoreau.[94]

Allusions to Hindu holy books and their many gods, avatars, and other sacred characters would have confounded most of Thoreau's American contemporaries (though not Emerson), whereas for many of them the Greek god Pan, the unruly lord of untamed forests whose attribute was his pipes, was an easily graspable alter ego for Thoreau. Louisa May Alcott, Bronson and Abigail May Alcott's second daughter, had grown up with Thoreau as a family friend. She published an elegiac poem in memory of Thoreau in the *Atlantic* in September 1863. Titled "Thoreau's Flute," it begins, "We sighing said, "Our Pan is dead; / His pipe hangs mute beside the river." But

> Then from the flute, untouched by hands,
> There came a low, harmonious breath:
> "For such as he there is no death;
> His life the eternal life commands."

For Alcott, Thoreau "Made one small spot a continent" while "Haunting the hills, the stream, the wild." To his flute's breath she ascribes the words of the concluding stanza:

> To him no vain regrets belong
> Whose soul, that finer instrument,
> Gave to the world no poor lament,
> But wood-notes ever sweet and strong.
> O lonely friend! he still will be
> A potent presence, though unseen,
> Steadfast, sagacious, and serene;
> Seek not for him—he is with thee.[95]

If, as I contend, aesthetics plays a vital role in Thoreau's thinking and practical philosophy, what he could hear was as important to him as what he could see and touch, whether in his collections or in the field. And the romantic in each of us might accept Louisa May Alcott's intuition, that Thoreau's flute, instrument of his "unpremeditated music," may yet be sensed by the attentive inner ear through the woods and across the waters of Walden, sounding—to paraphrase Keats—unheard melodies sweeter than those heard.

[CHAPTER EIGHT]

Conclusion

The intellect is a cleaver; it discerns and rifts its way into the secret of things.

Thoreau

The selective exploration of Thoreau's material worlds that I offer in this book does not admit of a neat conclusion. Thoreau's thinking changed during his short life as his ambitions changed. He progressed from wanting to be a poet after he graduated from Harvard College, through a long intellectual apprenticeship under Emerson in the principles of transcendentalism, to becoming his own man whose concerns encompassed natural history and human conduct and how they intertwine. He became a philosopher, the key move in that development being his experiment in deliberate living at Walden Pond. Initially, he was deeply embedded in a European-derived cultural tradition epitomized by Louisa May Alcott's affectionate elegy, "Thoreau's Flute." Yet he moved well beyond the boundaries of the settler worldview that gave currency to such classical references. He developed an extraordinary catholicity of intellectual engagement with other traditions, including Indian and Chinese texts and the orally transmitted knowledge of Native peoples. His respect for Native knowledge, condensed by his travels in the backwoods of Maine in 1853 and 1857, enhanced his perceptual acuity and aesthetic sensibility.

I have argued that Thoreau's life was profoundly shaped by aesthetics as a matter of sensibility. His aesthetic sensibility fostered his ethical principles, which found expression not only in his lectures and writings, such as "Resistance to Civil Government," "Slavery in Massachusetts," and "Life without Principle," but in his philosophically examined everyday life.[1] That continuous self-scrutiny entailed attending not simply to one world open to straightforward inspection and reflection but to worlds and the sensory apprehensions through which they might be known, however imperfectly. Those worlds in all their particularity contain mindprints, which project human presence across the ages and offer thoughts to the sensitive percipient.

Thoreau's aesthetic attention to the properties of material items prompted judgments in broader terms than beauty and sublimity. His aesthetics embraces perception by feeling involving the emotions. For Thoreau, aesthetics was a matter of sensibility. This sensibility allowed him to be aesthetically responsive to a wider range of phenomena than the fine arts. In particular, he initiated an environmental aesthetics and an everyday aesthetics. Thoreau's close contemporary, George Eliot, captures this sensitivity to "ordinary human life" when, in the first volume of *Middlemarch* (1871), she writes, "If we had a keen vision and feeling of all ordinary human life, it would be like hearing the grass grow and the squirrel's heart beat, and we should die of that roar which lies on the other side of silence." She continues, "As it is, the quickest of us walk about well wadded with stupidity."[2] Thoreau, surely, is among "the quickest of us." He is one who hears the grass grow, the squirrel's heart beat, and "the worm at work in this hardwood-pile on which I sit."[3]

Thoreau's work and thought provide an example of affective riches that can accrue when aesthetics does not ignore aspects of daily life that are often overlooked in favor of attending exclusively to the fine arts, whether visual, architectural, musical, theatrical, or literary. He shows that aesthetics can—and must—address the totality of human life experience. His statements and his life together demonstrate that a simple existence consisting of satisfying the necessities of life can provide aesthetic sustenance and allow humans to evade the bondage that follows the wasteful pursuit of luxury, power, and status. Such reticence need not result in the asceticism of a life bereft of enrichment or joy. Enrichment can derive from ordinary, overlooked, and even despised practices. Everyday aesthetics invites reflection on such practices, including, as Yuriko Saito has demonstrated, household chores.[4] Thoreau's emphasis on his daily tasks accords with critical moves to scrutinize environmental, social, and psychological problems associated with much contemporary life even if those problems can never be entirely avoided.

Attention to daily tasks is a constituent of the examined life that Thoreau espoused and led. Much contemporary philosophy fails to live up to the Socratic ideal of the examined life. Philosophy has largely become no more than an academic pursuit: exercises in thinking without any investment in their own lives on the part of the thinkers. Thoreau actually *lived* his philosophy, most explicitly, but far from exclusively, during his experiment at Walden Pond. Reflection on his surroundings prompted by direct experience of the natural environment, of his immediate circle and his extended society, and of utilitarian items of many kinds generated his philosophical thinking. In this work Thoreau makes no pretense of objectivity. Not for him the passive voice that signals evasion of personal responsibility. Instead, he always acknowledges himself in the first person as actor.

Thoreau as first person is not an outsider looking upon one world from on high, but an entangled participant in worlds whose experience and knowledge of reality and existence is relational. For Thoreau, relations between humans and items in the worlds through which they move are reciprocal. I am not suggesting an anachronistic equivalence between Thoreau's philosophy and contemporary agential theory, but Thoreau offers ideas that might help contemporary philosophers refine concepts of how humans and nonhumans act upon each other. Mindprints, for Thoreau, are never inert, lifeless, and mute objects but are tellers of tales, such as that of the arrowhead whose words he quotes speaking of how it will repeatedly be lost and found, cycling through generations of human hands and the dust.[5]

Such tales are beyond history proper—what humans in any given present make of pasts—but this does not mean that Thoreau had no interest in historical accounts of his hometown and beyond. As Thoreau asserted his intellectual independence from Emerson, who sought general principles and the unity of "one design," he increasingly attended to particularities discernible by profound empirical inspection of the specific characteristics of the worlds he scrutinized. Attention to particularities animates historical scholarship as a matter of principle. In historical practice, a priori claims—including those of philosophers—are always open to testing against the inferences historians draw from individual traces of the past. Those traces of the past include a plethora of varied material items, the interpretation of which for historical purposes presents considerable methodological challenges.[6] Through his respect for the individuality of phenomena and of a plurality of worlds, Thoreau points the way to what would become the practice of material culture history. I have therefore paired history and philosophy in this selective study.

We can consider history a form of poetry, as Thoreau implicitly does when he claims: "A true account of the actual is the rarest poetry."[7] In Thoreau's opinion, history approaches nature and truth so long as the historian feels "a human interest in his subject and to so express it."[8] Thoreau's sensitivity to the aesthetics of ordinary human—and natural—life initially led him to poetry and subsequently to philosophy as a means of exploring the human condition and proposing courses of action. Therefore, I conclude this selective exploration of some of Thoreau's worlds by acknowledging his belief—foreign to most philosophers now—that those two modes of thought, poetry and philosophy, are complementary, each inevitably incomplete. In a January 1852 journal entry, Thoreau sets out this idea succinctly: "Poetry *implies* the whole truth. Philosophy *expresses* a particle of it."[9] This is a realization that we philosophers—particularly prone to hubris within the community of scholars—might do well to keep in mind.

Acknowledgments

This text is closely informed by thoughts about Thoreau's work that I have published over a number of years. The chapters that derive from previously published work are all elaborations with extensive revisions and additions, in some cases scarcely recognizable when compared with their originals. Chapter 1, "Worlds," is new, written as an introduction to this book. Chapter 2, "Migrants," derives loosely from "Concord Migrations," in *Cultural Heritage, Ethics and Contemporary Migrations*, ed. Cornelius Holtorf, Andreas Pantazatos, and Geoffrey Scarre (London: Routledge, 2019) (reproduced with the permission of The Licensor through PLSclear). Chapter 3, "Buildings," is based on "Race, Aesthetics, and Shelter: Toward a Postcolonial Historical Taxonomy of Buildings," *Journal of Aesthetics and Art Criticism* 77 (2019) (reproduced with permission of the *Journal of Aesthetics and Art Criticism* and the American Society for Aesthetics). Chapter 4, "Shelter," is derived from "'To Build Still More Deliberately': Architectural Reconstruction and the House That Thoreau Built," in *The Routledge Companion to the Philosophy of Architectural Reconstruction*, ed. Lisa Giombini and Zoltán Somhegyi (London: Routledge, forthcoming) (reproduced with the permission of Routledge). Chapter 5, "Artistry," is entirely new, but draws on ideas about distinctions between tools and artworks that I first articulated in lectures I delivered at the Museo Nacional de Bellas Artes in Buenos Aires in 1998. Chapter 6, "Collections," includes some material, wholly reworked, that I included in "'Making a World': The Impact of Idealism on Museum Formation in Mid-Nineteenth-Century Massachusetts," in *The Impact of Idealism: The Legacy of Post-Kantian German Thought*, gen. ed. Nicholas Boyle and Liz Disley, vol. 3, *Aesthetics and Literature*, ed. Christoph Jamme and Ian Cooper (Cambridge: Cambridge University Press, 2013). Chapter 7, "Sounds," is entirely new and was inspired by conversations with, and papers by, a number of Indigenous scholars, among whom I should mention Butch Thunder Hawk (Húŋkpapȟa Lakȟóta), Jim Enote (A:shiwi), and Larissa Nez (Diné). I sum up the case I make for the importance of aesthetics in Thoreau's thinking in chapter 8, "Conclusion." I am grateful to all those scholars who prompted me, cajoled me, and saw the originals through to publication, and to the American Society for Aesthetics, Cambridge University Press, and Routledge.

Thinking about Thoreau incurs debts, and mine are many. In particular, I wish to acknowledge the importance of conversations about Thoreau's ideas and related matters with supportive friends and colleagues, some of whom are no longer with us: Michael Baxandall, Arnold Berleant, Laura Bieger, Pierre Bourdieu, Peter Burke, Sarah Anne Carter, Stanley Cavell, Arthur C. Danto, Anne Eaton, Martin van Gelderen, Reed Gochberg, Salim Kemal, Ann-Sophie Lehmann, Peter Miller, Yuriko Saito, Daniel Lord Smail, Nicholas Thomas, Laurel Thatcher Ulrich, David Ward, Richard Wollheim, and David Wood. The reader may find traces of their ideas—mindprints, if you like—throughout this book. I am especially indebted to Megan Marshall, who was kind enough to read a complete draft. Her generous notes saved me from several embarrassments. I am also indebted for their insights to the graduate students in my 2023 Thoreau seminar: Eliza Alsop, David Gassett, Joshua Massey, and Clara Murphy.

A number of institutions have been vitally supportive, among them Harvard Library (notably Tozzer Library), Cambridge, Massachusetts; Cary Memorial Library, Lexington, Massachusetts; Concord Free Public Library, Concord, Massachusetts; Fruitlands Museum (Trustees of Reservations), Harvard, Massachusetts; Lichtenberg-Kolleg (Advanced Study Institute), Georg-August University, Göttingen; Museum of Science, Boston, Massachusetts; Peabody Museum of Archaeology and Ethnology, Harvard University, Cambridge, Massachusetts; and the Sterling and Francine Clark Art Institute, Williamstown, Massachusetts. My colleagues at Bard Graduate Center have consistently encouraged me in my work on Thoreau and the Center generously provided a subvention to help cover costs of publication.

At the University of Chicago Press my editor, Kyle Wagner, and his team, including Kristin Rawlings, have been ceaselessly encouraging from the outset. Sharon Langworthy copyedited the text assiduously and graciously. Two anonymous readers made invaluable suggestions that prompted me to adduce further evidence and sharpen arguments.

The people who have put up with my Thoreau obsession—if such it is—with more patience than I deserve are my best interlocutor, editor, and fellow saunterer around, swimmer in, and skater on, Walden Pond, my beloved Jane Whitehead, and our curious and questioning son, Leo Gaskell. This book is for them.

Notes

Quotations from Thoreau's journals written between 1837 and much of 1854 are from the eight volumes published to date of the Princeton Edition (1981–2002). For the years not yet covered by the Princeton edition (late 1854 through 1861), quotations are from the fourteen-volume Riverside edition (1906).

PREFACE

1. William Wordsworth, "The Prelude, or Growth of a Poet's Mind: An Autobiographical Poem" (1850), in *Wordsworth Poetical Works*, ed. Thomas Hutchinson, rev. Ernest de Selincourt (London: Oxford University Press, 1936), 509 (Book III, lines 62–63) . Laura Dassow Walls confutes the widespread notion that Thoreau was alone in what she terms his *empirical holism*, which she compares with Alexander von Humboldt's conception of nature as moved by internal rather than external forces. Laura Dassow Walls, *Seeing New Worlds: Henry David Thoreau and Nineteenth-Century Natural Science* (Madison: University of Wisconsin Press, 1995), 84–93, 133–44.

2. F. O. Matthiessen pointed out differences long ago between the two men's ways of thinking that emerged as Thoreau reached maturity. F. O. Matthiessen, *American Renaissance: Art and Expression in the Age of Emerson and Whitman* (London: Oxford University Press, 1941), 83–92.

3. Henry D. Thoreau, *Journal*, gen. ed. Robert Sattelmeyer, vol. 4, *1851–1852*, ed. Leonard N. Neufeldt and Nancy Craig Simmons (Princeton, NJ: Princeton University Press, 1992), 310 (January 31, 1852).

4. Matthiessen, *American Renaissance*, 86. By "the thing" Matthiesson refers to what I term items of all kinds.

5. Ludwig Wittgenstein, *Tractatus Logico-Philosophicus* (London: Kegan Paul, Trench, Trubner; New York: Harcourt, Brace, 1922), 44:4.1121.

6. See bibliography in *Henry David Thoreau Online*, accessed January 8, 2023, https://www.thoreau-online.org/bibliography.htm. Henry David Thoreau, *A Week on the Concord and Merrimack Rivers* (Boston: J. Munroe; New York: G. P. Putnam, 1849).

7. See "Henry D. Thoreau," Princeton University Press, accessed January 8, 2023, https://press.princeton.edu/collected-works/collected-henry-d-thoreau.

8. Princeton University Press has published eight volumes of the journal, beginning with Henry D. Thoreau, *Journal*, gen. ed. John C. Broderick, vol. 1, *1837–1844*,

ed. Elizabeth Hall Witherell, William L. Howarth, Robert Sattelmayer, and Thomas Blanding (Princeton, NJ: Princeton University Press, 1981), and ending with Henry D. Thoreau, *Journal*, vol. 8, *1854*, ed. Sandra Harbert Petrulionis (Princeton, NJ: Princeton University Press, 2002). Also indispensable, though not comprehensive, is the edition published in fourteen volumes in 1906: *The Writings of Henry David Thoreau: Journal*, ed. Bradford Torrey (Boston: Houghton Mifflin; Cambridge, MA: Riverside, 1906), made available online by the Walden Woods Project, accessed January 8, 2023, https://www.walden.org/collection/journals/.

9. Wittgenstein, *Tractatus Logico-Philosophicus*: "a work that had been in print for seven years and was already regarded by many as a philosophical classic." Ray Monk, *Wittgenstein: The Duty of Genius* (London: Jonathan Cape, 1990), 271.

10. There is a brass memorial plaque in Trinity College Chapel. "Ludwig Josef Johann Wittgenstein," accessed July 24, 2023, http://trinitycollegechapel.com/about/memorials/brasses/wittgenstein/.

11. See, most famously, Gibbon's recollection of the genesis of *The Decline and Fall of the Roman Empire*: "It was at Rome, on the 15th of October, 1764, as I sat musing amidst the ruins of the Capitol, while the barefooted friars were singing vespers at the temple of Jupiter, that the idea of writing the decline and fall of the city first started to my mind." Edward Gibbon, "Memoirs of My Life and Writings," in *The Autobiography of Edward Gibbon*, ed. John Baker Holroyd, 1st Earl of Sheffield (London: Oxford University Press, 1907), 160. Gibbon's firsthand experience of many of the places about which he wrote underlies the vividness of his brilliant historical accounts.

12. Stanley Cavell, *The Senses of Walden: An Expanded Edition* (San Francisco: North Point Press, 1981); and Lawrence Buell, *The Environmental Imagination: Thoreau, Nature Writing, and the Formation of American Culture* (Cambridge, MA: Belknap Press of Harvard University Press, 1995).

13. I can find no trace of Keillor's BBC serial reading of *Walden*, but it must have been broadcast between 1983 and 1991 when I was living in Cambridge, England.

14. I read Monk, *Wittgenstein: The Duty of Genius* when it first came out while staying with a friend in Italy.

15. Henry D. Thoreau, *Walden and Other Writings of Henry David Thoreau*, ed. Brooks Atkinson (1937; New York: Modern Library, 1992); and Ludwig Wittgenstein, *Philosophical Investigations*, 3rd ed. (the German text with a revised English translation), ed. Gertrude Elizabeth Margaret Anscombe and Rush Rhees, trans. Gertrude Elizabeth Margaret Anscombe (Oxford: Blackwell, 2001).

16. My allusion to Edward Casaubon's project in George Eliot's *Middlemarch: A Study of Provincial Life* (Edinburgh: Blackwood, 1871) is only mildly facetious; whereas the fictional Casaubon's ambition was hopeless, Wittgenstein's was not. Thomas Wentworth Higginson, "Thoreau," in *Short Studies of American Authors* (Boston: Lee and Shepard; New York: Charles T. Dillingham, 1880), 25–26.

CHAPTER ONE

1. Henry D. Thoreau, *Walden: A Fully Annotated Edition*, ed. Jeffrey S. Cramer (New Haven, CT: Yale University Press, 2004), 89.

2. Robert D. Richardson, *Three Roads Back: How Emerson, Thoreau, and William*

James Responded to the Greatest Losses of Their Lives (Princeton, NJ: Princeton University Press, 2023), 29–64.

3. *The Writings of Henry David Thoreau: Journal XII*, ed. Bradford Torrey (Boston: Houghton Mifflin; Cambridge, MA: Riverside, 1906), 92 (March 28, 1859).

4. *Writings of Henry David Thoreau: Journal XII*, 91 (March 28, 1859). See also Curtis Runnels, "Henry David Thoreau, Archaeologist?," *Concord Saunterer*, n.s., 27 (2019): 42–67.

5. Thoreau, *Walden*, ed. Cramer, 216.

6. *The Writings of Henry David Thoreau: Journal I*, ed. Bradford Torrey (Boston: Houghton Mifflin; Cambridge, MA: Riverside, 1906), 374–75 (July 14[?], 1845).

7. Thoreau, *Walden*, ed. Cramer, 216.

8. Ralph Waldo Emerson, "The American Scholar," in *The Selected Writings of Ralph Waldo Emerson*, ed. Brooks Atkinson (New York: Modern Library, 1992), 57–58.

9. Henry D. Thoreau, *Journal*, vol. 7, *1853–1854*, ed. Nancy Craig Simmons and Ron Thomas (Princeton, NJ: Princeton University Press, 1999), 227–33 (January 8, 1854), referring to William Gilpin, *Three Essays: On Picturesque Beauty, on Picturesque Travel, and on Sketching Landscape; With a Poem, on Landscape Painting*, 3rd ed. (London: T. Cadell and W. Davies, 1808): "To these are now added two essays, giving an account of the principles and mode in which the author executed his own drawings."

10. Henry D. Thoreau, *Essays: A Fully Annotated Edition*, ed. Jeffrey S. Cramer (New Haven, CT: Yale University Press, 2013), 338–39.

11. *The Writings of Henry David Thoreau: Journal XI*, ed. Bradford Torrey (Boston: Houghton Mifflin; Cambridge, MA: Riverside, 1906), 166 (September 18, 1858).

12. *The Aesthetics of Everyday Life*, ed. Andrew Light and Jonathan M. Smith (New York: Columbia University Press, 2005); Yuriko Saito, *Everyday Aesthetics* (Oxford: Oxford University Press, 2007); Yuriko Saito, *Aesthetics of the Familiar: Everyday Life and World-Making* (Oxford: Oxford University Press, 2017); Yuriko Saito, "Aesthetics Is Everywhere," in *Aesthetic Literacy*, vol. 2, *Out of Mind*, ed. Valery Vinogradovs (n.p.: Mongrel Matter, 2023), 17–22; R. W. Hepburn, *"Wonder" and Other Essays: Eight Studies in Aesthetics and Neighbouring Fields* (Edinburgh: University of Edinburgh Press, 1984); R. W. Hepburn, *The Reach of the Aesthetic: Collected Essays on Art and Nature* (Aldershot: Ashgate, 2001); Allen Carlson, *Nature and Landscape: An Introduction to Environmental Aesthetics* (New York: Columbia University Press, 2009); Arnold Berleant, *The Aesthetics of Environment* (Philadelphia: Temple University Press, 1992); and *The Aesthetics of Natural Environments*, ed. Arnold Berleant and Allen Carlson (Peterborough, ON: Broadview, 2004). See also *Landscape, Natural Beauty and the Arts*, ed. Salim Kemal and Ivan Gaskell (Cambridge: Cambridge University Press, 1993).

13. Rick Anthony Furtak, "The Value of Being: Thoreau on Appreciating the Beauty of the World," in *Thoreau's Importance for Philosophy*, ed. Rick Anthony Furtak, Jonathan Ellsworth, and James D. Reid (New York: Fordham University Press, 2012), 118, 119, 126.

14. John Kaag, *Thinking through the Imagination: Aesthetics in Human Cognition* (New York: Fordham University Press, 2014), 204.

15. Thoreau, *Walden*, ed. Cramer, 150; and Kaag, *Thinking through the Imagination*,

205. Kaag attends to Thoreau's aesthetic imagination as a precedent for that of Charles Sanders Peirce, his principal focus of attention.

16. David F. Wood, *An Observant Eye: The Thoreau Collection at the Concord Museum* (Concord, MA: Concord Museum, 2006). I am grateful to David Wood for guiding me through examinations of many of Thoreau's personal possessions with associate curator Reed Gochberg at the Concord Museum.

17. Literary scholar Branka Arsić has proposed that Thoreau's metaphysics incorporates a vitalism that ascribes life—literally—to all manner of natural phenomena, including rocks and the items humans fashion from them. Branka Arsić, *Bird Relics: Grief and Vitalism in Thoreau* (Cambridge, MA: Harvard University Press, 2016). I cannot discuss vitalism here, but see Ivan Gaskell, "The Life of Things," in *The International Handbook of Museum Studies: Museum Media*, ed. Michelle Henning (Oxford: John Wiley, 2015), 167–90. Thoreau responded directly and indirectly to William Wordsworth's celebrated consideration of "the life of things" in, among other poems, "Lines Composed a Few Miles above Tintern Abbey" (1798): "While with an eye made quiet by the power / Of harmony, and the deep power of joy, / We see into the life of things. . . . A motion and a spirit, that impels / All thinking things, all objects of all thought, / And rolls through all things." *Wordsworth: Poetical Works*, ed. Thomas Hutchinson, rev. Ernest de Selincourt (Oxford: Oxford University Press, 1936), 163–65.

18. Henry D. Thoreau, *Journal*, gen. ed. Robert Sattelmayer, vol. 5, *1852–53*, ed. Patrick F. O'Connell (Princeton, NJ: Princeton University Press, 1997), 120 (June 21, 1852).

19. Ivan Gaskell, "Works of Art and Mere Real Things—Again," *British Journal of Aesthetics* 60, no. 2 (2020): 136. See also Arnold Berleant, *Sensibility and Sense: The Aesthetic Transformation of the Human World* (Springfield, IL: C. C. Thomas, 2010).

20. The works of Yuriko Saito cited note 12 have reinforced my conviction, notably *Everyday Aesthetics* and *Aesthetics of the Familiar*. The work of Arnold Berleant on environmental aesthetics, beginning with *Aesthetics of Environment* (cited in note 12) has helped me to consider Thoreau's concerns with nature in an aesthetic register.

21. Henry D. Thoreau, *A Week on the Concord and Merrimack Rivers*, ed. Carl F. Hovde, William L. Howarth, and Elizabeth Hall Witherell (Princeton, NJ: Princeton University Press, 2004), 49.

22. Thoreau had access to a translation of the *Bhagavad Gita* from 1845. Laura Dassow Walls, *Henry David Thoreau: A Life* (Chicago: University of Chicago Press, 2017), 230: "The Gita became the closest thing Thoreau had to a personal bible." Thoreau received his own copy, together with forty-two other volumes of mostly sacred texts in the Vedic tradition, as a gift sent from England by Thomas Cholmondeley in 1855. Wood, *Observant Eye*, 70–73. Stanley Cavell notes, "Like *Walden*, the *Bhagavad Gita* is a scripture in eighteen parts." Stanley Cavell, *The Senses of Walden: An Expanded Edition* (San Francisco: North Point Press, 1981), 117–18. See also Paul Friedrich, *The Gita within Walden* (Albany: State University of New York Press, 2008). Kevin Dann refers to Walden as "his own *gita*". Kevin Dann, *Expect Great Things: The Life and Search of Henry David Thoreau* (New York: Penguin Random House, 2018), 133.

23. See Clark A. Elliott, *Thaddeus William Harris (1795–1856): Nature, Science, and Society in the Life of an American Naturalist* (Bethlehem, PA: Lehigh University Press, 2008).

24. Thoreau, *Walden*, ed. Cramer, 1.

25. "Actant is a term from semiotics covering both humans and non-humans." Bruno Latour, *Politics of Nature*, trans. Catherine Porter (Cambridge, MA: Harvard University Press, 2004), 237. I mention physicist Karen Barad, sociologist Bruno Latour, archaeologist Lambros Malafouris, and anthropologist Nicholas Thomas as scholars who have explored reciprocal relations between humans and nonhuman entities in sophisticated manners.

26. *Writings of Henry David Thoreau: Journal XII*, 91, 92 (March 28, 1859).

27. *Writings of Henry David Thoreau: Journal XII*, 91.

28. Henry David Thoreau, *Cape Cod*, ed. Robert Pinsky and Joseph J. Moldenhauer (Princeton, NJ: Princeton University Press, 2010), 33. I completely reject the ill-considered term *New World* for the land of the Great Turtle.

29. Anthropologists use the term *peripatetic* to describe that subset of nomadic peoples who offer goods and services to sedentary communities. Michael J. Casimir and Aparna Rao, eds., *Mobility and Territoriality: Social and Spatial Boundaries among Foragers, Fishers, Pastoralists and Peripatetics* (New York: Berg, 1992); and Joseph C. Berland and Aparna Rao, eds., *Customary Strangers: New Perspectives on Peripatetic Peoples in the Middle East, Africa, and Asia* (Westport, CT: Praeger, 2004).

30. See Edward L. Glaeser, *Triumph of the City: How Our Greatest Invention Makes Us Richer, Smarter, Greener, Healthier, Happier* (New York: Penguin Books, 2011).

31. Thoreau, *Walden*, ed. Cramer, 12.

32. See, in the first instance, Richard B. Primack, *Walden Warming: Climate Change Comes to Thoreau's Woods* (Chicago: University of Chicago Press, 2014).

33. Out of respect for Native peoples, throughout the book I use endonyms for Native nations, followed by up-to-date settler equivalents in parentheses.

34. Henry David Thoreau, *The Maine Woods*, ed. Joseph J. Moldenhauer (Princeton, NJ: Princeton University Press, 2010), 136–37.

35. Thoreau, *Journal*, vol. 5, *1852–53*, 82–83 (June 9, 1852).

36. Thoreau, *Journal*, vol. 5, *1852–53*, 272 (August 3, 1852); and Thoreau, *Walden*, ed. Cramer, 209.

CHAPTER TWO

1. Robert A. Gross, "Thoreau and the Laborers of Concord," *Raritan* 33, no. 1 (2013): 57.

2. Among them was the woodcutter, identified as Alexander or Alek Therien, who felled trees in Walden Woods and on whom Thoreau reports at length. Henry D. Thoreau, *Walden: A Fully Annotated Edition*, ed. Jeffrey S. Cramer (New Haven, CT: Yale University Press, 2004), 139–45. See also Gross, "Thoreau and the Laborers of Concord," 57–58.

3. Gross, "Thoreau and the Laborers of Concord," 56.

4. I acknowledge that people moved to North America from Asia, Oceania, and South America during this period, but such emigration is beyond the bounds of this study.

5. Henry David Thoreau, *Cape Cod*, ed. Robert Pinsky and Joseph J. Moldenhauer (Princeton, NJ: Princeton University Press, 2010), 33.

6. Lemuel Shattuck, *A History of the Town of Concord, Middlesex County, Massachusetts: From Its Earliest Settlement to 1832* (Boston: Russell, Ordione; Concord: John Stacy, 1835).

7. Shattuck, *History of Concord*, 4–6.

8. Shattuck, *History of Concord*, 5n1.

9. Henry D. Thoreau, *A Week on the Concord and Merrimack Rivers*, ed. Carl F. Hovde, William L. Howarth, and Elizabeth Hall Witherell (Princeton, NJ: Princeton University Press, 2004), 5.

10. For a succinct account, see Brian Donahue, *The Great Meadow: Farmers and the Land in Colonial Concord* (New Haven, CT: Yale University Press, 2004), 35–53.

11. Shattuck, *History of Concord*, 3; and Shirley Blancke et al., "Clamshell Bluff, Concord, Massachusetts," *Bulletin of the Massachusetts Archaeological Society* 56, no. 2 (1995): 29–84.

12. Donahue, *Great Meadow*, 40.

13. Donahue, *Great Meadow*, 41.

14. On early Native uses of European metal objects, see Laurier Turgeon, "The Tale of a Kettle: Odyssey of an Intercultural Object," *Ethnohistory* 44, no. 1 (1997): 1–29.

15. See Alfred A. Cave, *The Pequot War* (Amherst: University of Massachusetts Press, 1996) on the 1636–37 conflict; and Jill Lepore, *The Name of War: King Philip's War and the Origins of American Identity* (New York: Vintage, 1998). Pequot is the preferred name of the contemporary Mashantucket (Western) Pequot Tribal Nation. "About the Mashantucket (Western) Pequot Tribal Nation," accessed March 31, 2023, https://www.mptn-nsn.gov/default.aspx.

16. John Milton Earle, *Report to the Governor and Council Concerning the Indians of the Commonwealth under the Act of April 6, 1859* (Boston: William White, Printer to the Senate, 1861), lxxviii, Senate Document no. 96, Massachusetts State Library, Special Collections, State House, Boston, MA, cited in Ann Marie Plane and Gregory Button, "The Massachusetts Indian Enfranchisement Act: Ethnic Contest in Historical Context, 1849–1869," *Ethnohistory* 40, no. 4 (1993): 589.

17. Plane and Button, "Massachusetts Indian Enfranchisement Act," 589–90.

18. Plane and Button, "Massachusetts Indian Enfranchisement Act," 588.

19. "Indian Entities Recognized by and Eligible to Receive Services from the United States Bureau of Indian Affairs," *Federal Register* 85, no. 20 (January 30, 2020): 5462–67, accessed December 30, 2022, https://www.federalregister.gov/documents/2020/01/30/2020-01707/indian-entities-recognized-by-and-eligible-to-receive-services-from-the-united-states-bureau-of.

20. These include the Massachusett Tribe at Ponkapoag website, accessed December 30, 2022, https://massachusetttribe.org/; and the Praying Indians of Natick and Ponkapoag website, accessed December 30, 2022, http://natickprayingindians.org/history.html.

21. See the Wôpanâak Language Reclamation Project website, accessed December 30, 2022, http://www.wlrp.org/.

22. Some of what follows on Thoreau's collection of Indigenous artifacts is derived from my "'Making a World': The Impact of Idealism on Museum Formation in

Mid-Nineteenth-Century Massachusetts," in *The Impact of Idealism: The Legacy of Post-Kantian German Thought*, gen. ed. Nicholas Boyle and Liz Disley, vol. 3, *Aesthetics and Literature*, ed. Christoph Jamme and Ian Cooper (Cambridge: Cambridge University Press, 2013), 245–63.

23. Shattuck, *History of Concord*, 3.

24. Henry David Thoreau, *Journal*, gen. ed. John C. Broderick, vol. 1, *1837–1844*, ed. Elizabeth Hall Witherell, William L. Howarth, Robert Sattelmayer, and Thomas Blanding (Princeton, NJ: Princeton University Press, 1981), 380–81 (March 19, 1842).

25. Thoreau, *Walden*, ed. Cramer, 151.

26. Thomas Jefferson, *Notes on the State of Virginia* (1785; New York: Library of America, 1984), 223–26.

27. Franklin B. Sanborn, *The Life of Henry David Thoreau: Including Many Essays Hitherto Unpublished, and Some Account of His Family and Friends* (Boston: Houghton Mifflin, 1917), 206.

28. For an account of their friendship, see Earl J. Dias, "Daniel Ricketson and Henry Thoreau," *New England Quarterly* 26, no. 3 (1953): 388–96.

29. *The Writings of Henry David Thoreau: Journal VIII*, ed. Bradford Torrey (Boston: Houghton Mifflin; Cambridge, MA: Riverside, 1906), 390–92 (June 26, 1856).

30. "Family Tree of Henry David Thoreau (1817–1862)," The Thoreau Society, accessed December 30, 2022, http://www.thoreausociety.org/life-legacy/family-tree.

31. See Henry David Thoreau, *The Maine Woods*, ed. Joseph J. Moldenhauer (Princeton, NJ: Princeton University Press, 2010). See also Timothy Troy, "Ktaadn: Thoreau the Anthropologist," *Dialectical Anthropology* 15, no. 1 (1990): 74–81; and Corinne Hosfeld Smith, *Westward I Go Free: Tracing Thoreau's Last Journey* (Winnipeg, MB: Green Frigate Books, 2012).

32. See Robert F. Sayre, *Thoreau and the American Indians* (Princeton, NJ: Princeton University Press, 1977), 101–22, 217–20. For a breakdown of the "Indian Books," see 110, table 1. See also Richard F. Fleck, *The Indians of Thoreau: Selections from the Indian Notebooks* (Albuquerque, NM: Hummingbird Press, 1974); Richard F. Fleck, *Selections from the "Indian Notebooks" (1847–1861) of Henry D. Thoreau*, (Lincoln, MA: The Thoreau Institute at Walden Woods, 2007), accessed December 30, 2022, http://www.walden.org/documents/file/Library/Thoreau/writings/Notebooks/IndianNotebooks.pdf.

33. Sayre, *Thoreau and the American Indians*, 105, 106.

34. Sayre, *Thoreau and the American Indians*, 102, quoting a review of *The Maine Woods* reliably attributed to Sanborn in the *Commonwealth*, June 10, 1864, 1.

35. Sayre, *Thoreau and the American Indians*, 105–6.

36. Joshua David Bellin, "In the Company of Savagists: Thoreau's Indian Books and Antebellum Ethnology," the *Concord Saunterer*, n.s., 16 (2008): 1–32. Bellin argues that Thoreau shared many of the emerging racist beliefs about the supposed intractability of Native people.

37. This is the burden of the argument presented by Sayre, *Thoreau and the American Indians*.

38. Thoreau, "The Allegash and East Branch," in *Maine Woods*, ed. Moldenhauer, 162. "The Indian sat on the front seat, saying nothing to anybody, with a stolid

expression of face, as if barely awake to what going on. Again I was struck by the peculiar vagueness of his replies when addressed in the stage, or at the taverns. He really never said anything on such occasions. He was merely stirred up, like a wild beast, and passively muttered sonic insignificant response. His answer, in such cases, was never the consequence of a positive mental energy, but vague as a puff of smoke, suggesting no *responsibility*, and if you considered it, you would find that you had got nothing out of him."

39. Thoreau, *Maine Woods*, 185.

40. Ben Shattuck, *Six Walks in the Footsteps of Henry David Thoreau* (Portland, OR: Tin House, 2022), 197.

41. I repeat this statement verbatim from Ivan Gaskell, "Historical Distance, Historical Judgment," in *Rethinking Historical Distance*, ed. Mark Salber Phillips, Barbara Caine, and Julia Adeney Thomas (New York: Palgrave Macmillan, 2013), 34.

42. Steven Conn, *History's Shadow: Native Americans and Historical Consciousness in the Nineteenth Century* (Chicago: University of Chicago Press, 2004).

43. Frank B. Sanborn, "Emerson and His Friends in Concord," *New England Magazine* 3 (1890): 430–31. The person "*not known to this audience*" was Walt Whitman. Sanborn reports that Emerson omitted the sentence referring to Whitman from the published version at Sophia Thoreau's request, which may have led to the omission of Polis's and Brown's names, too, where the only mention of Polis reads: "In his last visit to Maine he had great satisfaction from Joseph Polis, an intelligent Indian of Oldtown, who was his guide for some weeks." Ralph Waldo Emerson, "Thoreau," *Atlantic Monthly*, August 1862, 246. See also Sayre, *Thoreau and the American Indians*, 184.

44. Sayre, *Thoreau and the American Indians*, 184.

45. See, for example, Joyce Lee Malcolm, *Peter's War: A New England Slave Boy and the American Revolution* (New Haven, CT: Yale University Press, 2009).

46. Alexandra A. Chan, *Slavery in the Age of Reason: Archaeology at a New England Farm* (Knoxville: University of Tennessee Press, 2007); and C. S. Manegold, *Ten Hills Farm: The Forgotten History of Slavery in the North* (Princeton, NJ: Princeton University Press, 2010).

47. Elise Lemire, *Black Walden: Slavery and Its Aftermath in Concord, Massachusetts* (Philadelphia: University of Pennsylvania Press, 2009).

48. Lemire, *Black Walden*, 10. See also Sharon V. Salinger and Cornelia H. Dayton, *Robert Love's Warnings: Searching for Strangers in Colonial Boston* (Philadelphia: University of Pennsylvania Press, 2014); and Josiah Henry Benton, *Warning Out in New England* (Boston: W. B. Clarke, 1911), 46–62.

49. See Joanne Pope Melish, *Discovering Slavery: Gradual Emancipation and "Race" in New England, 1780–1860* (Ithaca, NY: Cornell University Press, 1998), 132–35.

50. H. D. Thoreau, "Resistance to Civil Government; a Lecture Delivered in 1847," in *Æsthetic Papers*, ed. Elizabeth P. Peabody (Boston: the editor; New York: G. P. Putnam, 1849), 189–211; Henry D. Thoreau, "Slavery in Massachusetts: An Address, Delivered at the Anti-Slavery Celebration at Framingham, July 4th, 1854," *Liberator*, July 21, 1854, 116; repr., *New-York Daily Tribune*, August 2, 1854, 3 (with a preface by Horace Greeley); and Henry D. Thoreau, "A Plea for Capt. John Brown," in *Echoes of Harper's Ferry*, ed. James Redpath (Boston: Thayer and Eldridge, 1860), 17–42 ("read to the

citizens of Concord, Mass., Sunday evening, October 30, 1859; also as the Fifth Lecture of the Fraternity Course, in Boston, November 1").

51. Thoreau, *Walden*, ed. Cramer, 246.

52. Robert A. Gross, *The Transcendentalists and Their World* (New York: Farrar, Straus and Giroux, 2021), 100.

53. Thoreau, *Walden*, ed. Cramer, 247. Lemire identifies the "old frequenter" as George Minot (Lemire, *Black Walden*, 135).

54. Gross, *Transcendentalists and Their World*, 101n35, with references. In the main text Gross states that she died at aged seventy-two, but in the note he states her age at death as eighty-two.

55. Thoreau, *Walden*, ed. Cramer, 248.

56. Lemire, *Black Walden*, 108.

57. Gross, *Transcendentalists and Their World*, 100–101.

58. Gross, *Transcendentalists and their World*, 101.

59. Thoreau, *Walden*, ed. Cramer, 248.

60. Lemire, *Black Walden*, 110–11.

61. Lemire, *Black Walden*, 141–42.

62. Thoreau, *Walden*, ed. Cramer, 247.

63. Thoreau, *Walden*, ed. Cramer, 248.

64. Robert Gross points out that Black families continued to live in Concord throughout Thoreau's lifetime (Gross, *Transcendentalists and Their World*, 102–7), but Thoreau mentions them only in his journal, not in his published writings, taking no account of their race. Robert A. Gross, "Thoreau and the Laborers of Concord," *Raritan* 33, no. 1 (2013): 63–64.

65. Although measures had been put in place in various Canadian provinces to inhibit or end slavery from the 1790s onward, the institution was not finally abolished until after the passage of the Slavery Abolition Act of 1833. See, in the first instance, Robin W. Winks, *The Blacks in Canada: A History*, 2nd ed. (Montreal: McGill-Queen's University Press, 1997), 142–77. I am grateful to Charmaine Nelson for discussions of slavery in Canada.

66. See, in the first instance, J. Blaine Hudson, *Encyclopedia of the Underground Railroad* (Jefferson, NC: McFarland, 2006); and William Still, *The Underground Railroad Records: Narrating the Hardships, Hairbreadth Escapes, and Death Struggles of the Slaves in Their Efforts for Freedom*, ed. Quincy T. Mills (New York: Modern Library, 2019).

67. A carefully considered account of the August 1, 1846, gathering and its place in the developing rift between Thoreau and Emerson is given by Randall Conrad, "Realizing Resistance: Thoreau and the First of August, 1846, at Walden," *Concord Saunterer* 12/13 (2004/2005): 164–93.

68. Thoreau, *Walden*, ed. Cramer, 146–47.

69. Henry D. Thoreau, *Journal*, gen ed. Robert Sattelmeyer, vol. 4, *1851–1852*, ed. Leonard N. Neufeldt and Nancy Craig Simmons (Princeton, NJ: Princeton University Press, 1992), 113 (October 1, 1851).

70. Moncure Daniel Conway, *Autobiography, Memories and Experiences of Moncure Daniel Conway* (London: Cassell, 1904), 1:127. See also Laura Dassow Walls, *Thoreau: A Life* (Chicago: University of Chicago Press, 2017), 319.

71. The project was made possible by Institute of Museum and Library Services Grant # MH-00-17-0030.

72. *The Robbins House: Concord's African American History*, accessed January 2, 2023, https://robbinshouse.org/.

73. Helen Lojek, "Thoreau's Bog People," *New England Quarterly* 67, no. 2 (1994): 280.

74. Thoreau, *Walden*, ed. Cramer, 41.

75. Thoreau, *Walden*, ed. Cramer, 42.

76. Thoreau, *Walden*, ed. Cramer, 42–43.

77. *The Correspondence of Henry D. Thoreau*, vol. 1, *1834–1848*, ed. Robert N. Hudspeth (Princeton, NJ: Princeton University Press, 2013), 320n19.

78. *Correspondence*, vol. 1, *1834–1848*, ed. Hudspeth, 337–39 (letter dated January 12, 1848).

79. *The Correspondence of Henry D. Thoreau*, vol. 2, *1849–1856*, ed. Robert N. Hudspeth, with Elizabeth Hall Witherell and Lihong Xie (Princeton, NJ: Princeton University Press, 2013), 175–77 (letters dated October 12, 1853, announcing the compensation sum raised and the loan of $50 due on November 1, 1854).

80. Henry D. Thoreau, *Journal*, vol. 7, *1853–1854*, ed. Nancy Craig Simmons and Ron Thomas (Princeton, NJ: Princeton University Press, 1999), 102–13 (October 12, 1853) (emphasis in original).

81. *Correspondence*, vol. 2, *1849–1856*, ed. Robert N. Hudspeth et al., 200 (Thoreau to Elijah Wood, February 26, 1854); and Bradley P. Dean, "Thoreau and Michael Flannery," *Concord Saunterer* 17, no. 3 (1984): 27–33.

82. Henry D. Thoreau, *Journal*, vol. 8, *1854*, ed. Sandra Harbert Petrulionis (Princeton, NJ: Princeton University Press, 2002), 33–34 (March 8, 1854); and Walls, *Thoreau: A Life*, 329.

83. Henry David Thoreau, *Cape Cod* (Boston: Ticknor and Fields, 1865).

84. "Cape Cod," *Putnam's Monthly: A Magazine of American Literature, Science, and Art*, June 1855, 632–40. No contributor was accorded a byline.

85. "Cape Cod," 633.

86. "Cape Cod," 633.

87. "Cape Cod," 635.

88. "Cape Cod," 634.

89. There is a considerable literature on the Know Nothings. For a succinct account, see James M. McPherson, *Battle Cry of Freedom: The Civil War Era* (Oxford: Oxford University Press, 1988), 135–44. For the Massachusetts election, see Tyler Anbinder, *Nativism and Slavery: The Northern Know Nothings and the Politics of the 1850s* (Oxford: Oxford University Press, 1992), 87–94.

90. "Secret Societies—the Know Nothings," *Putnam's Monthly: A Magazine of American Literature, Science, and Art*, January 1855, 88–97; "America for the Americans," *Putnam's Monthly: A Magazine of American Literature, Science, and Art*, May

1855, 533–41; and Parke Godwin, *Political Essays* (New York: Dix, Edwards, 1856), 175–209.

91. The passage of the Kansas-Nebraska Act in 1854 marked the end of the compromise affecting those areas of westward expansion where slavery could or could not be introduced, while the presidential election of 1856 (won by the Democrat James Buchanan) saw the emergence of the new Republican Party, which was to triumph with the election of Abraham Lincoln to the presidency in 1860. This in turn precipitated the secession of eleven slave states, the foundation of the Confederate States of America, and the disastrous civil war that ensued. The Thirteenth Amendment to the US Constitution, abolishing slavery in most circumstances, was ratified in December 1865.

92. See note 17. Emphasis in original.

93. Among the most widely reported incidents are those at Wounded Knee on the Pine Ridge Indian Reservation (Wazí Aháŋhaŋ Oyáŋke) of the Oglála Lakȟóta (Oglala Lakota) in South Dakota in 1973; and the St. Regis Mohawk or Akwesasne Reservation, New York, and the Akwesasne Reserve, Ontario and Quebec (an Indigenous entity that spans the US-Canadian border across the St. Lawrence River) in 1990.

94. In conversation at the Harvard University Native American Program, Cambridge, Massachusetts.

95. See University of Manitoba, National Centre for Truth and Reconciliation, "Reports," accessed January 2, 2023, https://nctr.ca/records/reports/.

96. A Joint Resolution to Acknowledge the 100th Anniversary of the January 17, 1893 Overthrow of the Kingdom of Hawaii, and to Offer an Apology to Native Hawaiians on Behalf of the United States for the Overthrow of the Kingdom of Hawaii, 103rd Cong. (1993–94), congress.gov, accessed January 2, 2023, https://www.congress.gov/bill/103rd-congress/senate-joint-resolution/19#:~:text=19%20%2D%20A%20joint%20resolution%20to,103rd%20Congress%20(1993%2D1994).

97. John D. McKinnon, "U.S. Offers an Official Apology to Native Americans," *Wall Street Journal*, December 22, 2009, accessed January 2, 2023, http://blogs.wsj.com/washwire/2009/12/22/us-offers-an-official-apology-to-native-americans/.

98. For example, Ta-Nehisi Coates, "The Case for Reparations," *Atlantic*, June 2014, accessed January 2, 2023, http://www.theatlantic.com/magazine/archive/2014/06/the-case-for-reparations/361631/. See also Ta-Nehisi Coates, *Between the World and Me* (New York: Spiegel & Grau, 2015). Among philosophical discussions, see Charles W. Mills, *The Racial Contract* (Ithaca, NY: Cornell University Press, 1997), 37–40.

99. Sarah Lyall, "Past as Prologue: Blair Faults Britain in Irish Potato Blight," *New York Times*, June 3, 1997, accessed January 2, 2023, http://www.nytimes.com/1997/06/03/world/past-as-prologue-blair-faults-britain-in-irish-potato-blight.html.

100. Roberta Smith, "Critic's Notebook; A Memorial Remembers the Hungry," *New York Times*, July 16, 2002, accessed January 2, 2023, http://www.nytimes.com/2002/07/16/arts/critic-s-notebook-a-memorial-remembers-the-hungry.html.

CHAPTER THREE

1. D. Graham Burnett, *Trying Leviathan: The Nineteenth-Century New York Court Case That Put the Whale on Trial and Challenged the Order of Nature* (Princeton, NJ: Princeton University Press, 2007).

2. Henry D. Thoreau, *Journal*, vol. 8, *1854*, ed. Sandra Harbert Petrulionis (Princeton, NJ: Princeton University Press, 2002), 98 (May 6, 1854).

3. *The Correspondence of Henry D. Thoreau*, vol. 1, *1834–1848*, ed. Robert N. Hudspeth (Princeton, NJ: Princeton University Press, 2013), 294 (Thoreau to Cabot, May 8, 1847). See also Patrick H. Vincent, "The Professor and the Fox: Louis Agassiz, Henry David Thoreau and the 'Two Cultures,'" *Spell: Swiss Papers in English Language and Literature* 19 (2007): 100–103.

4. Thoreau, *Journal* vol. 8, *1854*, 98.

5. *The Writings of Henry David Thoreau: Journal VII*, ed. Bradford Torrey (Boston: Houghton Mifflin; Cambridge, MA: Riverside, 1906), 503 (October 20, 1855).

6. *Writings of Henry David Thoreau: Journal VIII*, , 390 (June 26, 1856). The Narragansett Indian Tribe is a federally recognized sovereign nation (since 1983). Narragansett Indian Tribe, accessed April 13, 2023, https://narragansettindiannation.org/#.

7. Charles C. Mann, *1491: New Revelations of the Americas before Columbus* (New York: Knopf, 2005).

8. V. Gordon Childe, "Changing Methods and Aims in Prehistory: Presidential Address for 1935," *Proceedings of the Prehistoric Society* 1 (1935): 1–15; and V. Gordon Childe, *Man Makes Himself* (London: Watts, 1936). For preagricultural settlements in southern Mesopotamia, see James C. Scott, *Against the Grain: A Deep History of the Earliest States* (New Haven, CT: Yale University Press, 2017).

9. See the discussion of James Russell Lowell's criticism of Thoreau—"Thoreau," in *My Study Window* (Boston: J. R. Osgood, 1871), 208—in the following chapter.

10. For the latter, see Innocent Pikirayi, *The Zimbabwe Culture: Origins and Decline of Southern Zambezian States* (Walnut Creek, CA: AltaMira Press, 2001); Joost Fontein, *The Silence of Great Zimbabwe: Contested Landscapes and the Power of Heritage* (Abingdon: UCL Press, 2006); and Innocent Pikirayi, "Great Zimbabwe as Power-Scape: How the Past Locates Itself in Contemporary Southern Africa," in *Cultural Landscape Heritage in Sub-Saharan Africa*, ed. John Beardsley (Washington, DC: Dumbarton Oaks, 2016), 89–117.

11. Lewis H. Morgan, *Ancient Society: or, Researches in the Line of Human Progress from Savagery, through Barbarism to Civilization* (Chicago: C. H. Kerr, 1877). Scottish Enlightenment thinkers such as Adam Smith had earlier proposed a progression of human societies known as stadial theory: "There are four distinct states which mankind pass thro:—1st, the Age of Hunters; 2dly, the Age of Shepherds; 3dly, the Age of Agriculture; and 4thly, the Age of Commerce." Adam Smith, *Lectures on Jurisprudence*, ed. R. L. Meek, D. D. Raphael, and Peter Stein, Glasgow Edition of the Works and Correspondence of Adam Smith no. 5 (Oxford: Oxford University Press, 1978), 14 (December 24, 1762).

12. "Jonathan F. P. Rose," accessed December 29, 2022, http://www.welltemperedcity.com.

13. Edward L. Glaeser, *Triumph of the City: How Our Greatest Invention Makes Us Richer, Smarter, Greener, Healthier, Happier* (New York: Penguin Books, 2011), 1.

14. Glaeser, "Introduction: Our Urban Species," in *Triumph of the City*, 1–15.

15. Glaeser, "Introduction: Our Urban Species," 13–14.

16. "Current World Population," Worldometer, accessed December 29, 2022, http://www.worldometers.info/world-population.

17. See Scott, *Against the Grain*. See also Owen Lattimore, "On the Wickedness of Being Nomads," in *Studies in Frontier History: Collected Papers, 1928–1958* (London: Oxford University Press, 1962), 415–26; and Andrew Sherratt, "Reviving the Grand Narrative: Archaeology and Long-Term Change; The Second David L. Clarke Memorial Lecture," *Journal of European Archaeology* 3, no. 1 (1995): 1–32.

18. Charles Lane, "Life in the Woods," *Dial: A Magazine for Literature, Philosophy, and Religion* 4, no. 4 (1843–44): 415.

19. Henry David Thoreau, "A Winter Walk," *Dial: A Magazine for Literature, Philosophy, and Religion* 4, no. 2 (1843–44): 211–26.

20. Lane, "Life in the Woods," 415–16.

21. Henry D. Thoreau, *Walden: A Fully Annotated Edition*, ed. Jeffrey S. Cramer (New Haven, CT: Yale University Press, 2004), 12.

22. Laura Dassow Walls, *Henry David Thoreau: A Life* (Chicago: University of Chicago Press, 2017), 139.

23. *The Correspondence of Henry David Thoreau*, ed. Walter Harding and Carl Bode (New York: New York University Press, 1958), 621 (Thoreau, from Redwing, Minnesota, to Franklin Sanborn, June 25, 1861).

24. See Micheal Clodfelter, *The Dakota War: The United States Army versus the Sioux, 1862–1865* (Jefferson, NC: McFarland, 1998); and Scott W. Berg, *38 Nooses: Lincoln, Little Crow, and the Beginning of the Frontier's End* (New York: Pantheon, 2012).

25. Thoreau, *Walden*, ed. Cramer, 12.

26. Vitruvius (Marcus Vitruvius Pollo), *Ten Books on Architecture*, trans. Ingrid D. Rowland (Cambridge: Cambridge University Press, 1999).

27. Leon Battista Alberti, *De re aedificatoria: On the Art of Building in Ten Books*, trans. Joseph Rykwert, Robert Tavernor, and Neil Leach (Cambridge, MA: MIT Press, 1988). See also Rudolf Wittkower, *Architectural Principles in the Age of Humanism*, 4th ed. (London: Academy; New York: St. Martin's Press, 1988).

28. James S. Ackerman, *The Architecture of Michelangelo*, 2nd ed. (Harmondsworth: Penguin, 1986).

29. See Pekka Hämäläinen, *The Comanche Empire* (New Haven, CT: Yale University Press, 2009), who stresses not only the political, diplomatic, military, and economic acumen of the Numunuu (Comanche) peoples but also their nomadism, which he suggests led minority world historians to underestimate the sophistication of their institutions and actions.

30. Thoreau, *Walden*, ed. Cramer, 214–27.

31. Henry D. Thoreau, *Journal*, gen. ed. Robert Sattelmayer, vol. 5, *1852–53*, ed. Patrick F. O'Connell (Princeton, NJ: Princeton University Press, 1997), 154–55 (June 26, 1852).

32. Thoreau, *Journal*, vol. 5, *1852–53*, 154.

33. Jennifer Sherwood and Nikolaus Pevsner, *The Buildings of England: Oxfordshire* (Harmondsworth: Penguin. 1974).

34. Annemarie Jaeggi, *Fagus: Industrial Culture from Werkbund to Bauhaus*, trans. Elizabeth M. Schwaiger (New York: Princeton Architectural Press, 2000).

35. Tadao Ando & Associates, accessed December 29, 2022, http://www.tadao-ando.com.

36. Gensler, accessed December 29, 2022, https//www.gensler.com.

37. William L. MacDonald, *The Pantheon: Design, Meaning, and Progeny* (Cambridge, MA: Harvard University Press, 1976), 12.

38. MacDonald, *Pantheon*, 11–24.

39. Felicia G. Bock, "The Rites of Renewal at Ise," *Monumenta Nipponica* 29, no 1 (1974): 55–68.

40. Young-Tsu Wong, *A Paradise Lost: The Imperial Garden Yuanming Yuan* (Honolulu: University of Hawai'i Press, 2001).

41. Thoreau, *Journal*, vol. 5, *1852–53*, 155 (June 26, 1852).

42. Daniel M. Abramson, *Obsolescence: An Architectural History* (Chicago: University of Chicago Press, 2016), 20–37.

43. Abramson, *Obsolescence*, 1–2, 17.

44. "14 Wall Street Building: New York City Landmarks Preservation Commission Designation List 276 LP-1949 (January 14, 1997)," accessed December 29, 2022, http://s-media.nyc.gov/agencies/lpc/lp/1949.pdf.

45. Joseph J. Korom, *The American Skyscraper, 1850–1940: A Celebration of Height* (Boston: Branden Books, 2008), 219–21.

46. Matthew A. Postal, *Guide to New York City Landmarks*, 4th ed. (Hoboken, NJ: John Wiley & Sons, 2009), 14.

47. "Bankers Trust Company Building," Skyscraper Museum, New York, accessed December 29, 2022, https://old.skyscraper.org/EXHIBITIONS/FAVORITES/fav_bankers.htm.

48. Thoreau, *Journal*, vol. 5, *1852–53*, 155.

49. See, for example, "Board of Regulation of Architects," Mass.gov, accessed December 29, 2022, https://www.mass.gov/orgs/board-of-registration-of-architects.

50. See, for example, Construction Certification Institute, Inc., accessed December 29, 2022, https://www.statecertification.com/mass/class/faqs.html.

51. Vernacular Architecture Forum, accessed December 29, 2022, http://www.vernaculararchitectureforum.org/.

52. Henry David Thoreau, *The Maine Woods*, ed. Joseph J. Moldenhauer (Princeton, NJ: Princeton University Press, 2010): "Ktaadn," 19 (an empty logger's camp on the West Branch of the Penobscot River), 25–26 (their guide, George McCauslin's log house), and 27 (Thomas Fowler's log house); and *The Writings of Henry David Thoreau III: The Maine Woods* (Boston: Houghton Mifflin; Cambridge, MA: Riverside, 1906): "Chesuncook," 138–40 (Ansell Smith's house).

53. Thoreau, *Walden*, ed. Cramer, 41–43.

54. See Dibyendu Banerjee, "Ruins of Calcutta—Tagore Castle of Pathuriaghata," *NoiseBreak*, May 29, 2017, accessed December 29, 2022, https://noisebreak.com/ruins-calcutta-tagore-castle-pathurighata/.

55. Ian Hacking, *The Social Construction of What?* (Cambridge, MA: Harvard University Press, 1999), 29.

56. Yuriko Saito, *Everyday Aesthetics* (Oxford: Oxford University Press, 2007); and Yuriko Saito, *Aesthetics of the Familiar: Everyday Life and World-Making* (Oxford: Oxford University Press, 2017).

57. Walls, *Thoreau: A Life*, 199.

58. Ralph Waldo Emerson, *The Letters of Ralph Waldo Emerson*, ed. Ralph L. Rusk (New York: Columbia University Press, 1939), 3:262–63 (October 4, 1844); discussed in detail by W. Barksdale Maynard, "'Wyman's Lot': Forgotten Context for Thoreau's House at Walden," *Concord Saunterer*, n.s., 12/13 (2004–5): 58–84 with a detailed plan of the lot. See also W. Barksdale Maynard, *Walden Pond: A History* (Oxford: Oxford University Press, 2004), 60–61.

59. Casimir and Rao, *Mobility and Territoriality*, 3–8; and Tim Ingold, *The Appropriation of Nature: Essays on Human Ecology and Social Relations* (Manchester: Manchester University Press, 1986), 130.

60. See, for example, William Cronon, *Changes in the Land: Indians, Colonists, and the Ecology of New England*, rev. ed. (New York: Hill and Wang, 2003); and Stuart Banner, *Possessing the Pacific: Land, Settlers, and Indigenous People from Australia to Alaska* (Cambridge, MA: Harvard University Press, 2007).

61. See James Scott, *The Art of Not Being Governed: An Anarchist History of Upland Southeast Asia* (New Haven, CT: Yale University Press, 2009).

62. Henry David Thoreau, "Resistance to Civil Government [Civil Disobedience]," in Henry David Thoreau, *Essays: A Fully Annotated Edition*, ed. Jeffrey S. Cramer (New Haven, CT: Yale University Press, 2013), 145–71. Thoreau was arrested and jailed in 1846 for arrears in his annual poll tax contributions since 1842; he withheld payments as a matter of principle—at least in 1846—as a protest against the admission of Texas into the Union as a slave state in 1845 and the US invasion of México in 1846. See Walls, *Thoreau: A Life*, 208–13. Thoreau followed the example of Bronson Alcott and Charles Lane, Alcott's companion in the abortive 1843 "consociate family" at Fruitlands in Harvard, Massachusetts. Alcott had been detained in Concord in January, and Lane in December, 1843 for nonpayment of the poll tax. See Walter Harding, *The Days of Henry Thoreau: A Biography* (New York: Dover, 1982), 200–201.

63. See Joseph C. Berland and Aparna Rao, eds., *Customary Strangers: New Perspectives on Peripatetic Peoples in the Middle East, Africa, and Asia* (Westport, CT: Praeger, 2004).

64. See Y. C. Simhadri, *The Ex-Criminal Tribes of India* (New Delhi: National, 1979); and Dilip D'Souza, *Branded by Law: Looking at India's Denotified Tribes* (New Delhi: Penguin 2001).

65. *Report of the Committee on the Elimination of Racial Discrimination, Seventieth Session (19 February–9 March 2007; Seventy-first Session (30 July–17 August 2007); United Nations General Assembly Official Records, Sixty-second Session Supplement No. 18 (A/62/18)* (New York: United Nations, 2007), 36 para. 169. See also Nikita Sonavane and Ameya Bokil, "How Poverty-Struck Tribals Become 'Habitual Offenders,'" *Article 14: Justice, Constitution, Democracy*, May 28, 2020, accessed Janurary 24, 2023, https://article-14.com/post/born-a-criminal-how-poverty-struck-tribals-become-habitual-offenders.

66. See Günter Lewy, *The Nazi Persecution of the Gypsies* (Oxford: Oxford University Press, 2000).

67. Olav van Kappen, *Geschiedenis der Zigeuners in Nederland: De ontwikkeling van de rechtspositie der Heidens of Egyptenaren in de noordelijke Nederlanden (1420–1750)* (Assen: van Gorcum, 1965), 550.

68. Francis Parkman Jr., *The California and Oregon Trail: Being Sketches of Prairie and Rocky Mountain Life* (New York: Putnam, 1849), 240–41, 294, 297.

69. *Correspondence*, ed. Harding and Bode, 621 (Thoreau, from Redwing, Minnesota, to Franklin Sanborn, June 25, 1861).

70. Walls, *Thoreau: A Life*, 181–82, for the general circumstances; and Laura Dassow Walls, "'As You Are Brothers of Mine': Thoreau and the Irish," *New England Quarterly* 88, no. 1 (2015): 11 for the moving of an existing house to the new site.

71. For a photograph of railroad worker dugouts by Randolph Ravine House, ca. 1861, Gorham Historical Society, Gorham, New Hampshire, see Reuben Rajala, "Glimpses of Gorham's Past: Railroad Workers Endure Harsh Living Conditions," Irish Railroad Workers Museum, accessed January 24, 2023, https://www.irishshrine.org/big-pivot-posts/immigrant-irish-women-trackside-and-otherwise.

72. Mrs. R .P. Peabody, *History of Shelburne* (Gorham, NH: Mountaineer Print, 1882), 50.

73. Thoreau, *Walden*, ed. Cramer, 41–43.

74. See Ivan Gaskell, *Paintings and the Past: Philosophy, History, Art* (New York: Routledge, 2019).

75. See John Onians, *Bearers of Meaning: The Classical Orders in Antiquity, the Middle Ages, and the Renaissance* (Princeton, NJ: Princeton University Press, 1988).

76. See Vitruvius, *Ten Books on Architecture*; and Giacomo Barozzi da Vignola, *Canon of the Five Orders of Architecture*, trans. Branko Mitrović (New York: Acanthus Press, 1999).

77. Thoreau, *Walden*, ed. Cramer, 45–46.

CHAPTER FOUR

1. Henry D. Thoreau, *Walden: A Fully Annotated Edition*, ed. Jeffrey S. Cramer (New Haven, CT: Yale University Press, 2004), 12.

2. Roland Wells Robbins, *Discovery at Walden* (1947; Lincoln, MA: The Thoreau Society, 1999), 10.

3. W. Barksdale Maynard, "Thoreau's House at Walden," *Art Bulletin* 81, no. 2 (1999): 303–25, with extensive bibliography.

4. A replica of the house on its original site, incorporating some of its original materials, was opened in 2019. See the website of the Wittgenstein Foundation, Skjolden, accessed June 9, 2022, http://www.wittgenstein-foundation.com/. See also Ray Monk, *Ludwig Wittgenstein: The Duty of Genius* (London: Cape, 1990), 93–104, 361–84; and Jonathan Derbyshire, "A Place to Think: Wittgenstein's Norwegian Retreat Opens to Visitors," *Financial Times*, September 6, 2019.

5. One can gauge the depth of Thoreau's attachment from his actions immediately on learning of Fuller's drowning following a shipwreck off Fire Island in July 1850.

At Emerson's suggestion, and with his financial support, Thoreau rushed to the site, arriving five days after the disaster but, as he reported in a letter he wrote to Emerson the day after his arrival, he found little and could do nothing. See *The Writings of Henry David Thoreau VI: Familiar Letters*, ed. F. B Sanborn (Boston: Houghton Mifflin; Cambridge, MA: Riverside, 1906), 183–85. See also Laura Dassow Walls, *Henry David Thoreau: A Life* (Chicago: University of Chicago Press, 2017), 290–93; and Megan Marshall, *Margaret Fuller: A New American Life* (Boston: Houghton Mifflin Harcourt, 2013), 381–83.

6. S. M. Fuller, *Summer on the Lakes, in 1843* (Boston: Charles C. Little and James Brown; New York: Charles S. Francis, 1844), 59. For the origin and mode of construction of log cabins, see John May, *Buildings without Architects: A Global Guide to Everyday Architecture* (New York: Rizzoli, 2010), 132–33.

7. Fuller, *Summer on the Lakes*, 59.

8. Fuller, *Summer on the Lakes*, 59.

9. What Thoreau terms a *batteau* is a flat-bottomed, shallow-draft, doubled-ended boat used on backcountry rivers and lakes, derived from the French *bateau* (boat).

10. Henry David Thoreau, *The Maine Woods*, ed. Joseph J. Moldenhauer (Princeton, NJ: Princeton University Press, 2010): "Ktaadn," 19 (an empty logger's camp on the West Branch of the Penobscot River), 25–26 (their guide, George McCauslin's log house), and 27 (Thomas Fowler's log house); and "Chesuncook," 123–27 (Ansell Smith's house).

11. Thoreau, *Maine Woods*, 82.

12. Henry D. Thoreau, *Journal*, gen ed. Robert Sattelmeyer, vol. 4, *1851–1852*, ed. Leonard N. Neufeldt and Nancy Craig Simmons (Princeton, NJ: Princeton University Press, 1992), 110 (September 28, 1851).

13. In the Algonquian language of the Nipmuc peoples native to Musketaquid (the Concord area), *weekuwout* or *wekuwomut* denotes "in his house," and was reportedly corrupted to *wigwam*. James Hammond Trumbull, *Natick Dictionary*, Bureau of American Ethnology Bulletin 25 (Washington, DC: Government Printing Office, 1903), 191. The Alənapatəwéwakan (Eastern Abenaki) term *wigwôm* is also a possible source (the initial *w* in each instance denotes the third person).

14. Thoreau, *Walden*, ed. Cramer, 29, quoting Daniel Gookin, *Historical Collections of the Indians in New England* (Boston: Belknap and Hall, 1792), 10.

15. Henry D. Thoreau, *Journal*, gen. ed. John C. Broderick, vol. 1, *1837–1844*, ed. Elizabeth Hall Witherell, William L. Howarth, Robert Sattelmyer, and Thomas Blanding (Princeton, NJ: Princeton University Press, 1981), 304 (April 26, 1841).

16. *The Writings of Henry David Thoreau: Journal XII*, ed. Bradford Torrey (Boston: Houghton Mifflin; Cambridge, MA: Riverside, 1906), 192–93 (May 27, 1859).

17. Thoreau, *Walden*, ed. Cramer, 30.

18. Thoreau, *Walden*, ed. Cramer, 30.

19. Thoreau, *Walden*, ed. Cramer, 30.

20. Thoreau, *Walden*, ed. Cramer, 31.

21. Lemuel Shattuck, *A History of the Town of Concord, Middlesex County, Massachusetts: From Its Earliest Settlement to 1832* (Boston: Russell, Ordione; Concord: John Stacy, 1835).

22. For this development, see Andro Linklater, *Measuring America: How the United States Was Shaped by the Greatest Land Sale in History* (New York: Penguin, 2002).

23. Thoreau, *Journal*, vol. 1, *1837–1844*, 97–98 (November 11, 1840). For Thoreau's practice as a land surveyor, see David F. Wood, *An Observant Eye: The Thoreau Collection at the Concord Museum* (Concord, MA: Concord Museum, 2006), 74–83; and Patrick Chura, *Thoreau the Land Surveyor* (Gainesville: University of Florida Press, 2010).

24. For a detailed discussion of Thoreau's observations on the Hunt house, see Wood, *Observant Eye*, 24–28.

25. Thoreau established this provenance with information received from the Concord physician Josiah Bartlett, correcting that given to him by Abel Hunt. Thoreau, *Journal*, vol. 4, *1851–1852*, 446 (April 14, 1852).

26. Thoreau, *Journal*, vol. 4, *1851–1852*, 429–30 (April 9, 1852).

27. *Writings of Henry David Thoreau: Journal XII*, 36–37 (March 11, 1859) and 46–48 (March 13, 1859).

28. The most comprehensive analysis of settler timber frame house construction in Massachusetts is Abbott Lowell Cummings, *The Framed Houses of Massachusetts Bay, 1625–1725* (Cambridge, MA: Belknap Press of Harvard University Press, 1979). Cummings (167–68) cites Thoreau's characteristically thorough description in his journal entry for March 13, 1859 of the construction of the cellar steps in the Hunt house; see *Writings of Henry David Thoreau: Journal XII*, 47.

29. Maynard, "Thoreau's House at Walden," 320–22.

30. Henry D. Thoreau, *Journal*, gen. ed. John C. Broderick, vol. 2, *1842–1848*, ed. Robert Sattelmayer (Princeton, NJ: Princeton University Press, 1984), 155 (July 5, 1845).

31. Henry D. Thoreau, *Journal*, gen. ed. John C. Broderick, vol. 3, *1848–1851*, ed. Robert Sattelmyer, Mark R. Patterson, and William Rossi (Princeton, NJ: Princeton University Press, 1990), 235 (May 25, 1851).

32. Maynard, "Thoreau's House at Walden," 303–25.

33. Thoreau, *Walden*, ed. Cramer, 14.

34. Ludwig Wittgenstein, *Tractatus Logico-Philosophicus*, trans. C. K. Ogden (1922; Mineola, NY: Dover, 1999), 1.1, 1.2.

35. Thoreau, *Journal*, vol. 2, *1842–1848*, 156 (July 6, 1845).

36. Thoreau, *Walden*, ed. Cramer, 88.

37. William Desmond, *Cynics* (Berkeley: University of California Press, 2008), 21, citing Diogenes Laërtius, *Lives of Eminent Philosophers*, trans. R. D. Hicks (Cambridge, MA: Harvard University Press; London: Heinemann, 1925), 2:6.23, 6.24, 6.25.

38. Transcribed by Walter Harding, "Thoreau and the Lexington Lyceum," *Thoreau Society Bulletin*, no. 161 (Fall 1982): 2. The letter is in the Cary Memorial Library, Lexington. Abigail May Alcott was a women's suffragist, abolitionist, and social worker, and the wife of Bronson Alcott.

39. *Boston Daily Courier*, October 10, 1859.

40. James Russell Lowell, "Thoreau," in *My Study Window* (Boston: J. R. Osgood, 1871), 208. Lowell was a poet, critic, Harvard professor, and diplomat.

41. Thomas Wentworth Higginson, "Thoreau," in *Short Studies of American Authors* (Boston: Lee and Shepard; New York: Charles T. Dillingham, 1880), 22–31. Higginson's wife was Mary Channing, Ellery Channing's sister, and the couple raised Margaret Fuller Channing, the eldest daughter of Channing and Ellen Fuller, Margaret Fuller's sister. See Brenda Wineapple, *White Heat: The Friendship of Emily Dickinson and Thomas Wentworth Higginson* (New York: Knopf, 2008).

42. Higginson, "Thoreau," 25–26.

43. Thoreau, *Walden*, ed. Cramer, 28.

44. Thoreau, *Walden*, ed. Cramer, 27–28.

45. Thoreau, *Walden*, ed. Cramer, 39.

46. Thoreau, *Journal*, vol. 2, *1842–1848*, 155 (July 5, 1845, the day after moving into his house at Walden Pond); and Maynard, "Thoreau's House at Walden," 320–22.

47. *The Correspondence of Henry D. Thoreau*, vol.1, *1834–1848*, ed. Robert D. Hudspeth (Princeton, NJ: Princeton University Press, 2013), 268.

48. Thoreau, *Walden*, ed. Cramer, 39. Thoreau probably, as Laura Dassow Walls notes, borrowed the axe from Bronson Alcott, but as she adds, "Once the axe became famous, both Channing and Emerson laid claim to it." Walls, *Thoreau: A Life*, 203.

49. Thoreau, *Walden*, ed. Cramer, 69.

50. Thoreau, *Walden*, ed. Cramer, 39.

51. Whether the slaveholding Republic of Texas should be admitted to the Union was a major policy question at this time. It was settled by the election of the expansionist James K. Polk to the US presidency in 1844. Texas joined the Union the following year. Like the new state, from a metropolitan viewpoint the Thoreaus' new house was remote and in the southwest.

52. Laura Dassow Walls, "'As You Are Brothers of Mine': Thoreau and the Irish," *New England Quarterly* 88, no. 1 (2015): 11, notes that it had long been assumed that the Thoreaus built the house themselves, but that a newly discovered letter dated April 16, 1844, from Concord resident Jane Hallett Prichard to her mother, Jane Thompson Hallett Prichard (Concord Free Library), makes it clear that the Thoreau family acquired the house and had it moved to the new site.

53. Walter Harding, *The Days of Henry Thoreau: A Biography* (1962; New York: Dover Publications, 1982), 178. A photograph of the Texas house (demolished in 1954) is reproduced in Wood, *Observant Eye*, 131, who notes that an eighteenth-century door, salvaged from the house, is in the Concord Museum (130, 132 ill.).

54. Harding, *Days of Henry Thoreau*, 178.

55. Harding, *Days of Henry Thoreau*, 267.

56. Wood engraving, *Alcott's Summer House*, by Richardson and Cox after Richards. *Homes of American Authors; Comprising Anecdotical, Personal, and Descriptive Sketches, by Various Writers* (New York: G. P. Putnam, 1853), 233.

57. Harding, *Days of Henry Thoreau*, 216–19; and *Correspondence*, vol. 1, *1834–1848*, ed. Hudspeth, 313–18, esp. 314–15.

58. *The Writings of Henry David Thoreau: Journal X*, ed. Bradford Torrey (Boston: Houghton Mifflin; Cambridge, MA: Riverside, 1906), 61 (October 4, 1857).

59. Thoreau, *Walden*, ed. Cramer, 41–43.

60. Thoreau, *Walden*, ed. Cramer, 34.

61. Helen Lojek, "Thoreau's Bog People," *New England Quarterly* 67, no. 2 (1994): 279–97; Ivan Gaskell, "Concord Migrations," in *Cultural Heritage, Ethics and Contemporary Migrations*, ed. Cornelius Holtorf, Andreas Pantazatos, and Geoffrey Scarre (London: Routledge, 2019), 89–109, esp. 100–103. Laura Dassow Walls cogently suggests that Thoreau's equivocal attitude to the newly arrived Irish immigrants was colored by his identification with them as fellow outsiders. Walls, "'As You Are Brothers of Mine,'" 5–36.

62. Thoreau, *Walden*, ed. Cramer, 41.

63. Thoreau, *Walden*, ed. Cramer, 42.

64. Thoreau, *Walden*, ed. Cramer, 42, 43.

65. Joseph Hosmer, "Henry D. Thoreau: Some Recollections and Incidents Concerning Him," *Concord Freeman: Thoreau Annex* (1880): 1.

66. Harding, *Days of Henry Thoreau*, 183.

67. Thoreau, *Walden*, ed. Cramer, 47. Maynard points out that "there is a note of parody here" for the "catalog of costs is appropriated from the villa books," such as John Claudius Loudon, *An Encyclopedia of Cottage, Farm, and Villa Architecture* (1833; rev. ed., London: Longman, 1839), 127–32. Maynard, "Thoreau's House at Walden," 308.

68. Lisa Goff, *Shantytown, USA: Forgotten Landscapes of the Working Poor* (Cambridge, MA: Harvard University Press, 2016), 11. I owe this reference to Meredith Linn.

69. Thoreau, *Walden*, ed. Cramer, 44.

70. Thoreau, *Walden*, ed. Cramer, 44.

71. Thoreau, *Walden*, ed. Cramer, 39.

72. Properly, the title page is a stereotype incorporating an image derived from a wood engraving after the drawing. The wood engraving was made by the short-lived Boston firm of Baker and Andrew (William Jay Baker and John Andrew). Wood, *Observant Eye*, 43.

73. See Gerri L. Herrick, "Sophia Thoreau—'Cara Sophia,'" *Concord Saunterer* 13, no. 3 (1978): 5–12, esp. 9; and, more generally, Kathy Fedorko, "'Henry's Brilliant Sister': The Pivotal Role of Sophia Thoreau in Her Brother's Posthumous Publications," *New England Quarterly* 89, no. 2 (2016): 222–54.

74. W. Barksdale Maynard, *Walden Pond: A History* (Oxford: Oxford University Press, 2004), 118, quoting F. B. Sanborn, *Recollections of Seventy Years* (Boston: Richard G. Badger, 1909), 2:321, describing "Mr. E's [i.e. Emerson's] woodland, where he has had wood lately cut off—oak and pine. There are no beeches here—few maples, if any." This was on a walk on November 2, 1854. Although it concerns Emerson's land on the south side of the pond, it also applies to the north side.

75. Anne Whiston Spirn, *The Language of Landscape* (New Haven, CT: Yale University Press, 1998), 17. "A coherence of human vernacular landscapes emerges from dialogues between builders and place, fine-tuned over time. They tell of the congruence of snowfall and roof pitch." Thoreau would subsequently propose a theory—foundational in ecology—of the succession of trees through the dispersion of seeds in an address, published widely, in 1860. Henry David Thoreau, "An Address on the

Succession of Forest Trees," in *Essays: A Fully Annotated Edition*, ed. Jeffrey S. Cramer (New Haven, CT: Yale University Press, 2013), 225–42. See Lawrence Buell, *The Environmental Imagination: Thoreau, Nature Writing, and the Formation of American Culture* (Cambridge, MA: Harvard University Press, 1995), 136–37; and Walls, *Thoreau: A Life*, 470–72.

76. William Gilpin, *Three Essays: On Picturesque Beauty, on Picturesque Travel, and on Sketching Landscape; With a Poem, on Landscape Painting*, 3rd ed. (London: T. Cadell and W. Davies, 1808). "To these are now added two essays, giving an account of the principles and mode in which the author executed his own drawings." Gilpin had published the first three essays in 1792.

77. Henry D. Thoreau, *Journal*, vol. 7, *1853–1854*, ed. Nancy Craig Simmons and Ron Thomas (Princeton, NJ: Princeton University Press, 1999), 229–33 (January 8, 1854).

78. Book title pages by Peter Paul Rubens are particularly sophisticated examples; see J. Richard Judson and Carl Van de Velde, *Corpus Rubenianum Ludwig Burchard*: *Book Illustrations and Title Pages*, 2 vols. (London: Harvey Miller; Philadelphia: Heyden, 1978); and Gitta Bertram, *Peter Paul Rubens as a Designer of Title Pages: Title Page Production and Design in the Beginning of the Seventeenth Century* (Heidelberg: Arthistoricum.net, 2018).

79. Thoreau, *Journal*, vol. 7, *1853–1854*, 230 (January 8, 1854).

80. Marc-Antoine Laugier, *Essai sur l'architecture* (1753; 2nd ed., Paris: N.-B. Duchesne, 1755).

81. Vitruvius, Book II, i, "The Origin of the Dwelling House," in *The Ten Books on Architecture*, trans. Morris Hicky Morgan (Cambridge, MA: Harvard University Press, 1914), 38–42.

82. For the primitive hut, see Wolfgang Herrmann, *Laugier and Eighteenth Century French Theory* (London: A. Zwemmer, 1962; repr. 1985); and Joseph Rykwert, *On Adam's House in Paradise: The Idea of the Primitive Hut in Architectural History*, 2nd ed. (Cambridge, MA: MIT Press, 1981).

83. Thoreau, *Walden*, ed. Cramer, 45.

84. Thoreau, *Walden*, ed. Cramer, 45–46.

85. Thoreau, *Walden*, ed. Cramer, 198.

86. Thoreau, *Walden*, ed. Cramer, 198.

87. Thoreau, *Walden*, ed. Cramer, 198.

88. Walls, "'As You Are Brothers of Mine,'" 20–23; and Thoreau, "Higher Laws," in *Walden*, ed. Cramer, 202–13.

89. Stanley Cavell, *The Senses of Walden: An Expanded Edition* (San Francisco: North Point Press, 1981), 117–18. For Walden as an emulation of the *Bhagavad Gita*, see also Kevin Dann, *Expect Great Things: The Life and Search of Henry David Thoreau* (New York: Penguin Random House, 2018), 133. Thoreau had made his admiration of the *Bhagavad Gita* and other Hindu scriptures abundantly clear in the "Monday" episode of *A Week on the Concord and Merrimack Rivers*, ed. Carl F. Hovde, William L. Howarth, and Elizabeth Hall Witherell (Princeton, NJ: Princeton University Press, 2004), 135–54.

90. Cavell, *Senses of Walden*, 14, 17–35, elaborates on the argument that Thoreau conceived of the book as Scripture. Thoreau, "Reading," in *Walden*, ed. Cramer, 97–107.

91. The German naturalist Ernst Haeckel introduced the term *Oecologie* (ecology) in 1866 in his *Generelle Morphologie der Organismen: Allgemeine Grundzüge der organischen Formen-Wissenschaft, mechanisch begründet durch die von Charles Darwin reformirte Descendenztheorie*. Zweiter Band, *Allgemeine Entwicklungsgeschichte der Organismen* (Berlin: G. Reimer, 1866), 286. "By 'ecology' we understand the complete science of the relationships of the organism to its surrounding environment, in which, in a broad sense, we can include all 'conditions of existence.'"

92. Thoreau, *Walden*, ed. Cramer, 298.

93. Thoreau, *Walden*, ed. Cramer, 234.

94. *Bede's Ecclesiastical History of England*, trans. A. M. Sellar (London: George Bell, 1907), bk. II, ch. 13, 117 (written ca. 731); John M. Kemble, *A Translation of the Anglo-Saxon Poem of Beowulf, with a Copious Glossary, Preface, and Philological Notes* (London: William Pickering, 1837); and A. Diedrich Wackerbarth, *Beowulf: An Epic Poem Translated from the Anglo-Saxon into English Verse* (London: William Pickering, 1849). Grímur Jónssen Thorkelin had published the old English text with a Latin translation in parallel in 1815. Grim. Johnson Thorkelin, *De Danorum rebus gestis secul. III & IV: Poëma Danicum dialecto Anglosaxonica; Ex Bibliotheca Cottoniana Musaei Britannici* (Copenhagen: Th. H. Rangel, 1815). Set in the sixth century, the earliest manuscript (British Library) is late tenth or early eleventh century.

95. William Wordsworth, "Persuasion," in *Ecclesiastical Sketches* (London: Longman, Hurst, Rees, Orme, and Brown, 1822). Wordsworth consistently sanctioned the eremetic life, notably in his poem "Inscription for the Spot Where the Hermitage Stood on St. Herbert's Island, Derwent-water," in W. Wordsworth and S. T. Coleridge, *Lyrical Ballads, with Other Poems: In Two Volumes*, 2nd ed. (London: T. N. Longman and O. Rees, 1800), vol. 2. See Jessica Fay, "Wordsworth's Northumbria: Bede, Cuthbert, and Northern Medievalism," *Modern Language Review* 111, no. 4 (2016): 917–35, esp. 917–20. Wordsworth's attitude may have informed Thoreau.

96. William Ellery Channing, *Thoreau the Poet-Naturalist, with Memorial Verses*, ed. F. B. Sanborn (Boston: Charles E. Goodspeed, 1902), 188–90.

97. On Nutting, see Thomas Andrew Denenberg, *Wallace Nutting and the Invention of Old America* (New Haven, CT: Yale University Press in association with the Wadsworth Atheneum, 2003). William Sumner Appleton Jr. founded The Society for the Preservation of New England Antiquities (renamed Historic New England) in 1910.

98. Thoreau, *Walden*, ed. Cramer, 313; and Robert B. Ray, *Walden X 40: Essays on Thoreau* (Bloomington: Indiana University Press, 2012), 84–87.

99. Harding, *Days of Henry Thoreau*, 221; and Walls, *Thoreau: A Life*, 231.

100. *Correspondence*, vol. 1, *1834–1848*, ed. Hudspeth, 313 (Thoreau to Emerson, November 14, 1847).

101. Harding, *Days of Henry Thoreau*, 222–24; and Jeanne M. Zimmer, "A History of Thoreau's Hut and Hut Site," *ESQ: A Journal of the American Renaissance* 68 (1972): 134–40, reprinted as *Concord Saunterer*, supp. no. 3 (December 1973).

102. *Correspondence*, vol. 1, *1834–1848*, ed. Hudspeth, 327–29 (December 15, 1847) and 337–40 (January 12, 1848).

103. Thoreau mentions Whelan's ambition as an "open secret" in his letter to Emerson of November 14. *Correspondence*, vol. 1, *1834–1848*, ed. Hudspeth, 317.

104. *Correspondence*, vol. 1, *1834–1848*, ed. Hudspeth, 327, 328.

105. In Channing's annotated copy of *Walden*, transcribed by Frank Sanborn. F.B. Sanborn, *Recollections of Seventy Years* (Boston: R.G. Badger, 1909), 2:392. "The stones that were brought up from the pond for the chimney were carried away, I think, by the Scotch gardener, Hugh Whelan, for his intended house on the Bean-field." In light of his discovery of the foundation in 1945, Robbins points out that the removal would have been limited to the top section and the hearth. Robbins, *Discovery at Walden*, 11, 30–31.

106. *Correspondence*, vol. 1, *1834–1848*, ed. Hudspeth, 38.

107. *Correspondence*, vol. 1, *1834–1848*, ed. Hudspeth, 339.

108. Harding, *Days of Henry Thoreau*, 224; and Zimmer, "History of Thoreau's Hut and Hut Site," 134. See also Randall Conrad, "Road to the Golden Age: Thoreau's Old Carlisle Road," *Nineteenth Century Prose* 40, no. 1 (2013): 91.

109. Mary P. Sherwood, "Where Can I See Thoreau's Hut?," *Concord Town*, July 1964, 9–12, cited by Zimmer, "History of Thoreau's Hut and Hut Site," 135.

110. For James and Daniel Brooks Clark see FamilySearch, accessed July 13, 2023, https://ancestors.familysearch.org/en/MN13-F66/james-clark-1815-1854.

111. *Daniel Ricketson and His Friends: Letters, Poems, Sketches, Etc.*, ed. Anna Ricketson and Walton Ricketson (Boston: Houghton, Mifflin; Cambridge, MA: Riverside Press, 1902), 159.

112. Maynard, *Walden Pond*, 156–157.

113. Sanborn, *Recollections of Seventy Years*, 2:390, 392.

114. Maynard, *Walden Pond*, 159–60. Alcott proposed as an alternative: "I can raise a column on the spot, of rude workmanship—some grotesque shaft cut from the woods in the neighborhood, perhaps, and inscribed with his name."

115. Sanborn, *Recollections of Seventy Years*, 2:391.

116. Sanborn, *Recollections of Seventy Years*, 2:392.

117. Maynard, *Walden Pond*, 165n24.

118. Harding, *Days of Henry Thoreau*, 224; Zimmer, "History of Thoreau's Hut and Hut Site," 134; and Maynard, *Walden Pond*, 165.

119. Wood, *Observant Eye*, 125.

120. Wood, *Observant Eye*, 125–27, ill. The nails may be those collected at the Sullivan farm by Anna and Walton Ricketson with Channing in October 1868. Roland Wells Robbins donated various nails and fragments of brick and plaster from the house site he excavated in 1945. Wood, *Observant Eye*, 126.

121. Maynard, *Walden Pond*, 165.

122. *Writings of Henry David Thoreau: Journal XII*, 91–92 (March 28, 1859).

123. Henry D. Thoreau, "Resistance to Civil Government [Civil Disobedience]," in Thoreau, *Essays*, ed. Cramer, 170.

124. For the Fugitive Slave Act and the Burns case, see Albert J. Von Frank, *The Trials of Anthony Burns: Freedom and Slavery in Emerson's Boston* (Cambridge, MA: Harvard University Press, 1998), with details of Thoreau's involvement.

125. Henry D. Thoreau, "Slavery in Massachusetts," in Thoreau, *Essays*, ed. Cramer, 186 (emphases in original).

126. Thoreau, "Slavery in Massachusetts," 188.

127. Thoreau, "Slavery in Massachusetts," 184.

128. Walls, *Thoreau: A Life*, 314.

129. Thoreau, *Walden*, ed. Cramer, 246; and Joanne Pope Melish, *Disowning Slavery: Gradual Emancipation and "Race" in New England, 1780–1860* (Ithaca, NY: Cornell University Press, 2016), 64–65.

130. Thoreau, *Walden*, ed. Cramer, 246–52; Elise Lemire, *Black Walden: Slavery and Its Aftermath in Concord, Massachusetts* (Philadelphia: University of Pennsylvania Press, 2009), 108, 110–11, 136; and Robert A. Gross, *The Transcendentalists and Their World* (New York: Farrar, Straus and Giroux, 2021), 99–102.

131. See Walls, *Thoreau: A Life*, 318–19, with references.

132. Tao Tao Holmes, "Protesters Are Rebuilding Thoreau's Cabin to Block a Gas Pipeline," *Atlas Obscura*, April 8, 2016, accessed June 20, 2022, https://www.atlasobscura.com/articles/protesters-are-rebuilding-thoreaus-cabin-to-block-a-gas-pipeline. See also Ashfield Gas Pipeline Resistance, Facebook, June 20, 2022, https://www.facebook.com/NoFrackGasAshfield/.

133. As noted by Peter Funken, "Tobias Hauser: 'Walden,'" in *Hauser-Werke: Ausgewählte Besprechungen zum Werk von Tobias Hauser*, accessed June 20, 2022, http://www.hauser-werke.de/sites-main/essays.html. I am grateful to Laura Bieger for bringing Hauser's project (also installed in other locations) to my attention.

134. "Governors Island: Public Art," accessed June 20, 2022, https://www.govisland.com/things-to-do/public-art/cabin. See also Ivan Gaskell, "Display Displayed," in *The Agency of Display: Objects, Framings and Parerga*, ed. Johannes Grave, Christiane Holm, Valérie Kobi, and Caroline van Eck (Dresden: Sandstein Verlag, 2018), 28–29, ill.

135. Cavell, *Senses of Walden*, 131.

136. Martin Heidegger, "Building Dwelling Thinking," in *Poetry, Language, Thought*, trans. Albert Hofstader (1971; New York: Harper & Row, 1975), 148.

137. Thoreau, *Walden*, ed. Cramer, 125.

138. Heidegger, "Building Dwelling Thinking," 149.

139. Thoreau, *Walden*, ed. Cramer, 12.

CHAPTER FIVE

1. On the lure of German thought for thinkers in greater Boston, see Mark Peterson, *The City-State of Boston: The Rise and Fall of an Atlantic Power, 1630–1865* (Princeton, NJ: Princeton University Press, 2019), 486–539.

2. Elizabeth P. Peabody, "The Word Æsthetic," in *Æsthetic Papers*, ed. Elizabeth P. Peabody (Boston: The Editor; New York: G. P. Putnam, 1849), 3. Peabody conceived of *Æsthetic Papers* as a periodical, but only one volume was published.

3. J. B. Stallo, *General Principles of the Philosophy of Nature: With an Outline of Some of Its Recent Developments among the Germans, Embracing the Philosophical Systems of Schelling and Hegel, and Oken's System of Nature* (London: Chapman; Boston: W. Crosby and H. P. Nichols, 1848), 187–520; noted by Robert Sattelmeyer, *Thoreau's Reading* (Princeton, NJ: Princeton University Press, 2014), 46. Emerson read Stallo's

book enthusiastically and copied many passages. *Journals of Ralph Waldo Emerson*, [vol. 8,] *1849–1855*, ed. Edward Waldo Emerson and Waldo Emerson Forbes (Boston: Houghton Mifflin; Cambridge, MA: Riverside Press, 1912), 77.

4. Laura Dassow Walls, *Henry David Thoreau: A Life* (Chicago: University of Chicago Press, 2017), 144.

5. Elizabeth P. Peabody, "Exhibition of Allston's Paintings in Boston in 1839," reprinted in Elizabeth P. Peabody, *Last Evening with Allston, and Other Papers* (Boston: D. Lothrop, 1886), 30–61; and Margaret Fuller, "A Record of Impressions Produced by the Exhibition of Mr. Allston's Pictures in the Summer of 1839," *Dial: A Magazine for Literature, Philosophy, and Religion* 1, no. 1 (July 1840): 73–83.

6. Eliza Palmer Peabody copybook, letter 24, Peabody Family Papers, 1790–1880, Massachusetts Historical Society, Boston, quoted in Megan Marshall, *The Peabody Sisters: Three Women Who Ignited American Romanticism* (Boston: Houghton Mifflin, 2005), 119.

7. The only synthetic account of Doggett's Repository of the Arts is the Wikipedia entry, accessed February 3, 2023, https://en.wikipedia.org/wiki/Doggett%27s_Repository_of_Arts.

8. See Mabel Munson Swan, *The Athenæum Gallery 1827–1873: The Boston Athenæum as an Early Patron of Art* (Boston: The Boston Athenæum, 1940).

9. *Exhibition of Pictures, Painted by Washington Allston, at Harding's Gallery, School Street* (Boston: John H. Eastburn, 1839).

10. Leah Lipton, "Harding, Chester," in *Grove Art Online*, 2003, accessed February 3, 2023, https://www-oxfordartonline-com.ezp-prod1.hul.harvard.edu/groveart/display/10.1093/gao/9781884446054.001.0001/oao-9781884446054-e-7000036624#oao-9781884446054-e-7000036624.

11. The building also housed the Boston Artists' Association, which existed between 1841 and 1851, with Washington Allston as its president until 1845. Leah Lipton, "The Boston Artists' Association, 1841–1851," *American Art Journal* 15, no. 4 (1983): 45–57, esp. 50.

12. [Margaret Fuller], "The Atheneum Exhibition of Painting and Sculpture," *Dial: A Magazine for Literature, Philosophy, and Religion* 1, no. 2 (October 1840): 260–64.

13. Fuller, "Atheneum Exhibition," 261.

14. Ann Hostetler, "Emerson and the Visual Arts: Private Response and Public Pressure," *ESQ: A Journal of the American Renaissance* 33, no. 3 (1987): 121n2 gives the details of the lectures and subsequent publications. "Michel Angelo Buonaroti" is reprinted in *The Early Lectures of Ralph Waldo Emerson*, ed. Stephen E. Whicher and Robert E. Spiller (Cambridge, MA: Belknap of Harvard University Press, 1959–72), 1, 98–117; "Thoughts on Art," *Dial: A Magazine for Literature, Philosophy, and Religion* 1, no. 3 (January 1841): 367–78; and Ralph Waldo Emerson, "Essay XII: Art," in *Essays* (Boston: James Munroe, 1841), 287–303.

15. *The Journals and Miscellaneous Notebooks of Ralph Waldo Emerson*, ed. William H. Cilman et al. (Cambridge, MA: Belknap of Harvard University Press, 1960–82), 4, 139, quoted in Hostetler, "Emerson and the Visual Arts," 123. Neil Harris gives a perceptive account of the transcendentalists' attitudes to visual art. Neil Harris, *The Artist in American Society: The Formative Years, 1790–1860* (Chicago: University of Chicago

Press, 1982), 169–86. My analysis differs from his in emphasis. My thanks to Megan Marshall for bringing this book to my attention.

16. Ralph Waldo Emerson, *The Letters of Ralph Waldo Emerson*, vol. 2, ed. Ralph L. Rusk (New York: Columbia University Press, 139), 275.

17. Ralph Waldo Emerson, "Essay II: Self-Reliance," in *Essays* (Boston: James Munroe, 1841), 37.

18. C. P. Seabrook Wilkinson, "Emerson and the 'Eminent Painter,'" *New England Quarterly*, 71, no. 1 (1998): 126.

19. Emerson, "Essay XII: Art," 303.

20. Ralph Waldo Emerson, *The Letters of Ralph Waldo Emerson*, vol. 7, ed. Eleanor M. Tilton (New York: Columbia University Press, 1990), 314.

21. [Samuel Gray Ward], "The Gallery," *Dial: A Magazine for Literature, Philosophy, and Religion* 3, no. 2 (October 1842): 269–72.

22. Ward, "Gallery," 272.

23. Ward, "Gallery," 269, referring to the prominent fine art authority Gustav Friedrich Waagen, director of the Berlin Museum and author of the three-volume *Kunstwerke und Künstler in England und Paris* (Berlin: In der Nicolaischen Buchhandlung, 1837–39), who would gain greater exposure later by means of the expanded translation, *Treasures of Art in Great Britain: Being an Account of the Chief Collections of Paintings, Drawings, Sculptures, Illuminated Mss, &c. &c.*, trans. Elizabeth, Lady Eastlake, 3 vols (London: John Murray, 1854), and the supplementary volume, *Galleries and Cabinets of Art in Great Britain* (London: John Murray, 1857).

24. [Samuel Gray Ward], "Notes on Art and Architecture," *Dial: A Magazine for Literature, Philosophy, and Religion* 4, no. 1 (July 1843): 107–15.

25. Emerson's study has been reconstructed with much of its contents, including the copy of the *Three Fates*, in the Concord Museum, on long-term loan from the Ralph Waldo Emerson Association. I am grateful to David Wood for giving me information about it in situ.

26. *The Correspondence of Henry D. Thoreau*, vol. 1, *1834–1848*, (Princeton, NJ: Princeton University Press, 2013), 170 (Thoreau to Sophia Thoreau, May 22, 1843). "I also saw the Great Western, the Croton Waterworks, and the picture gallery of the National Academy of Design." The works of Leutze and Durand are mentioned as having been in this exhibition by Walls, *Thoreau: A Life*, 153. Leutze's painting is in the Dr. and Mrs. Robert B. Pamplin, Jr. International Collection of Art and History, Petersburg, VA.

27. *The Writings of Henry David Thoreau: Journal VII*, ed. Bradford Torrey (Boston: Houghton Mifflin; Cambridge, MA: Riverside, 1906), 432 (July 4, 1855).

28. Richard J. Schneider, "Thoreau and American Landscape Painting," *ESQ* 31, no. 2 (1985): 69. Neither panorama is extant.

29. "File: 1849 Champney Rhine HorticulturalHall Boston.png," Wikipedia: accessed February 23, 2023, https://en.m.wikipedia.org/wiki/File:1849_Champney_Rhine_HorticulturalHall_Boston.png.

30. Henry D. Thoreau, *Journal*, gen. ed. John C. Broderick, vol. 3, *1848–1851*, ed. Robert Sattelmeyer, Mark R. Patterson, and William Rossi (Princeton, NJ: Princeton University Press, 1990), 181 (undated entry, after January 10, 1851).

31. Schneider, "Thoreau and American Landscape Painting," 69–70.

32. [Ralph Waldo Emerson], "Ode to Beauty," *Dial: A Magazine for Literature, Philosophy, and Religion* 4, no. 2 (October 1843): 257. He refers to the seventeenth-century Italian artists Salvatore Rosa and Giovanni Francesco Barbieri, called Guercino; and the eighteenth-century Italian Giovanni Battista Piranesi, celebrated for his etchings of Roman ruins and fantastic prison interiors.

33. Henry David Thoreau, *Poems of Nature*, ed. Henry S. Salt and Frank B. Sanborn (Boston: Houghton Mifflin; London: John Lane, The Bodley Head, 1895), 19n1.

34. Much reproduced, the best-known print after the fresco (D. Stephen Pepper, *Guido Reni: A Complete Catalogue of His Works* [Oxford: Phaidon, 1984], no. 40) is the large-scale work (45.4 x 90.5 cm) produced in 1787 by Raphael, or Raffaello, Morghen after the intermediary drawing by Antonio Cavallucci. The British Museum purchased a proof in 1843: 1843,0513.1089, accessed February 2, 2023, https://www.britishmuseum.org/collection/object/P_1843-0513-1089. The impression in the Emerson House is later, for it bears the name of Pietro Fontana ("Petrus Fontana sculp"). Fontana was a former student of Morghen. Perhaps control of the plate passed to him after Morghen's death in 1833. It was a celebrated print, and copies were produced for much of the nineteenth century; see the unattributed version sold at Skinner, Marlborough, Massachusetts, February 16, 2012, lot 1540, accessed February 13, 2023, https://www.skinnerinc.com/auctions/2583M/lots/1540.

35. I am grateful to Ellen Emerson, secretary of the Ralph Waldo Emerson Association, for taking the trouble to examine the print in the Emerson House and for sending me her detailed observations.

36. Amy Golahny, "Poe's References to the Visual Arts," *Edgar Allan Poe Review* 22, no. 1 (2021): 9.

37. Thoreau, *Poems of Nature*, 19–20. A note to the poem (19n1) states that it was "suggested by the print of Guido's 'Aurora,' sent by Mrs. Carlyle as a wedding gift to Mrs. Emerson," presumably in 1835, but Carlyle's letter cited above suggests the gift was made in 1839, the likely date of Thoreau's poem.

38. Megan Marshall, *The Peabody Sisters: Three Women Who Ignited American Romanticism* (Boston: Houghton Mifflin, 2005), 4, 434, citing George Frisbie Hoar, *Autobiography of Seventy Years* (New York: Charles Scribner's Sons, 1903), 69 ("exquisite light figures and horses and youths and maidens flying through the air"); and Caroline Healey's 1842 description of furniture painted by Sophia Peabody, including, "On her bedstead—was Guido's Night—and his day break—Aurora—lighting up the East with her torch the morning star—above-and Apollo with his coursers—and retinue." Dall Papers, Massachusetts Historical Society, Boston. I am grateful to Megan Marshall, who in *The Peabody Sisters* (206–12) describes Sophia Peabody's formation as an artist, for mentioning her painted bedstead to me in conversation.

39. Emerson, "Essay XII: Art," 289.

40. *The Writings of Henry David Thoreau: Journal XII*, ed. Bradford Torrey (Boston: Houghton Mifflin; Cambridge, MA: Riverside, 1906), 367–368 (October 3, 1859).

41. *The Writings of Henry David Thoreau: Journal XIV*, ed. Bradford Torrey (Boston: Houghton Mifflin; Cambridge, MA: Riverside, 1906), 117 (October 13, 1860).

42. Henry D. Thoreau, "Autumnal Tints," in Henry D. Thoreau, *Essays: A Fully Annotated Edition*, ed. Jeffrey S. Cramer (New Haven, CT: Yale University Press, 2013), 301 (who points out that paper-stainers are wallpaper makers); originally published in *Atlantic Monthly* October 1862, 395. The passage derives from Thoreau's journal entry for October 18, 1858. *The Writings of Henry David Thoreau: Journal XI*, ed. Bradford Torrey (Boston: Houghton Mifflin; Cambridge, MA: Riverside, 1906), 220.

43. Hugh Miller, *The Old Red Sandstone: or, New Walks in an Old Field* (Boston: Gould and Lincoln, 1851), 88, quoted in Henry D. Thoreau, *Journal*, gen. ed. Robert Sattelmeyer, vol. 4, *1851–1852*, ed. Leonard N. Neufeldt and Nancy Craig Simmons (Princeton, NJ: Princeton University Press, 1992), 106 (September 28, 1851).

44. Thoreau, *Journal*, vol. 4, *1851–1852*, 107.

45. Henry D. Thoreau, *Journal*, gen. ed. John C. Broderick, vol. 1, *1837–1844*, ed. Elizabeth Hall Witherell, William L. Howarth, Robert Sattelmeyer, and Thomas Blanding (Princeton, NJ: Princeton University Press, 1981), 155 (July 11, 1840).

46. Henry D. Thoreau, "The Service," in Henry D. Thoreau, *Reform Papers*, ed. Wendell Glick (Princeton, NJ: Princeton University Press, 1974), 16, repeating the same passage in Thoreau, *Journal*, vol. 1, *1837–1844*, 155. Thoreau wrote and submitted the article to the *Dial* in 1840, but Margaret Fuller rejected it, and it was not published until 1902.

47. Henry D. Thoreau, *A Week on the Concord and Merrimack Rivers*, ed. Carl F. Hovde, William L. Howarth, and Elizabeth Hall Witherell (Princeton, NJ: Princeton University Press, 2004), 318. He repeats this claim, and the passage that follows it, from his journal entry for August 13, 1841. Thoreau, *Journal*, vol. 1, *1837–1844*, 320.

48. Thoreau, *Week on the Concord and Merrimack Rivers*, 318.

49. Henry David Thoreau, *Journal*, gen. ed. Robert Sattelmeyer, vol. 6, *1853*, ed. William Rossi and Heather Kirk Thomas (Princeton, NJ: Princeton University Press, 2000), 174 (June 2, 1853).

50. Henry D. Thoreau, *Journal*, gen. ed. John C. Broderick, vol. 2, *1842–1848*, ed. Robert Sattelmeyer (Princeton, NJ: Princeton University Press, 1984), 162 (July 14, 1845).

51. Henry D. Thoreau, *Walden: A Fully Annotated Edition*, ed. Jeffrey S. Cramer (New Haven, CT: Yale University Press, 2004), 36–37.

52. Thoreau, *Walden*, ed. Cramer, 37.

53. Thoreau, *Journal*, vol. 2, *1842–1848*, 172 (after August 6, 1845).

54. Plato, *Sophist*, in *The Collected Dialogues of Plato*, ed. Huntington Cairns and Edith Hamilton (Princeton, NJ: Princeton University Press, 1961), 978–79: 235d–37; and Plato, *Republic*, in *Collected Dialogues of Plato*, 823–28: X, 598b–603b.

55. [Ralph Waldo Emerson], *Nature* (Boston: James Munroe, 1836), and subsequent editions.

56. Thoreau, *Walden*, ed. Cramer, 295.

57. Thoreau, *Walden*, ed. Cramer, 294–298.

58. Thoreau, *Journal*, vol. 4, *1851–1852*, 230 (December 31, 1851).

59. Thoreau, *Walden*, ed. Cramer, 295.

60. Thoreau, *Journal*, vol. 4, *1851–1852*, 230.

61. Thoreau, *Walden*, ed. Cramer, 295.

62. Thoreau, *Journal*, vol. 4, *1851–1852*, 45 (September 4, 1851).

63. An admittedly anachronistic but suggestive thought is that Thoreau's perception of the tree in the pine board is akin to what Italian sculptor Giuseppe Penone (b. 1947), associated with the *arte povera* movement, makes literally apparent in his sculptures recovering trees from within lumber in his various installations from the 1980s and 1990s, titled *Ripetere il bosco*.

64. *Writings of Henry David Thoreau: Journal VII*, 62 (September 30, 1854).

65. Thoreau, *Journal*, vol. 4, *1851–1852*, 102 (September 27, 1851).

66. Thoreau, *Journal*, vol. 4, *1851–1852*, 102.

67. Henry D. Thoreau, *Journal*, gen. ed. Robert Sattelmayer, vol. 5, *1852–1853*, ed. Patrick F. O'Connell (Princeton, NJ: Princeton University Press, 1997), 318 (August 29, 1852). For Thoreau's service as an officer of the Lyceum between 1839 and 1842 and his declining reappointment in 1844, see Walls, *Thoreau: A Life*, 102, 141, 185.

68. Thoreau, *Walden*, ed. Cramer, 106. Cf. Thoreau, *Journal*, vol. 5, *1852–53*, 319 (August 29, 1852). "As the Nobleman of cultivated taste surrounds himself with whatever conduces to his culture—books—paintings—statuary &c—So let the village do.... Instead of noblemen let us have noble towns or villages of men."

69. See William Templeman, "Thoreau, Moralist of the Picturesque," *Proceedings of the Modern Language Association* 49, no. 3 (1932): 864–89; and Gordon Boudreau, "Henry David Thoreau, William Gilpin, and the Metaphysical Ground of the Picturesque," *American Literature* 45, no. 3 (1973): 357–69.

70. Thoreau, *Journal*, vol. 4, *1851–1852*, 408 (April 1, 1852); and Thoreau, *Journal*, vol. 5, *1852–53*, 380 (October 21, 1852).

71. *The Correspondence of Henry David Thoreau*, vol. 2, *1849–1856*, ed. Robert N. Hudspeth, with Elizabeth Hall Witherell and Lihong Xie (Princeton, NJ: Princeton University Press, 2013), 357 (Thoreau to Daniel Ricketson, October 12, 1855). "They told me at Little Brown & Co's that his works (not complete) in 12 vols 8vo, were imported & sold in this country 5 or 6 years ago for about 15 dollars. Their terms for importing are 10 per cent on the cost." Such a sum would presumably have been beyond Thoreau's means.

72. William Gilpin, *An Essay on Prints*, 3rd ed. (London: Printed by G. Scott for R. Blamire, B. Law, and R. Faulder, 1781), xii.

73. William Gilpin, *Observations on the River Wye, and Several Parts of South Wales, &c. Relative Chiefly to Picturesque Beauty; Made in the Summer of the Year 1770* (London: Printed for R. Blamire, sold by B. Law and R. Faulder, 1782); and Edmund Burke, *A Philosophical Enquiry into the Origin of Our Ideas of the Sublime and Beautiful* (London: R. and J. Dodsley, 1757).

74. William Gilpin, *Three Essays: On Picturesque Beauty; On Picturesque Travel; and on Sketching Landscape: To which is Added a Poem on Landscape Painting* (London: R. Blamire, 1792). By this date, Gilpin, vicar of Boldre, had been promoted a prebendary of Salisbury Cathedral.

75. Henry D. Thoreau, *Journal*, vol. 7, *1853–1854*, ed. Nancy Craig Simmons and Ron Thomas (Princeton, NJ: Princeton University Press, 1999), 229 (January 8, 1854).

76. Thoreau, *Journal*, vol. 5, *1852–53*, 389 (November 1, 1852).

77. Thoreau, *Journal*, vol. 7, *1853–1854*, 230 (January 8, 1854)

78. Thoreau, *Journal*, vol. 7, *1853–1854*, 231, 232 (January 8, 1854).

79. Thoreau, *Journal*, vol. 7, *1853–1854*, 232.

80. Thoreau, *Journal*, vol. 7, *1853–1854*, 232.

81. Thoreau, *Walden*, ed. Cramer, 46 (emphasis in original).

82. Thoreau, *Journal*, vol. 7, *1853–1854*, 233.

83. Thoreau, *Journal*, vol. 7, *1853–1854*, 271 (February 6, 1854), quoting Uvedale Price, *An Essay on the Picturesque, as Compared with the Sublime and the Beautiful; and, on the Use of Studying Pictures, for the Purpose of Improving Real Landscape* (London: J. Robson, 1796), 195, 202.

84. Price, *Essay on the Picturesque*, 195–196.

85. Lawrence Buell, *The Environmental Imagination: Thoreau, Nature Writing, and the Formation of American Culture* (Cambridge, MA: Harvard University Press, 1995), 131.

86. Thoreau, *Journal*, vol. 4, *1851–1852*, 307–8 (January 30, 1852).

87. Giorgio Vasari, *Lives of the Most Eminent Painters, Sculptors, and Architects*, trans. Gaston du C. de Vere (London: Macmillan, 1912–14), 4:112–13.

88. Thoreau, *Journal*, vol. 4, *1851–1852*, 490 (April 25, 1852).

89. Johann Joachim Winckelmann, *The History of Ancient Art*, trans. G. Henry Lodge, vol. 1 (Boston: Little, Brown, 1856); vol. 2 (Boston: J. Munro, 1849); vol. 3 (Boston: J. R. Osgood, 1872); and vol. 4 (Boston: J. R. Osgood, 1873).

90. See Alex Potts, *Flesh and the Ideal: Winckelmann and the Origins of Art History* (New Haven, CT: Yale University Press, 1994), esp. 11–46, "Inventing a History of Art."

91. *The Writings of Henry David Thoreau: Journal IX*, ed. Bradford Torrey (Boston: Houghton Mifflin; Cambridge, MA: Riverside, 1906), 288 (March 8, 1857), quoting Winckelmann, *History of Ancient Art*, 2:27.

92. Robert D. Richardson Jr., *Henry Thoreau: A Life of the Mind* (Berkeley: University of California Press, 1986), 358–62, draws particular attention to Thoreau's reading of Ruskin.

93. [John Ruskin], *Modern Painters: Their Superiority in the Art of Landscape Painting to All the Ancient Masters, Proved by Examples of the True, the Beautiful, and the Intellectual, from the Works of Modern Artists, Especially from Those of J.M.W. Turner*, 5 vols. (London: Smith, Elder, 1843–60); and John Ruskin, *The Seven Lamps of Architecture* (London: Smith, Elder, 1849). See Timothy Hilton, *John Ruskin*, vol. 1, *The Early Years, 1819–1859* (New Haven, CT: Yale University Press, 1985).

94. *The Writings of Henry David Thoreau: Journal X*, ed. Bradford Torrey (Boston: Houghton Mifflin; Cambridge, MA: Riverside, 1906), 69 (October 6, 1857).

95. *Correspondence*, vol. 2, *1849–1856*, ed. Hudspeth et al., 497 (Thoreau to Harrison Blake, November 16, 1857).

96. John Ruskin, *The Elements of Drawing: In Three Letters to Beginners* (New York: Wiley & Halsted, 1858); and Richardson, *Thoreau: A Life of the Mind*, 359. For a succinct account of Ruskin (and Gilpin) in relation to art instruction in the first half of

the nineteenth century, see Peter Bicknell and Jane Munro, *Gilpin to Ruskin: Drawing Masters and Their Manuals, 1800–1860*, exhibition catalog, Fitzwilliam Museum, Cambridge, and Dove Cottage and the Wordsworth Museum, Grasmere, 1987–88 (London: Christie's, 1987), esp. 19–22, 115–18.

97. Ruskin, *Elements of Drawing*, 22n1.

98. Ruskin, *Elements of Drawing*, 129 (emphasis in original).

99. *Writings of Henry David Thoreau: Journal X*, 210 (November 27, 1857).

100. *Writings of Henry David Thoreau: Journal X*, 96–97 (October 14, 1857) (emphasis in original).

101. Schneider, "Thoreau and American Landscape Painting," 78–79.

102. Henry David Thoreau, "Autumnal Tints," in Thoreau, *Essays*, 281–316, esp. 316.

103. *Writings of Henry David Thoreau: Journal X*, 146 (October 29, 1857).

104. CPC [Christopher Pearse Cranch], "The Artist," *Dial: A Magazine for Literature, Philosophy, and Religion* 3, no. 2 (October 1842): 226.

105. Henry D. Thoreau, *Walden: A Fully Annotated Edition*, ed. Jeffrey S. Cramer (New Haven and London: Yale University Press, 2004), 12.

106. Emerson, "Essay XII: Art," 289.

107. Emerson, "Essay XII: Art," 289.

108. Emerson, "Essay XII: Art," 292.

109. Emerson, "Essay XII: Art," 294.

110. Emerson, "Essay XII: Art," 301.

111. Emerson, "Essay XII: Art," 301.

112. Emerson, "Essay XII: Art," 303.

113. Emerson, "Essay XII: Art," 302.

114. Emerson, "Essay XII: Art," 303.

115. Thoreau, *Journal*, vol. 2, *1842–1848*, 162 (July 16, 1845); repeated verbatim in Thoreau, *Walden*, ed. Cramer, 36.

116. Thoreau, *Walden*, ed. Cramer, 36.

117. Richard H. Davis, "Henry David Thoreau, Yogi," *Common Knowledge* 24, no. 1 (2018): 81–82.

118. Thoreau, *Walden*, ed. Cramer, 317.

119. Thoreau, *Walden*, ed. Cramer, 318.

120. Thoreau, *Walden*, ed. Cramer, 318.

121. Discussed in chapter 6, "Collections."

122. Patrick Chura, *Thoreau the Land Surveyor* (Gainesville: University Press of Florida, 2010), 81, 84, referring to the broadside advertising Thoreau's services as a professional surveyor, ca. 1850 (Berg Collection, New York Public Library), 85, ill.

123. Thoreau, *Journal*, vol. 4, *1851–1852*, 201–2 (December 12, 1851). The Concord Free Public Library holds 195 items. "Henry David Thoreau Land & Property Surveys," accessed February 28, 2023, https://concordlibrary.org/special-collections/thoreau-surveys. The Concord Museum holds a further five surveys. David F. Wood,

An Observant Eye: The Thoreau Collection at the Concord Museum (Concord, MA: Concord Museum, 2006), 78–83.

124. Thoreau, *Journal*, vol. 4, *1851–1852*, 70 (September 11, 1851).

125. Thoreau, *Journal*, vol. 4, *1851–1852*, 71 (September 11, 1851).

126. *The Writings of Henry David Thoreau: Journal VIII*, ed. Bradford Torrey (Boston: Houghton Mifflin; Cambridge, MA: Riverside, 1906), 26–27 (November 17, 1855).

127. *Writings of Henry David Thoreau: Journal VIII*, 26.

128. Wood, *Observant Eye*, 74–83.

129. Wood, *Observant Eye*, 76. A rod is sixteen feet and six inches.

130. Walls, *Thoreau: A Life*, 205–7. The manuscript survey is in the "Henry David Thoreau Land & Property Surveys" collection, Concord Free Public Library, no. 133a, accessed February 28, 2023, https://concordlibrary.org/special-collections/walden/1.

131. Walls, *Thoreau: A Life*, 206.

132. Thoreau, *Journal*, vol. 7, *1853–1854*, 180 (November 29, 1853).

133. For Joseph Hosmer, who wrote various reminiscences of Thoreau, see Richard O'Connor, "Reminiscences of Thoreau by Joseph Hosmer," *Concord Saunterer* 19, no. 2 (1987): 12–17.

134. Thoreau, *Journal*, vol. 7, *1853–1854*, 180 (November 29, 1853).

135. Duncan Caldwell, "A Possible New Class of Prehistoric Musical Instruments from New England: Portable Cylindrical Lithophones," *American Antiquity* 78, no. 3 (2013): 520–35; Duncan Caldwell, "Mind Prints, Arrowheads, the Indians & Thoreau" (paper delivered at the symposium Uses and Abuses of Thoreau at 200, University of Gothenburg, 2018), 15–16, accessed March 7, 2023, https://www.duncancaldwell.com/Site/Duncan_Caldwell_files/ARTICLE%202018,%20Mind%20Prints,%20Arrowheads,%20the%20Indians%20and%20Thoreau,%20Duncan%20Caldwell,%20University%20of%20Gothenberg.pdf.

136. Peabody Museum of Archaeology and Ethnology 69-34-10/2382; discussed further in Chapter 6, "Collections."

137. *Writings of Henry David Thoreau: Journal XII*, 91 (March 28, 1859).

138. Henry D. Thoreau, "Ktaadn, and the Maine Woods: No. IV, The Ascent of Ktaadn," *Union Magazine of Literature and Art* 3, no. 4 (1848): 177–82. He did not reach the summit.

139. Lawrence Buell, *The Environmental Imagination: Thoreau, Nature Writing, and the Formation of American Culture* (Cambridge, MA: Belknap Press of Harvard University Press, 1995), 180.

140. An example is the economist Edward Glaeser in *Triumph of the City: How Our Greatest Invention Makes Us Richer, Smarter, Greener, Healthier, Happier* (New York: Penguin, 2011), 199–202. In contrast, a thoughtful assessment of the incident is given by Walls in *Thoreau: A Life*, 170–74, who maintains: "From that day forward, Thoreau knew a truth few others fully understood: human beings are not separate from nature but fully involved in natural cycles, agents who trigger change and are vulnerable to the changes they trigger" (173).

141. Thoreau, *Journal*, vol. 5, *1852–53*, 120 (June 21, 1852).

142. *Writings of Henry David Thoreau: Journal XI*, 166 (September 18, 1858).

143. *Writings of Henry David Thoreau: Journal XII*, 367 (October 3, 1859).

144. Thoreau, *Journal*, vol. 2, *1842–1848*, 172 (after August 6, 1845).

145. Arnold Berleant, "The Aesthetics of Art and Nature," in *The Aesthetics of Natural Environments*, ed. Allen Carlson and Arnold Berleant (Peterborough, ON: Broadview Press, 2004), 76.

146. Berleant, "Aesthetics of Art and Nature," 86.

147. Berleant, "Aesthetics of Art and Nature," 86.

148. Ronald Hepburn, "Contemporary Aesthetics and the Neglect of Natural Beauty," in *British Analytical Philosophy*, ed. Bernard Williams and A. Montefiore (London: Routledge and Kegan Paul, 1966), 285–310, reprinted in *Aesthetics of Natural Environments*, ed. Carlson and Berleant, 43–62.

149. Thoreau, *Walden*, ed. Cramer, 295.

150. Ralph Waldo Emerson, "Essay I: History," in *Essays* (Boston: James Munroe, 1841), 3.

151. Thoreau, *Week on the Concord and Merrimack Rivers*, 325.

152. Thoreau, *Walden*, ed. Cramer, 295.

153. Yuriko Saito, *Everyday Aesthetics* (Oxford: Oxford University Press, 2007); and Yuriko Saito, *Aesthetics of the Familiar: Everyday Life and World-Making* (Oxford: Oxford University Press, 2017); see also Thomas Leddy, *The Extraordinary in the Ordinary: The Aesthetics of Everyday Life* (Peterborough, ON: Broadview Press, 2012).

CHAPTER SIX

1. Steven Conn, *Museums and American Intellectual Life, 1876–1926* (Chicago: University of Chicago Press, 1998), 16.

2. Ralph Waldo Emerson, "Experience," in *The Selected Writings of Ralph Waldo Emerson*, ed. Brooks Atkinson (New York: Modern Library, 1992), 309.

3. Ralph Waldo Emerson, "The American Scholar," in *The Selected Writings of Ralph Waldo Emerson*, ed. Brooks Atkinson (New York: Modern Library, 1992), 57–58.

4. Emerson, "American Scholar," 58.

5. Richard J. Schneider, "Walden," in *The Cambridge Companion to Henry David Thoreau*, ed. Joel Myerson (Cambridge: Cambridge University Press, 1995), 100.

6. Henry D. Thoreau, *Walden: A Fully Annotated Edition*, ed. Jeffrey S. Cramer (New Haven, CT: Yale University Press, 2004), 216.

7. *The Writings of Henry David Thoreau: Journal I*, ed. Bradford Torrey (Boston: Houghton Mifflin; Cambridge, MA: Riverside, 1906), 374–75 (July 14[?], 1845).

8. See Nelson Goodman, *Ways of Worldmaking* (Indianapolis, IN: Hackett, 1978).

9. William Ellery Channing, *Thoreau the Poet-Naturalist with Memorial Verses*, enlarged ed., ed. F. B. Sanborn (Boston: Charles E. Goodspeed, 1902), 66.

10. Channing, *Thoreau*, 66.

11. For Thoreau's attic room, see Walter Harding, *The Days of Henry Thoreau: A Biography* (New York: Dover Publications, 1982), 264–65.

12. The locus classicus of discussion is Susan Stewart, "Objects of Desire," in *On Longing: Narratives of the Miniature, the Gigantic, the Souvenir, the Collection* (Durham, SC: Duke University Press, 1993), 132–73.

13. Thoreau, *Walden*, ed. Cramer, 64.

14. Harding, *Days of Henry Thoreau*, 265.

15. William Wordsworth, "The Prelude, or Growth of a Poet's Mind: An Autobiographical Poem" (1850), in *Wordsworth Poetical Works*, ed. Thomas Hutchinson, rev. Ernest de Selincourt (London: Oxford University Press, 1936), 536 (Book VI, line 639).

16. Laura Dassow Walls, *Seeing New Worlds: Henry David Thoreau and Nineteenth-Century Natural Science* (Madison: University of Wisconsin Press, 1995), 121. Among the works by Humboldt that Thoreau read are *Cosmos: Sketch of a Physical Description of the Universe*, trans. Elizabeth J. L. Sabine, vols. 1–3 (London: Longman, Brown, Green and Longmans, and John Murray, 1845–52), likely in the sixth edition, including part 1 of vol. 4 (1849–58); *Views of Nature: Or, Contemplations on the Sublime Phenomena of Creation; with Scientific Illustrations*, trans. E. C. Otté and Henry G. Bohn (London: H. G. Bohn, 1850); and *Personal Narrative of Travels to the Equinoctial Regions of America: During the Years 1799–1804, by Alexander von Humboldt and Aimé Bonpland*, trans. Thomasina Ross, 3 vols. (London: H. G. Bohn, 1852–53).

17. Andrea Wulf, *The Invention of Nature: Alexander von Humboldt's New World* (New York: Penguin Random House, 2015), 305.

18. I appeal, admittedly casually, to the formulation proposed by Claude Lévi-Strauss, *Le Cru et le cuit* (Paris: Plon, 1964).

19. See Clark A. Elliott, *Thaddeus William Harris (1795–1856): Nature, Science, and Society in the Life of an American Naturalist* (Bethlehem, PA: Lehigh University Press, 2008).

20. Laura Dassow Walls, *Henry David Thoreau: A Life* (Chicago: University of Chicago Press, 2017), 68.

21. Ralph Waldo Emerson, "Biographical Sketch," in Henry David Thoreau, *Miscellanies* (Boston: Houghton, Mifflin; Cambridge, MA: Riverside Press, 1894), 19.

22. Emerson, "Biographical Sketch," 18–19.

23. Harvard University Herbaria, "Thoreau's Herbarium," accessed January 4, 2023, https://www.flickr.com/photos/huh/sets/72157680747810871.

24. Asa Gray, *A Manual of the Botany of the Northern United States: From New England to Wisconsin and South to Ohio and Pennsylvania Inclusive* (Boston: James Munroe; London: John Chapman, 1848). See also Harvard University Herbaria, "Thoreau's Herbarium."

25. George B. Emerson, *Report on Trees and Shrubs Growing Naturally in the Forests of Massachusetts* (Boston: Dutton and Wentworth, 1846). The importance of these two books to Thoreau is pointed out by Ray Angelo, "Thoreau as Botanist: An Appreciation and a Critique," *Thoreau Quarterly* 15 (1983): 15–31, reprinted in *Arnoldia* 45, no. 3 (1985): 13–23. I am indebted to Reed Gochberg for bringing Angelo's work to my attention.

26. Emerson, "Biographical Sketch," 2.

27. Henry D. Thoreau, *Journal*, gen ed. Robert Sattelmeyer, vol. 4, *1851–1852*, ed. Leonard N. Neufeldt and Nancy Craig Simmons (Princeton, NJ: Princeton University Press, 1992), 310 (January 31, 1852).

28. Thoreau, *Journal*, vol. 4, *1851–1852*, 345 (February 13, 1852). Reuben Rice the farmer is not to be confused with Reuben N. Rice, the first station agent of the Fitchburg Railroad in Concord, who went on to have a career in railroad administration that would bring him considerable wealth and social prominence.

29. Thoreau, *Walden*, ed. Cramer, 1.

30. John G. T. Anderson, *Deep Things out of Darkness* (Berkeley: University of California Press, 2012), 211.

31. *The Writings of Henry David Thoreau: Journal X*, ed. Bradford Torrey (Boston: Houghton Mifflin; Cambridge, MA: Riverside, 1906), 164–65 (November 5, 1857). Walls, pointing out the importance of this passage in the development of Thoreau's thought, notes that the 1906 edition omits contextual material included in *The Maine Woods*. Walls, *Thoreau: A Life*, 426n58. Thoreau's phrase, "a waking thought or dream remembered," may be a transmuted recollection of William Beckford, *Dreams, Waking Thoughts, and Incidents: In a Series of Letters, from Various Parts of Europe* (London: J. Johnson and P. Elmsly, 1783).

32. Arnold Berleant, *Aesthetics Beyond Art: New and Recent Essays* (Farnham, UK: Ashgate, 2012), viii. See also Arnold Berleant, *The Aesthetic Field: A Phenomenology of Aesthetic Experience* (Springfield, IL: C. C. Thomas, 1970); and Arnold Berleant, *Sensibility and Sense: The Aesthetic Transformation of the Human World* (Exeter: Imprint Academic, 2010).

33. *Proceedings of the Boston Society of Natural History* 9 (1862–63): 152.

34. Walls, *Thoreau: A Life*, 306. Samuel Cabot was Louis Agassiz's assistant, James Elliot Cabot's, brother.

35. *The Writings of Henry David Thoreau VI: Familiar Letters*, ed. F. B. Sanborn (Boston: Houghton Mifflin; Cambridge, MA: Riverside, 1906), 188 (Cabot to Thoreau, December 18, 1849). Sanborn also records Thoreau's acceptance into the society as a corresponding member "with all the *honores, privilegia, etc., ad gradum tuum pertinentia*, without the formality of paying any entrance fee, or annual subscription" (letter from Cabot to Thoreau dated December 27, 1850) (emphasis in original). See also Walls, *Seeing New Worlds*, 122.

36. Henry D. Thoreau, *Journal*, gen. ed. John C. Broderick, vol. 3, *1848–1851*, ed. Robert Sattelmeyer, Mark R. Patterson, and William Rossi (Princeton, NJ: Princeton University Press, 1990), 81 (June 4, 1850). He does not say whether he removed them.

37. Channing, *Thoreau*, 265. For Thoreau's initial reservations about the use of a spyglass and his acquisition of one in 1854 and use thereof, see David F. Wood, *An Observant Eye: The Thoreau Collection at the Concord Museum* (Concord, MA: Concord Museum, 1996), 51–53.

38. Alexander Wilson, *American Ornithology, or, the Natural History of the Birds of the United States: Illustrated with Plates Engraved and Colored from Original Drawings Taken from Nature*, 9 vols.; vols. 8 and 9, ed. George Ord (Philadelphia: Bradford and Inskeep, 1808–14).

39. *Wilson's American Ornithology, with Notes by Jardine, to Which Is Added a Synopsis of American Birds, Including Those Described by Bonaparte, Audubon, Nuttall, and Richardson*, ed. Thomas M. Brewer (New York: H. S. Samuels, 1852).

40. Henry David Thoreau, *Journal*, gen. ed. Robert Sattelmeyer, vol. 6, *1853*, ed. Leonard N. Neufeldt and Nancy Craig Simmons (Princeton, NJ: Princeton University Press, 2000), 48 (March 29, 1853).

41. Henry D. Thoreau, *Journal*, vol. 8, *1854*, ed. Sandra Harbert Petrulionis (Princeton, NJ: Princeton University Press, 2002), 41 (March 13, 1854).

42. Spyglass (telescope), made in England, Concord Museum, Concord: Th41, Thoreau Collection, accessed February 27, 2023, https://concordmuseum.org/collection/thoreaus-spyglass/; and Wood, *Observant Eye*, 50–54.

43. Thoreau, *Journal*, vol. 8, *1854*, 278 (August 18, 1854).

44. In her discussion of this journal entry, Reed Gochberg stresses the inconsistency of Thoreau's "poetic perception" with what might "serve science." Reed Gochberg, *Useful Objects: Museums, Science, and Literature in Nineteenth-Century America* (Oxford: Oxford University Press, 2021), 162–63.

45. The collection is in the Fruitlands Museum, Harvard, Massachusetts. I am grateful to Anna Thompson, collections manager of the Trustees of Reservations, for giving me access to Thoreau's minerals and one arrowhead reportedly from Thoreau's collection.

46. Robert M. Thorson, *Walden's Shore: Henry David Thoreau and Nineteenth-Century Science* (Cambridge, MA: Harvard University Press, 2014), 46.

47. Lemuel Shattuck, *A History of the Town of Concord, Middlesex County, Massachusetts: From Its Earliest Settlement to 1832* (Boston: Russell, Ordione; Concord: John Stacy, 1835), 196–208. "Natural History.—Climate.—Geology.—Botany.—Ponds.—Rivers.—Brooks.—Fish.—Quadrupeds.—Birds." The paragraphs on geology are on pages 197–199.

48. Thorson, *Walden's Shore*, 46; and Edward Hitchcock, *Final Report on the Geology of Massachusetts: In Four Parts; I. Economical Geology, II. Scenographical Geology, III. Scientific Geology, IV. Elementary Geology, with an Appended Catalogue of the Rocks and Minerals in the State Collection* (Amherst: J. S. & C. Adams; Northampton: J. H. Butler, 1841).

49. Thorson, *Walden's Shore*, 47.

50. Warren Miles, who bought the rights to the process from Cynthia Thoreau after Henry Thoreau's death, describes the mill in an interview with Edward Waldo Emerson in 1890. Edward Waldo Emerson Papers, Concord Free Public Library, William Munroe Special Collections. Only the finest milled particles would settle on a shelf toward the top of a seven-foot-high cylinder blown by a bellows. The remainder would be milled again. See Wood, *Observant Eye*, 87–88.

51. Henry Petrovski, "H. D. Thoreau, Engineer," *Invention and Technology* 5, no. 2 (1989), accessed January 6, 2023, https://www.inventionandtech.com/content/h-d-thoreau-engineer-1; and Walls, *Thoreau: A Life*, 94.

52. Letter dated June 1844, quoted in Petrovski, "H. D. Thoreau, Engineer"; and Walls, *Thoreau: A Life*, 165.

53. Harding, *Days of Henry Thoreau*, 197; Thorson, *Walden's Shore*, 47; and Walls, *Thoreau: A Life*, 230. In a letter from Nantucket to Lidian Emerson, Emerson writes, "I think you had better open any letters that come to me & then send any through the mail that are important. I asked Susan J. if the Doctor [Charles Jackson] had any offer to make Henry T." *The Letters of Ralph Waldo Emerson*, ed. Ralph L. Rusk (New York: Columbia University Press, 1939), 3:397 (May 4, 1847). Jackson would read the announcement of Thoreau's death and the donation of his plant, bird, and Indian implements collections by his mother and sister at the May 21, 1862, meeting of the Boston Society for Natural History. *Proceedings of the Boston Society of Natural History* 9 (1862–63): 70–72, 152.

54. Emerson, "Biographical Sketch," 1–2.

55. Petrovski, "H. D. Thoreau, Engineer."

56. As recorded in Henry D. Thoreau, *Journal*, vol. 7, *1853–1854*, ed. Nancy Craig Simmons and Ron Thomas (Princeton, NJ: Princeton University Press, 1999), 176 (November 28, 1853). Thoreau informed Harrison Gray Otis Blake in a letter dated February 27, 1853, that he was using his surveying earnings to pay off his debt to James Munroe. *The Correspondence of Henry D. Thoreau*, vol. 2, *1849–1856*, ed. Robert N. Hudspeth, with Elizabeth Hall Witherell and Lihong Xie (Princeton, NJ: Princeton University Press, 2013), 140.

57. Wood, *Observant Eye*, 87.

58. Petrovski, "H. D. Thoreau, Engineer"; Walls, *Thoreau: A Life*, 283–84, 438; and Kathy Fedorko, "'Henry's Brilliant Sister': The Pivotal Role of Sophia Thoreau in Her Brother's Posthumous Publications," *New England Quarterly* 89, no. 2 (2016): 228–29.

59. Thoreau, *Walden*, ed. Cramer, 50; see also Laurel Thatcher Ulrich, Ivan Gaskell, Sara Schechner, and Sarah Anne Carter, *Tangible Things: Making History through Objects* (Oxford: Oxford University Press, 2015), 118–19.

60. See Sedgwick Museum of Earth Sciences, accessed July 12, 2022, http://www.sedgwickmuseum.org/index.php?page=dr-woodward-s-study.

61. Wood, *Observant Eye*, 60–62.

62. Reed Gochberg, "In 19th-Century New England, This Amateur Geologist Created Her Own Cabinet of Curiosities," *Smithsonian Magazine*, November, 19, 2021, accessed January 9, 2023, https://www.smithsonianmag.com/history/in-19th-century-new-england-this-amateur-geologist-created-her-own-cabinet-of-curiosities-180979083/?no-cache.

63. Walls, *Thoreau: A Life*, 102–6, 111–14.

64. Walls, *Thoreau: A Life*, 112.

65. Gochberg, "In 19th-Century New England." "There is a rock labeled opal that was sent to Ellen Sewall Osgood by John Thoreau. This opal is mentioned in the letter from John Thoreau to Ellen's brother, George, on Dec. 31, 1839 (HM 64928)." Online Archive of California, Huntington Library Manuscript Collections, Thoreau and Sewall Family Papers, Finding Aid, accessed January 9, 2023, https://oac.cdlib.org/findaid/ark:/13030/c8ws900x/admin/.

66. *Proceedings of the Boston Society of Natural History* 9 (1862–63): 72.

67. Thoreau, *Journal*, vol. 3, *1848–1851*, 140 (November 16, 1850).

68. Nathaniel Hawthorne, "The Old Manse," in *Mosses from an Old Manse* (Boston: Houghton Mifflin, 1884), 1:19.

69. Emerson, "Biographical Sketch," 13.

70. Yuriko Saito, "Aesthetics Is Everywhere," in *Aesthetic Literacy*, vol. 2, *Out of Mind*, ed. Valery Vinogradovs (n.p.: Mongrel Matter, 2023), 17.

71. *The Writings of Henry David Thoreau: Journal XIV*, ed. Bradford Torrey (Boston: Houghton Mifflin; Cambridge, MA: Riverside, 1906), 58–60, ill. 59 (August 22, 1860).

72. Peabody Museum of Archaeology and Ethnology 69-34-10/2405, accessed December 30, 2022, https://collections.peabody.harvard.edu/objects/details/175338?ctx=51866ea0f8e9d04a60d7a74a24c4e9426f0ec24f&idx=0.

73. Henry David Thoreau, *Journal*, gen. ed. John C. Broderick, vol. 2, *1842–1848*, ed. Robert Sattelmayer (Princeton, NJ: Princeton University Press, 1984), 58–59 (October 30, 1842). Part of a lengthy consideration of Indian lithic tools.

74. *The Writings of Henry David Thoreau: Journal XII*, ed. Bradford Torrey (Boston: Houghton Mifflin; Cambridge, MA: Riverside, 1906), 90–91 (March 28, 1859).

75. *Writings of Henry David Thoreau: Journal XII*, 92.

76. Thorson, *Walden's Shore*, 163.

77. *Writings of Henry David Thoreau: Journal XII*, 92.

78. *Writings of Henry David Thoreau: Journal XII*, 92.

79. *Writings of Henry David Thoreau: Journal XII*, 92.

80. *Writings of Henry David Thoreau: Journal XII*, 93. "What reck I?" is archaic or Scots usage for "What do I care?" (compare Robert Burns, "I Reign in Jeanie's Bosom": "Louis, what reck I by thee, / Or Geordie on his ocean?").

81. Christine DeLucia, "Recovering Material Archives in the Native Northeast," *Early American Literature* 55, no. 2 (2020): 369.

82. Thorson, *Walden's Shore*, 163.

83. Ivan Gaskell, *Paintings and the Past: Philosophy, History, Art* (London: Routledge, 2019), 24–25.

84. Gaskell, *Paintings and the Past*, 24.

85. Henry D. Thoreau, *Journal*, gen. ed. John C. Broderick, vol. 1, *1837–1844*, ed. Elizabeth Hall Witherell, William L. Howarth, Robert Sattelmayer, and Thomas Blanding (Princeton, NJ: Princeton University Press, 1981), 9 (October 29, 1837). Laura Dassow Walls perceptively grounds her biography of Thoreau on this incident and how, in her account, it colored Thoreau's thought thereafter. Walls, *Thoreau: A Life*, 3–4.

86. Duncan Caldwell, "Mind Prints, Arrowheads, the Indians & Thoreau" (paper delivered at the symposium Uses and Abuses of Thoreau at 200, University of Gothenburg, 2018), 2, accessed March 7, 2023, https://www.duncancaldwell.com/Site/Duncan_Caldwell_files/ARTICLE%202018,%20Mind%20Prints,%20Arrowheads,%20the%20Indians%20and%20Thoreau,%20Duncan%20Caldwell,%20University%20of%20Gothenberg.pdf.

87. Caldwell, "Mind Prints, Arrowheads, the Indians & Thoreau," 2. See also Branka Arsić, *Bird Relics: Grief and Vitalism in Thoreau* (Cambridge, MA: Harvard University Press, 2016), 30–31, 226. Literary scholar Branka Arsić's controversial reading of

Thoreau as propounding a nonmetaphorical vitalism in nature such that arrowheads, for example, are literally alive, takes us from aesthetics to metaphysics, which is beyond what I can consider in this book. See also Ross Martin, "Fossil Thoughts: Thoreau, Arrowheads, and Radical Paleontology," *ESQ: A Journal of Nineteenth-Century American Literature and Culture* 65, no. 3 (2019): 424–68.

88. Channing, *Thoreau*, 66.

89. Thoreau, *Journal*, vol. 4, *1851–1852*, 170–171 (November 9, 1851) (emphases in original).

90. Channing, *Thoreau*, 65.

91. In addition to many scholarly articles, Agassiz is the subject of two biographies: Edward Lurie, *Louis Agassiz: A Life in Science* (Chicago: University of Chicago Press, 1960); and Christoph Irmscher, *Louis Agassiz: Creator of American Science* (Boston: Houghton Mifflin Harcourt, 2013).

92. Louis Agassiz, *Recherches sur les poissons fossils*, 5 vols. (Neuchâtel: Petitpierre, 1833–43); and Louis Agassiz, *Études sur les glaciers* (Neuchâtel: Author; Soleure: Jent et Gassmann, 1840).

93. Louis Agassiz, "Autobiographical Review of School and University Life," in Elizabeth Cary Agassiz, *Louis Agassiz: His Life and Correspondence*, 5th ed., 2 vols. (Boston: Houghton Mifflin, 1885), 1:150–51.

94. Lurie, *Louis Agassiz*, 60.

95. Wulf, *Invention of Nature*, 250.

96. Agassiz discharged his debt in an *Address Delivered on the Centennial Anniversary of the Birth of Alexander von Humboldt, under the Auspices of the Boston Society of Natural History* (Boston: Boston Society of Natural History, 1869).

97. Louis Agassiz, "Discours prononcé à l'ouverture des séances de la Société Helvétique des Sciences naturelles," *Actes de la Société Helvétique des Sciences naturelles* 2 (1837): v–xxxii.

98. Walls, *Seeing New Worlds*, 114.

99. James Teller mentions their relationship briefly. James D. Teller, "Louis Agassiz and Men of Letters," *Scientific Monthly* 65, no. 5 (1947): 428. Patrick Vincent describes key aspects of their relationship. Patrick H. Vincent, "The Professor and the Fox: Louis Agassiz, Henry David Thoreau and the 'Two Cultures,'" *Spell: Swiss Papers in English Language and Literature* 19 (2007): 95–110. So does John G. T. Anderson, in "Naturalists in New England: Thoreau, Agassiz, and Gray," in *Deep Things out of Darkness*, 208–25. Robert Thorson touches on the relationship. Robert M. Thorson, *Walden's Shore: Henry David Thoreau and Nineteenth-Century Science* (Cambridge, MA: Harvard University Press, 2014), 96, 289, 292, 302, 304–5. In more general terms, Alfred Tauber discusses the shift from amateur naturalist to professional scientist, Thoreau's and Agassiz's stances respectively. Alfred I. Tauber, *Henry David Thoreau and the Moral Agency of Knowing* (Berkeley: University of California Press, 2001), 121–25.

100. Vincent, "Professor and the Fox," 103. To be clear, Vincent hedges this claim with the phrase, "I would like to imagine . . ." but continues, "Sending Agassiz a fox is Thoreau's final act of parody, an anomalous act, that, like anomalies in science, violates prevailing paradigms and forces us to look at nature in a fresh manner."

101. *The Correspondence of Henry D. Thoreau*, vol. 1, *1834–1848*, ed. Robert N. Hudspeth (Princeton, NJ: Princeton University Press, 2013), 290–92, 299–300, 303–4 (Cabot to Thoreau, May 3, May 27, and June 1, 1847); 292–95, 302–3 (Thoreau to Cabot, May 8 and June 1, 1847).

102. *Correspondence*, vol. 2, *1849–1856*, ed. Hudspeth et al., 23–24 (June 30, 1849). "You may recognize in your correspondent the individual who forwarded to you through Mr Cabot many firkins of fishes and turtles a few years since and who also had the pleasure of an introduction to you at Marlboro' Chapel." Marlboro Chapel was a center of antislavery activity where in 1841 abolitionists founded the first Boston Vigilance Committee. National Park Service: "Marlboro Church: Boston African American National Historic Site," accessed January 13, 2023, https://www.nps.gov/places/marlboro-church.htm. See also Walls, *Thoreau: A Life*, 287.

103. *Correspondence*, vol. 1, *1834–1848*, 333 (December 29, 1847).

104. Harding and Bode note that Frank Sanborn had identified "your Professor" as Agassiz, which is confirmed by Thoreau's mention in the same letter that "he was complimented at the conclusion of his course in Boston by the Mayor moving the appointment of a committee to draw up resolutions expressive of &c &c which was done." *The Correspondence of Henry David Thoreau*, ed. Walter Harding and Carl Bode (New York: New York University Press, 1958), 200. See also Thorson, *Walden's Shore*, 289.

105. *Correspondence*, vol. 2, *1849–1856*, ed. Hudspeth et al., 24 (June 30, 1849).

106. *Correspondence*, vol. 2, *1849–1856*, ed. Hudspeth et al., 25–26 (July 5, 1849).

107. Henry D. Thoreau, *A Week on the Concord and Merrimack Rivers*, ed. Carl F. Hovde, William L. Howarth, and Elizabeth Hall Witherell (Princeton, NJ: Princeton University Press, 2004), 28, 33. One consequence of Agassiz's denial of evolutionary change in species was a proliferation of what he regarded as separate species often peculiar to small geographical locations.

108. Louis Agassiz, *Contributions to the Natural History of the United States of America*, vol. 1 (Boston: Little, Brown, 1857), xii, 442.

109. Henry D. Thoreau, *Journal*, vol. 8, *1854*, ed. Sandra Harbert Petrulionis (Princeton, NJ: Princeton University Press, 2002), 277 (August 18, 1854); and *Museum of Comparative Zoology: MCZBase: The Database of the Zoological Collections*. "This is the specimen that Thoreau's journal entry (Journal VI: 452, 18 August 1854) refers to," presumably referencing "my large one" rather than the small turtle that Thoreau saw that day whose dimensions do not accord with the specimen in the museum; the entry also states "date unknown" for collection date, confirming this supposition. MCZ:Herp:R-1501, accessed January 14, 2023, https://mczbase.mcz.harvard.edu/guid/MCZ:Herp:R-1501. See also Ulrich et al., *Tangible Things*, 78–79, 204, ill.

110. *The Writings of Henry David Thoreau: Journal IX*, ed. Bradford Torrey (Boston: Houghton Mifflin; Cambridge, MA: Riverside, 1906), 298–99 (March 20, 1857) and 300–301 (March 24, 1857). "If we have recently met and talked with a man, and would report our experience, we commonly make a very partial report at first, failing to seize the most significant, picturesque, and dramatic points; we describe only what we have had time to digest and dispose of in our minds, without being conscious that there were other things really more novel and interesting to us, which will not fail to recur to us and impress us suitably at last. How little that occurs to us in any way are we prepared

at once to appreciate! We discriminate at first only a few features, and we need to reconsider our experience from many points of view and in various moods, to preserve the whole fruit of it."

111. Harding, *Days of Henry Thoreau*, 429. See also Randall Fuller, *The Book That Changed America: How Darwin's Theory of Evolution Ignited a Nation* (New York: Viking, 2017). I owe this reference to Megan Marshall.

112. John Wheeler Clarkson Jr., *An Annotated Checklist of the Letters of Franklin Benjamin Sanborn (1831–1917)* 72–73, no. 134 (January 2, 1860), Concord Free Public Library, Concord, Massachusetts, accessed January 14, 2023, https://www.proquest.com/docview/302477818?parentSessionId=pw7VNJJjuQxiCzgWVpX3gPb4HQ3sAoI4V5bjAG02g70%3D&pq-origsite=primo&accountid=11311.

113. Clarkson, *Letters of Franklin Benjamin Sanborn*, 75, no. 142 (March 11–12, 1860), Concord Free Public Library, Concord, Massachusetts.

114. *Journals of Ralph Waldo Emerson, with Annotations*, vol. 9, ed. Edward Waldo Emerson and Waldo Emerson Forbes (Boston: Houghton Mifflin; Cambridge, MA: Riverside Press, 1913), 270 (May 1860).

115. Lurie, *Agassiz*, 146.

116. For example, the fold-out plate of the jellyfish *Cyanea arctica* by Auguste Sonrel after Jaques Burkhardt, in Louis Agassiz, *Contributions to the Natural History of the United States of America*, vol. 3 (Boston: Little, Brown, 1860), plate III.

117. Carlos Baker, *Emerson among the Eccentrics: A Group Portrait* (New York: Penguin Books, 1996), 426.

118. See Conn, *Museums and American Intellectual Life*; and Kathleen Curran, *The Invention of the American Art Museum: From Craft to Kulturgeschichte, 1870–1930* (Los Angeles: Getty Research Institute, 2016).

119. These were not the only museums in the area; for instance, the physician John Collins Warren had founded the Warren Anatomical Museum at the Harvard Medical School in 1847. Harvard Countway Library, *History of the Warren Anatomical Museum*, accessed January 16, 2023, https://countway.harvard.edu/center-history-medicine/warren-anatomical-museum/history-warren-anatomical-museum. Jeffries Wyman, Hersey Professor of Anatomy at Harvard from 1847, founded the Museum of Comparative Anatomy after 1858 in the newly built Boylston Hall. Toby A. Appel, "A Scientific Career in the Age of Character: Jeffries Wyman and Natural History at Harvard," in *Science at Harvard University: Historical Perspectives*, ed. Clarke A. Elliott and Margaret W. Rossiter (Bethlehem, PA: Lehigh University Press, 1992), 105–7.

120. Thoreau, *Journal*, vol. 1, *1837–1844*, 465 (September 24, 1843).

121. Thoreau, *Journal*, vol. 1, *1837–1844*, 472 (September 29, 1843)

122. Thoreau, *Journal*, vol. 3, *1848–1851*, 349 (July 31, 1851). Pilgrim Hall Museum now contains five early settlement-era great or armchairs associated with the first leaders of the colony. Pilgrim Hall Museum: America's Museum of Pilgrim Possessions, "Furniture: Chairs," https://pilgrimhall.org/ce_funiture.htm. Henry Sargent painted the monumental canvas, *The Landing of the Pilgrims*, between 1818 and 1822 to replace the damaged ca. 1815 version, and donated it to the Pilgrim Society in 1835. Pilgrim Hall Museum: America's Museum of Pilgrim Possessions, "History Paintings," https://

pilgrimhall.org/ce_history_paintings.htm. "Standish's sword" is a Solingen-made rapier reputedly owned by the settlers' military leader, Myles Standish. Pilgrim Hall Museum, https://pilgrimhall.org/ce_arms_armor.htm. The only firearm currently in the museum collection is an English-lock pistol that belonged to John Thompson, who was promoted to lieutenant during King Philip's War (1675–76). Pilgrim Hall Museum, https://pilgrimhall.org/ce_arms_armor.htm. Myles Standish's cast iron cooking pot descended in the Standish family prior to its acquisition by the Pilgrim Society. Pilgrim Hall Museum, https://pilgrimhall.org/ce_17_century.htm (all Web pages accessed February 8, 2023). I have been unable to identify the other items that Thoreau mentions.

123. See David Jaffe, *New York Crystal Palace 1853 Digital Publication* (New York: Bard Graduate Center, 2017), accessed February 27, 2023, https://crystalpalace.visualizingnyc.org/digital-publication/.

124. Greeley had promoted the *Dial*, welcomed Thoreau when he visited him in New York in 1843, placed Thoreau's article about Thomas Carlyle in the well-paying *Graham's Magazine* in 1846, and championed his writings thereafter. Walls, *Thoreau: A Life*, 155, 244–48.

125. Walls, *Thoreau: A Life*, 366–67.

126. *The Writings of Henry David Thoreau: Journal VII*, ed. Bradford Torrey (Boston: Houghton Mifflin; Cambridge, MA: Riverside, 1906), 76 (November 22, 1854).

127. *Writings of Henry David Thoreau: Journal VII*, 76.

128. *Writings of Henry David Thoreau: Journal VII*, 96 (December 28, 1854).

129. The East India Marine Society, founded in 1799, is a predecessor institution of the Peabody Essex Museum, Salem, Massachusetts. The museum has more than twenty thousand Oceanian items in its collection. For the East India Marine Society, Melville's Spouter-Inn, and Oceanian items in Massachusetts collections more generally, see Ivan Gaskell, "Joining the Club: A Tongan *'akau* in New England," in *Curatopia: Museums and the Future of Curatorship*, ed. Philipp Schorch and Conal McCarthy (Manchester: Manchester University Press, 2019), 176–90, with further references.

130. Thoreau, *Week on the Concord and Merrimack Rivers*, 55, 65, 71; and Henry David Thoreau, *Cape Cod*, ed. Robert Pinsky and Joseph J. Moldenhauer (Princeton, NJ: Princeton University Press, 2010), 169–70, noted by Richard F. Fleck, *Selections from the "Indian Notebooks" (1847–1861) of Henry D. Thoreau* (online edition under the auspices of the Thoreau Institute at Walden Woods, 2007), 38, accessed February 10, 2023, https://www.walden.org/wp-content/uploads/2016/03/IndianNotebooks-1.pdf. "Thoreau was fascinated with Cook's account of Tahitian culture."

131. *The Writings of Henry David Thoreau: Journal XI*, ed. Bradford Torrey (Boston: Houghton Mifflin; Cambridge, MA: Riverside, 1906), 170–71 (September 21, 1858, with an addition concerning September 24).

132. *The Writings of Henry David Thoreau: Journal XIII*, ed. Bradford Torrey (Boston: Houghton Mifflin; Cambridge, MA: Riverside, 1906), 153 (February 18, 1860).

133. Quy Nguyen, "Concord Museum," *Clio: Your Guide to History*, July 30, 2018, accessed January 16, 2023, http://www.theclio.com/entry/12798.

134. See Wood, *Observant Eye*, 32–34, for Thoreau's interest in Davis's museum. For Thoreau's gift of the nine-round cartridge box, see 34 and ill. Wood reports it as having been stolen from the Concord Museum in about 1973. Thoreau mentions the cartridge

box in his journal. *Writings of Henry David Thoreau: Journal XIV*, 307 (January 3, 1861).

135. Wood, *Observant Eye*, 34. For the Canada lynx, see *Writings of Henry David Thoreau: Journal XIV*, 78–81 (September 11, 1860), and 83–87 (September 13, 1860), where he gives a detailed account of the slaying and appearance of the Canada lynx. See also 142 (October 17, 1860), 231 (November 10, 1860), and 282–83 (November 29, 1860).

136. *Writings of Henry David Thoreau: Journal XIV*, 87–88 (September 15, 1860).

137. Wood, *Observant Eye*, 33–34, citing *Daniel Ricketson and His Friends; Letters, Poems, Sketches, etc.*, ed. Anna Ricketson and Walton Ricketson (Boston: Houghton Mifflin, 1902), 320, quoting Daniel Ricketson's journal. "Visited an antiquarian collection of a Mr. Davis in company with Miss Sophia Thoreau and Mr. Thoreau."

138. Angelo, "Thoreau as Botanist," 21.

139. Richard I. Johnson, "The Rise and Fall of the Boston Society of Natural History," *Northeastern Naturalist* 11, no. 1 (2004): 81–108.

140. *Proceedings of the Boston Society of Natural History* 9 (1862–63): 72, 152 ("by the bequest of Mr. H.D. Thoreau"); and Harding, *Days of Henry Thoreau*, 268–269.

141. Harvard University Herbaria, "Thoreau's Herbarium"; and Harvard University Herbaria & Libraries, "New England Botanical Club Herbarium (NEBC)," accessed January 5, 2023, https://huh.harvard.edu/pages/new-england-botanical-club-herbarium-nebc.

142. Harvard University Herbaria, "Thoreau's Herbarium."

143. Harvard Museum of Natural History, *In Search of Thoreau's Flowers: An Exploration of Change and Loss* (exhibition, 2022–2023), accessed January 4, 2023, https://hmnh.harvard.edu/search-thoreau-flowers, with extensive bibliography.

144. Charles G. Willis, Brad Ruhfel, Richard B. Primack, Abraham J. Miller-Rushing, and Charles C. Davis, "Phylogenetic Patterns of Species Loss in Thoreau's Woods Are Driven by Climate Change," *Proceedings of the National Academy of Sciences of the United States of America* 105, no. 44 (2008): 17029–33. See also Richard B. Primack, *Walden Warming: Climate Change Comes to Thoreau's Woods* (Chicago: Chicago University Press, 2014). This climatological work relies on Thoreau's notes rather than on his specimens, regarding which Angelo pointed out that the absence of precise location information for many of them limited their scientific usefulness. Angelo, "Thoreau as Botanist," 20.

145. Thoreau, *Journal*, vol. 4, *1851–1852*, 170 (November 9, 1851); and *Writings of Henry David Thoreau: Journal X*, 164–65 (November 5, 1857).

146. Karen A. Rader and Victoria E. M. Cain, *Life on Display: Revolutionizing U.S. Museums of Science and Natural History in the Twentieth Century* (Chicago: University of Chicago Press, 2014), 126n171, with further references; they describe the collections concerned as "exotic."

147. Katie Barrett, email to author, February 7, 2023. I am grateful to Katie Barrett for conducting an exhaustive, though in the end fruitless, search of the museum's remaining records.

148. Victoria Cain, "Present Tense: Locating History in Boston's Museums of Science," *Isis* 108, no. 2 (2017): 385–86. I am indebted to Reed Gochberg for drawing my attention to this article.

149. Katie Barrett, email to author, February 7, 2023.

150. F. B. Sanborn, *H.D. Thoreau* (Boston : Houghton, Mifflin ; Cambridge, MA: Riverside Press, 1882), the absence is noted by Thorson, *Walden's Shore*, 47; and John W. Clarkson Jr., "Mentions of Emerson and Thoreau in the Letters of Franklin Benjamin Sanborn," *Studies in the American Renaissance* (1978): 400–420. "A Calendar of the Letters of Franklin Benjamin Sanborn with Mentions of Emerson and Thoreau, 1854–1916."

151. As reported by Thorson, *Walden's Shore*, 46, citing correspondence from the museum. This was confirmed by Anna M. Thompson, collections manager of the Trustees of Reservations, which now administers Fruitlands Museum, and who kindly made the collection available to me for examination.

152. Franklin Parker, *George Peabody: A Biography* (Nashville, TN: Vanderbilt University Press, 1995). See also Curtis M. Hinsley, "The Museum Origins of Harvard Anthropology, 1866–1915," in *Science at Harvard University: Historical Perspectives*, ed. Clarke A. Elliott and Margaret W. Rossiter (Bethlehem, PA: Lehigh University Press, 1992), 121–45.

153. Appel, "Scientific Career in the Age of Character," 96–120.

154. Jeffries Wyman, "Report of the Curator," in *Third Annual Report of the Trustees of the Peabody Museum of American Archaeology and Ethnology, Presented to the President and Fellows of Harvard College, Dec. 1, 1870* (Boston: A. A. Kingman, 1870), 6–7.

155. Frederic Ward Putnam, *Guide to the Peabody Museum of Harvard University, with a Statement Relating to Instruction in Anthropology, Complementary to the American Association for the Advancement of Science, Fiftieth Anniversary* (Cambridge, MA: Peabody Museum, 1898), 16.

156. Caldwell, "Mind Prints, Arrowheads, the Indians & Thoreau," 9.

157. Peabody Museum of Archaeology and Ethnology 69-34-10/2412.

158. The Metropolitan Museum of Art, New York, has five bannerstones in its collection: 1979.206.403, 1979.206.1129, 2011.154.13, 2011.154.14, and 2011.154.15.

159. Peabody Museum of Archaeology and Ethnology 69-34-10/2382, included in Collection of Historical Scientific Instruments and other Harvard venues, February–May 2011, organized by Laurel Thatcher Ulrich and Ivan Gaskell, with Sara Schechner and Sarah Anne Carter.

160. Laurel Thatcher Ulrich, Ivan Gaskell, Sara J. Schechner, and Sarah Anne Carter, with photographs by Samantha van Gerbig, *Tangible Things: Making History through Objects* (Oxford: Oxford University Press, 2015), 25, 79 fig. 65.

161. Three projectile points for spear or arrow fashioned from rhyolite from Mount Kineo or from another of two outcrops of the same rock in Maine. Peabody Museum of Archaeology and Ethnology, 69-34-10/2424.39.3, 69-34-10/2424.39.6, and 69-34-10/2424.40.3. Tools up to and over ten thousand years old made by Indians from this Maine rock have been found across New England and beyond, and in Canada.

162. Henry David Thoreau, *The Maine Woods*, ed. Joseph J. Moldenhauer (Princeton, NJ: Princeton University Press, 2010), 84–156, "Chesuncook"; and 157–297, "The Allegash and the East Branch."

163. Steven Conn, *History's Shadow: Native Americans and Historical Consciousness in the Nineteenth Century* (Chicago: University of Chicago Press, 2004).

164. Caldwell, "Mind Prints, Arrowheads, the Indians & Thoreau," 15–25.

165. Recent examples include the current exhibition *Wiyohpiyata: Lakota Images of the Contested West*, Peabody Museum of Archaeology and Ethnology, Harvard University (curated by Castle McLaughlin and Butch Thunder Hawk, Hunkpapa Lakota professor of traditional tribal arts at United Tribes Technical College in Bismarck, North Dakota), accessed January 16, 2023, https://peabody.harvard.edu/wiyohpiyata-lakota-images-contested-west; *The Story Box: Franz Boas, George Hunt and the Making of Anthropology*, Bard Graduate Center, New York, and the U'mista Cultural Centre, Alert Bay, British Columbia, 2019 (in collaboration with the Kwakwa̱ka̱'wakw artist, Corinne Hunt, and other members of the Kwakwa̱ka̱'wakw community), accessed January 16, 2023, https://www.bgc.bard.edu/exhibitions/exhibitions/88/the-story-box; and *Jules Tavernier and the Elem Pomo*, Metropolitan Museum of Art, New York, and the Fine Arts Museums of San Francisco, 2021 (in collaboration with Elem Pomo cultural leader and regalia maker Robert Joseph Geary, and Dry Creek Pomo/Bodega Miwok scholar Sherrie Smith-Ferri, PhD), accessed January 16, 2023, https://www.metmuseum.org/exhibitions/listings/2021/jules-tavernier.

166. See Wood, *Observant Eye*.

167. I owe this point to Jane Whitehead.

CHAPTER SEVEN

1. The issue is discussed by Martin Jay, *Downcast Eyes: The Denigration of Vision in Twentieth-Century French Thought* (Berkeley: University of California Press, 1993).

2. Although long aware of this issue, I was particularly stimulated by a paper by Diné (Navajo) scholar Larissa Nez, "We Are Alive: Restoring Meaning and Life to Navajo Weavings" (paper presented at symposium Ecologies of Making: Knowledge and Process in Navajo Weaving, Bard Graduate Center, New York, February 17, 2023). One of the few thinkers to have considered the importance of sound to Thoreau recently is literary scholar Branka Arsić, in "What Music Shall We Have? Thoreau on the Aesthetics and Politics of Listening," in *American Impersonal: Essays with Sharon Cameron* (New York: Bloomsbury, 2014), reprinted in *Belgrade Journal of Media and Communications* 11 (2017): 67–81.

3. Henry D. Thoreau, *Journal*, gen. ed. John C. Broderick, vol. 2, *1842–1848*, ed. Robert Sattelmayer (Princeton, NJ: Princeton University Press, 1984), 158 (July 7, 1845).

4. Henry D. Thoreau, *Journal*, gen ed. Robert Sattelmeyer, vol. 4, *1851–1852*, ed. Leonard N. Neufeldt and Nancy Craig Simmons (Princeton, NJ: Princeton University Press, 1992), 468 (April 18, 1852).

5. See, in the first instance, Ian Hodder, *Entangled: An Archaeology of the Relationships between Humans and Things* (Malden, MA: Wiley-Blackwell, 2012); and Lambros Malafouris, *How Things Shape the Mind: A Theory of Material Engagement* (Cambridge, MA: MIT Press, 2013).

6. *The Writings of Henry David Thoreau: Journal IX*, ed. Bradford Torrey (Boston: Houghton Mifflin; Cambridge, MA: Riverside, 1906), 275 (February 20, 1857).

7. *Writings of Henry David Thoreau: Journal IX*, 274–75 (February 20, 1857).

8. Out of respect for Native peoples, I use endonyms for Native nations.

9. Henry D. Thoreau, *Journal*, gen. ed. John C. Broderick, vol. 3, *1848–1851*, ed. Robert Sattelmeyer, Mark R. Patterson, and William Rossi (Princeton, NJ: Princeton University Press, 1990), 152–54 (November 26, 1850).

10. Thoreau, *Journal*, vol. 3, *1848–1851*, 154.

11. In describing Aitteon's use of the birchbark horn moose lure, Thoreau incorporates his journal observations about the moose lure from three years earlier. Henry David Thoreau, *The Maine Woods*, ed. Joseph J. Moldenhauer (Princeton, NJ: Princeton University Press, 2010), 102. He notes that the user produces the sound with the voice (137).

12. Thoreau, *Maine Woods*, 118.

13. Thoreau, *Maine Woods*, 103.

14. Thoreau, *Maine Woods*, 103–4.

15. Thoreau, *Maine Woods*, 136–37. Paugus was the leader of the Pekquawket people on the Saco River in present-day New Hampshire and Maine; he was killed in battle by settlers invading up the Kennebec River in 1725.

16. Fannie Hardy Eckstorm, "Notes on Thoreau's 'Maine Woods,'" *Thoreau Society Bulletin* 51 (Spring, 1955): 1, 3. For Eckstorm, see "Fannie Hardy Eckstorm," Maine Folklife Center, University of Maine, accessed March 31, 2023, https://umaine.edu/folklife/women-folklorists/fannie-hardy-eckstorm/.

17. Thoreau, *Maine Woods*, 137.

18. The Eliot Bible (*Mamusse wunneetupanatamwe Up-Biblum God naneeswe Nukkone Testament kah wonk Wusku Testament*, trans. John Eliot [Cambridge, MA: Samuel Green and Marmaduke Johnson, 1663]) is a vital resource in the Wôpanâak Language Reclamation Project of the Wampanoag Tribe of Gay Head (Aquinnah) on Noepe (called by settlers Martha's Vineyard), mentioned in chapter 2.

19. Henry D. Thoreau, *A Week on the Concord and Merrimack Rivers*, ed. Carl F. Hovde, William L. Howarth, and Elizabeth Hall Witherell (Princeton, NJ: Princeton University Press, 2004), 151.

20. See Philip F. Gura, "Elizabeth Palmer Peabody and the Philosophy of Language," *ESQ* 23, no. 3 (1977): 154–63. I owe this idea and this reference to Megan Marshall.

21. Thoreau, *Week on the Concord and Merrimack Rivers*, 174–75.

22. Henry D. Thoreau, *Journal*, gen. ed. John C. Broderick, vol. 1, *1837–1844*, ed. Elizabeth Hall Witherell, William L. Howarth, Robert Sattelmayer, and Thomas Blanding (Princeton, NJ: Princeton University Press, 1981), 38 (March 14, 1838).

23. Henry D. Thoreau, *Walden: A Fully Annotated Edition*, ed. Jeffrey S. Cramer (New Haven, CT: Yale University Press, 2004), 246. See also Elise Lemire, *Black Walden: Slavery and Its Aftermath in Concord, Massachusetts* (Philadelphia: University of Pennsylvania Press, 2009).

24. Thoreau, *Walden*, ed. Cramer, 162. "Any news?" is often the first inquiry among the characters in E. F. Benson's novels known as the Mapp and Lucia series, beginning with *Queen Lucia* (London: Hutchinson, 1920).

25. Thoreau, *Walden*, ed. Cramer, 136.

26. Thoreau, *Journal*, vol. 3, *1848–1851*, 121 (after September 19, 1850).

27. Thoreau, *Journal*, vol. 4, *1851–1852*, 56 (September 7, 1851).

28. Jeff Todd Titon, "Thoreau's Ear," *Sound Studies* 1, no. 1 (2015): 144–54.

29. For instance, Sherman Paul, "The Wise Silence: Sound as Agency of Correspondence in Thoreau," *New England Quarterly* 22, no. 4 (1949): 511–27; Walter Harding, "A Bibliography of Thoreau in Music," *Studies in the American Renaissance* (1992): 291–315; and George Wolfe, "Henry Thoreau: 'True Musician and Harmonist,'" accessed March 14, 2023, https://cardinalscholar.bsu.edu/bitstream/handle/123456789/202391/Thoreau%20True%20Musician_WolfeG.pdf?sequence=1&isAllowed=y; Wai Chee Dimock, "Hearing Animals: Thoreau between Fable and Elegy," *J19: The Journal of Nineteenth-Century Americanists* 1, no. 2 (2013): 397–401; and Douglas Kahn, "The Aeolian and Henry David Thoreau's Sphere Music," in *Earth Sound Earth Signal: Energies and Earth Magnitude in the Arts* (Berkeley: University of California Press, 2013), 41–52.

30. Arsić, "What Music Shall We Have?," citing materials both published and unpublished (in the Walter Harding Collection, Thoreau Institute at Walden Woods, Lincoln, Massachusetts).

31. John Cage, "Preface to 'Lecture on the Weather,'" in John Cage, *Empty Words: Writings '73–'78* (Middletown, CT: Wesleyan University Press, 1979), 3.

32. Cage, "Preface to 'Lecture on the Weather,'" 3.

33. Titon, "Thoreau's Ear," 144.

34. Thoreau, *Journal*, vol. 1, *1837–1844*, 50 (August 5, 1838).

35. Henry D. Thoreau, *Journal*, gen. ed. Robert Sattelmayer, vol. 5, *1852–53*, ed. Patrick F. O'Connell (Princeton, NJ: Princeton University Press, 1997), 82–83 (June 9, 1852).

36. Thoreau, *Journal*, vol. 5, *1852–53*, 83.

37. This despite his September 7, 1851, journal statement, cited previously, that "the singing of men is something far grander than any natural sound." Thoreau, *Journal*, vol. 4, *1851–1852*, 56.

38. Thoreau, *Journal*, vol. 5: *1852–53*, 146 (June 25, 1852). Until the identification was refuted in 1896, it was believed that Dibdin wrote "Tom Bowling," who was a sailor whose "soul is gone aloft," to mourn the death of his brother, so for Thoreau the lyrics likely evoked his late brother, John. George Benson, "Tom Bowling, a York Worthy," in "Local Notes and Queries, Number 962," *Leeds Mercury*, October 3, 1896.

39. Edward Waldo Emerson, *Henry Thoreau, as Remembered by a Young Friend* (Boston: Houghton Mifflin; Cambridge, MA: Riverside, 1917), 88–89. Emerson recounts Walton Ricketson recalling Thoreau singing "Tom Bowling" at Louisa Ricketson's request during a two-week visit with Daniel and Louisa Ricketson in New Bedford in April 1857. Emerson, *Henry Thoreau*, 145–46.

40. Thoreau, *Journal*, vol. 4, *1851–1852*, 261 (July 27, 1852).

41. Thoreau, *Walden*, ed. Cramer, 109.

42. Thoreau, *Walden*, ed. Cramer, 114. The effect of "railroad time" on society, from the displacement of telling time locally by the sun to how synchrony affected theoretical physics, is much discussed; see, in particular, Peter Galison, *Einstein's Clocks, Poincaré's Maps: Empires of Time* (New York: Norton, 2003).

43. Thoreau, *Walden*, ed. Cramer, 113, 115, 120.

44. Thoreau, *Week on the Concord and Merrimack Rivers*, 176–77.

45. Thoreau's aeolian harp, made of rosewood, likely by Thoreau himself, is in the Concord Museum, Concord (TH68), and is discussed and illustrated by David F. Wood, *An Observant Eye: The Thoreau Collection at the Concord Museum* (Concord, MA: Concord Museum, 1996), 68–69. See "The Thoreau Collection," accessed April 12, 2023, http://www.concordcollection.org/mDetail.aspx?rID=TH68&db=objects&dir=PERMANENT.

46. Thoreau, *Week on the Concord and Merrimack Rivers*, 177.

47. Thoreau, *Journal*, vol. 4, *1851–1852*, 35 (September 3, 1851).

48. Thoreau, *Journal*, vol. 4, *1851–1852*, 92 (September 23, 1851).

49. Thoreau, *Journal*, vol. 4, *1851–1852*, 92.

50. Thoreau, *Journal*, vol. 4, *1851–1852*, 90 (September 22, 1851).

51. Thoreau, *Journal*, vol. 3, *1848–1851*, 137 (November 11, 1850).

52. Thoreau, *Journal*, vol. 3, *1848–1851*, 323 (July 21, 1851).

53. Thoreau, *Journal*, vol. 3, *1848–1851*, 360 (August 8, 1851).

54. Henry David Thoreau, *Journal*, gen. ed. Robert Sattelmeyer, vol. 6, *1853*, ed. William Rossi and Heather Kirk Thomas (Princeton, NJ: Princeton University Press, 2000), 237 (June 22, 1853). "Listen in every zephyr for some reproof. It is the sweetest strain of the music. It provokes by its proud remoteness. Its satire trembles round the world. We cannot touch a string–awake a sound but it reproves us. Many an irksome noise in our neighborhood–go a long distance off is heard as music and a proud sweet satire on the meanness of our life. Not a music to dance to, but to live by."

55. Henry D. Thoreau, *Journal*, vol. 7, *1853–1854*, ed. Nancy Craig Simmons and Ron Thomas (Princeton, NJ: Princeton University Press, 1999), 268–69 (February 5, 1854).

56. Thoreau, *Week on the Concord and Merrimack Rivers*, 184.

57. Thoreau, *Journal*, vol. 5, *1852–53*, 82–83 (June 9, 1852).

58. Thoreau, *Journal*, vol. 3, *1848–1851*, 305–6 (July 16, 1851).

59. Thoreau, *Journal*, vol. 3, *1848–1851*, 261 (June 13, 1851).

60. Thoreau, *Journal*, vol. 4, *1851–1852*, 23 (August 31, 1851).

61. Thoreau, *Journal*, vol. 5, *1852–53*, 146 (June 25, 1852)

62. Thoreau, *Journal*, vol. 5, *1852–53*, 272 (August 3, 1852).

63. Thoreau, *Journal*, vol. 1, *1837–1844*, 303 (April 24, 1841).

64. Thoreau, *Journal*, vol. 5, *1852–53*, 272 (August 3, 1852).

65. Thoreau, *Walden*, ed. Cramer, 209. For Thoreau's appeals to Confucian writings, including by Zengzi, see Lyman V. Cady, "Thoreau's Quotations from the Confucian Books in *Walden*," *American Literature* 33, no. 1 (1961), 20–32, esp. 20–23 (for Thoreau's sources), and 28–29 (for this quotation in question). Cady renders Zengzi as Tseng Tsan or Tseng Tzu.

66. Thoreau, *Journal*, vol. 5, *1852–53*, 272 (August 3, 1852).

67. Thoreau, *Week on the Concord and Merrimack Rivers*, 382.

68. Thoreau, *Journal*, vol. 5, *1852–53*, 413 (December 28, 1852).

69. Thoreau, *Journal*, vol. 7, *1853–1854*, 256 (January 30, 1854).

70. *The Writings of Henry David Thoreau: Journal XII*, ed. Bradford Torrey (Boston: Houghton Mifflin; Cambridge, MA: Riverside, 1906), 148 (April 17, 1859).

71. Thoreau, *Journal*, vol. 3, *1848–1851*, 301 (July 11, 1851).

72. Thoreau, *Journal*, vol. 3, *1848–1851*, 305 (July 14, 1851).

73. Thoreau, *Journal*, vol. 4, *1851–1852*, 155 (October 26, 1851).

74. Thoreau, *Journal*, vol. 7, *1853–1854*, 40 (September 12, 1853).

75. Thoreau, *Walden*, ed. Cramer, 317.

76. Thoreau, *Week on the Concord and Merrimack Rivers*, 173.

77. Thoreau, *Journal*, vol. 3, *1848–1851*, 359 (August 8, 1851).

78. Thoreau, *Journal*, vol. 4, *1851–1852*, 479 (April 21, 1852).

79. Thoreau, *Walden*, ed. Cramer, 301.

80. Laura Dassow Walls, *Henry David Thoreau: A Life* (Chicago: Chicago University Press, 2017), 419.

81. Tom Lynch, "The 'Domestic Air' of Wilderness: Henry Thoreau and Joe Polis in the Maine Woods," *Weber Studies* 14, no. 3 (1997): 39. For shamanism among the Pαnawáhpskewi, see Fannie H. Eckstorm, *Old John Neptune and Other Maine Indian Shamans* (Portland: Southworth-Anthoensen Press, 1945).

82. Walls, *Thoreau: A Life*, 419–20, with references.

83. See Robert F. Sayre, *Thoreau and the American Indians* (Princeton, NJ: Princeton University Press, 2014).

84. Boxwood and ivory flute with four brass keys by Meacham and Pond, Albany, New York, 1828–32, TH40. "The Thoreau Collection," accessed April 12, 20232, http://www.concordcollection.org/mDetail.aspx?rID=TH40&db=objects&dir=PERMANENT. It is inscribed on the mouthpiece section, "John Thoreau/+1835+/Henry D. Thoreau/+1845+" and on the ivory cap, in the center, "JT," surrounded by (in graphite) "+Henry+D+Thoreau." See Wood, *Observant Eye*, 66–67.

85. Thoreau, *Journal*, vol. 1, *1837–1844*, 311 (May 27, 1841); 320–21 (August 18, 1841). Wood states that John likely gave his flute to his younger brother. Wood, *Observant Eye*, 67.

86. Thoreau, *Journal*, vol. 1. *1837–1844*, 321.

87. Thoreau, *Walden*, ed. Cramer, 213.

88. Walls, *Thoreau: A Life*, 355.

89. Stanley Cavell, *The Senses of Walden: An Expanded Edition* (San Francisco: North Point Press, 1981), 14, 117–18. Thoreau discusses Hindu philosophy in his journal after June 20, 1846. Henry D. Thoreau, *Journal*, vol. 2, *1842–1848*, 253–261.

90. *The Vishṅu Puráṅa: A System of Hindu Mythology and Tradition*, trans. and ed. H. H. Wilson (London: John Murray, 1840); and *Le Bhâgavita Puráṇa, ou histoire poétique de Krichṇa*, vols. 1–3, trans. Eugène Burnouf (Paris: Imprimerie Royale, 1840–1847). Listed in a letter from the London publisher John Chapman to Thoreau, October 26, 1855: *The Correspondence of Henry D. Thoreau*, vol. 2, *1849–1856*, ed. Robert N. Hudspeth (Princeton, NJ: Princeton University Press, 2018), 371–72.

91. *Correspondence*, vol. 2, ed. Hudspeth, 378 (Thoreau to Thomas Cholmondeley, November 8, 1855).

92. See Paul Friedrich, *The Gita within Walden* (Albany: State University of New York Press, 2008).

93. *Correspondence*, vol. 2, ed. Hudspeth, 394 (Thoreau to Daniel Ricketson, December 25, 1855). See also Walls, *Thoreau: A Life*, 381–82.

94. David Wood was kind enough to discuss this connection with me, and although we are confident that Thoreau was aware of the association, we agree that it is unlikely that Thoreau might have gone so far as to identify with the Lord Krishna.

95. [Louisa May Alcott], "Thoreau's Flute," *Atlantic Monthly*, September 1863, 280–81.

CHAPTER EIGHT

1. Elizabeth Peabody published "Resistance to Civil Government; A Lecture Delivered in 1847" in her journal *Æsthetic Papers* (1849): 189–211. Henry D. Thoreau, *Essays*, ed. Jeffrey S. Cramer (New Haven, CT, 2013), xxv–xxx, 145–71. "Slavery in Massachusetts" was first published in William Lloyd Garrison's abolitionist paper, the *Liberator* (July 21, 1854), following Thoreau's delivery of an earlier version at an antislavery convention in Framingham, Massachusetts on July 4, 1854. Thoreau, *Essays*, ed. Cramer, xxx–xxxiii, 172–89. "Life Without Principle," derived from a lecture Thoreau delivered seven times from 1854 onward," was published posthumously in *Atlantic Monthly*, October 1863, 484–95. Thoreau, *Essays*, ed. Cramer, xlvii–xlix, 346–68.

2. George Eliot, *Middlemarch: A Study of Provincial Life*, vol. 1 (Edinburgh: Blackwood, 1871), 351.

3. Henry D. Thoreau, *Journal*, gen. ed. Robert Sattelmeyer, vol. 4, *1851–1852*, ed. Leonard N. Neufeldt and Nancy Craig Simmons (Princeton, NJ: Princeton University Press, 1992), 261 (July 27, 1852).

4. Yuriko Saito, *Aesthetics of the Familiar: Everyday Life and World-Making* (Oxford: Oxford University Press, 2017).

5. *The Writings of Henry David Thoreau: Journal XII*, ed. Bradford Torrey (Boston: Houghton Mifflin; Cambridge, MA: Riverside, 1906), 93 (March 28, 1859).

6. I address some of those challenges, often with valued colleagues, in Laurel Thatcher Ulrich, Ivan Gaskell, Sara J. Schechner, and Sarah Anne Carter, with photographs by Samantha S. B. van Gerbig, *Tangible Things: Making History through Objects* (Oxford: Oxford University Press, 2015); Ivan Gaskell, *Paintings and the Past: Philosophy, History, Art* (London : Routledge, 2019); and Ivan Gaskell and Sarah Anne Carter, eds., *The Oxford Handbook of History and Material Culture* (London : Oxford University Press, 2020).

7. Henry D. Thoreau, *Week on the Concord and Merrimack Rivers*, ed. Carl F. Hovde, William L. Howarth, and Elizabeth Hall Witherell (Princeton, NJ: Princeton University Press, 2004), 325.

8. *The Writings of Henry David Thoreau: Journal IX*, ed. Bradford Torrey (Boston: Houghton Mifflin; Cambridge, MA: Riverside, 1906), 75 (September 9, 1856).

9. Thoreau, *Journal*, vol. 4, *1851–1852*, 291 (January 26, 1852).

Index

Page numbers in italics refer to figures.

Abenaki (Aln8bak), 9, 140
Abramson, Daniel, 43
aeolian harp, 144, 145, 206n45
aesthetics, 3, 4–5, 6, 8, 10, 12, 37, 39, 46, 54, 78, 80–81, 93, 104–5, 112, 117, 120, 136, 153, 154–55, 156, 189n87; environmental, 3, 7–8, 9, 76, 80, 136, 148, 150, 155; everyday, 3, 5, 7–8, 9, 54, 58, 76, 80, 82, 89, 98–99, 102, 103, 105, 136, 148, 150, 155
Africa, sub-Saharan, 13, 21, 35, 48, 50
African Americans, 25–26, 31
Agassiz, Louis, 7, 33, 108, 111, 122–25, 127
Aitteon, Joseph, 57, 138–41
Alberti, Leon Battista, 39–40
Alcott, Abigail May, 62
Alcott, Amos Bronson, 36, 48, 64, *65*, 75, 125, 132, 149
Alcott, Louisa May, "Thoreau's Flute," 153
Allston, Washington, 81–82, 83
Aln8bak (Abenaki), 9, 140
American Anti-Slavery Society, 24
American Party (Know Nothings), 29, 31, 51
Anderson, John, 111
Ando, Tadeo, 40, 42, 71
Angelo, Ray, 131
antiquity, Greek and Roman, 9, 52, 92, 95, 137
Appleton, William Sumner, 73
architecture, 7, 32, 34, 39–40, 41–47, 50, 51–52, 54, 56, 62, 67, 69, *70*, 71, 72, 73, 79, 83, 95; vernacular, 45–46, 47
Aristotle, 137
arrowhead, 119; Native American, 1, 17, 18, 102, 109, 112, 117, 118–21, 151
Arsić, Branka, 142, 162n17, 196n87
art, 5, 8, 17, 40, 51–52, 58, 69, 80, 86, 87–90, 97–99, 101, 104, 105, 129; fine art, 3, 8, 80, 81–84, 86, 90, 91–95, 97–99; as imitation, 86, 89, 105; "true art," 87; useful arts, 8, 101, 102, 104, 105
artistry, 8, 54, 69, 80, 98, 99, 101, 105, 157
"Artist who made the world and me," 8, 89, 105
Ashfield, Massachusetts, 77
Assyrians, 1
Atlantic, 97, 153
atlatl weight (bannerstone), 134, *134*
Audubon, John James, 113

Baird, Jesse Little Doe, 17
Baird, Spencer Fullerton, 123
Bankers Trust Company Building (14 Wall Street), New York, 44
Barad, Karen, 5, 132, 136
Barbarelli, Giorgio, 94
barbarism, 35
Barnum, P. T., 129
Barrett, Katie, 132
Baumgarten, Alexander Gottlieb, 80
Baxandall, Michael, 158

beauty, 3, 4, 5, 8, 41, 52, 57, 71, 73, 76, 82, 84, 86, 91, 92, 95, 96, 98, 102, 103–4, 119, 141, 145, 148, 154
Bede, *Ecclesiastical History of England*, 72
Beowulf, 72
Berg, Charles I., 44
Berleant, Arnold, 3, 104, 112, 158
Berlin, Germany, 77–78, 123
Bhagavad Gita, 5, 72, 152
Bhagavata Purana, 152
Bieger, Laura, 158
Billings, Rebecca, 57
birdsong, 150, 151
Blair, Tony, 31
Blake, Harrison, 96, 195n56
body, human, as musical instrument, 149
Boston, Massachusetts, 8, 24–25, 26, 28, 76, 81–82, 83–84, 90, 91, 114, 115–16, 117, 122, 123, 124, 127, 158
Boston Athenaeum, 81–82, 83
Boston Society of Natural History, 9, 102, 113, 117, 127, 131, 132
Bourdieu, Pierre, 158
Brace, Charles, 125
Bradford, Mrs. M. L. B., 131
Bramante, Donato, 39
British Museum, London, 119
Brook Farm, 62
Brown, John, 21, 22
Brunelleschi, Filippo, 40
Buell, Lawrence, 93, 103
Bulkeley, Peter, 15
Burke, Edmund, *A Philosophical Enquiry into the Origin of Our Ideas of the Sublime and the Beautiful* (1757), 69, 91
Burke, Peter, 158
Burn, Mackintosh, 46

Cabot, James Elliot, 123–24, 125
Cabot, Samuel, 113
Cage, John, *Lecture on the Weather*, 143
Cain, Victoria, 132
Caldwell, Duncan, 121, 133
Cambridge, Massachusetts, 14, 24, 58, 81, 83, 84, 90, 97, 127, 140
Cambridge, UK, xii–xiii, 116
Cape Cod, Massachusetts, 13, 28, 29, 116
Carlson, Allen, 3

Carlyle, Jane, 84
Carlyle, Thomas, 84
Carter, Sarah Anne, 158
Catskill house, Scribner's, 60–61
Catskill Mountains, 56, 60–61, 63
Cavell, Stanley, 71–72, 78, 158
Champney, Benjamin, *The River Rhine*, 83–84
Channing, William Ellery, 9, 28, 56, 60, 63–64, 73, 74, 75, 83, 107, 109, 113, 116, 121, 122
Childe, V. Gordon, 34
Cholmondeley, Thomas, 152
civilization, 34, 35–36, 40, 41, 63, 66, 90
Clamshell Bluff, Concord, Massachusetts, 15, 117, 134
Clark, Daniel Brooks, 74–75
Clark, Edward H., 44
Clark, James, 74–75
Clark Art Institute, Williamstown, Massachusetts, 40, 42, 43, 158
Cohasset, Massachusetts, 28, 31, 116
collection, 8, 9, 17, 29, 81, 82, 102, 106, 108–10, 112–13, 114, 116–18, 123–24, 127, 129, 130, 131, 132–36, 137, 153
Collins, James, "shanty," 26–27, 51, 65, 66, 67
Comanche (Nʉmʉnʉʉ), 40
Conant house, Concord, Massachusetts, 57–58, 146
Conantum, 57
Concord (Musketaquid) River, 13, 14, 15, 18, 122, 124, 133, 138, 152
Concord, Massachusetts, xii, xiii, 1, 7, *11*, 12, 13, 14, 17, 18, 22, 23–27, 30, 31, 32, 50, 51, 56, 57, 59–60, 64, 74, 75, 77, 84, 90, 100, *103*, 109, 111, 112, 113, 114, 116, 117, *118*, 125, 127, 130, 131, 132, 133, *134*, 135, 138, 146, 150, 151
Concord Antiquarian Society, 130
Concord Free Public Library, 131, 158
Concord Lyceum, 90
Concord Museum, 75, 101, 114, 116, 130, 136, 152
Conn, Steven, 106, 135
Conté, Nicolas-Jacques, 115
Conway, Moncure, 25
Cook, James, 129

craft, 8, 89, 98, 99, 101
Cranch, Christopher Pearse, 97
Cuming, John, 23
Cuvier, Georges, 122, 123, 125

Dakȟóta (Dakota), 19, 37, 50
Dakota-US War, 1862, 37
Dana, Sebattis, 140, 141, 151
Danto, Arthur C., 158
Darwin, Charles, 125, 127
Davis, Cummings, 130
Davis, Richard, 99
DeLucia, Christine, 120
Dial, 36, 56, 80, 81–82, 83, 95, 97
Dibdin, Charles, "Tom Bowling," 143
Diogenes, 35, 62, 63
Doggett's Repository of Arts, Boston, Massachusetts, 81, 83
Döllinger, Ignaz, 122
Drinking Gourd Project, 25
Dugan house, Concord, Massachusetts, 89
Dunbar, Charles, 114
Durand, Asher, 83

Eastham, Massachusetts, 13–14
East India Marine Society, Salem, Massachusetts, 129–30
Eaton, Anne, xiii, 158
Eckstorm, Fannie Hardy, 140
ecology, 2, 41, 72, 78
Eisen, Charles, 69, *70*
ekphrasis, 86
electrotyping (stereotyping), 115–16
Eliot, George, *Middlemarch*, 155
Eliot, John, 15, 140
emblem, 8, 69
Emerson, Edward, 143
Emerson, George, 111
Emerson, Lidian, 73, 106, 124
Emerson, Ralph Waldo, xi, 1, 4, 21, 24, 25, 27, 56, 64, 73, 74, 81, 82–83, 84, 95, 99, 107, 108, 111, 115, 116, 117, 123, 124, 125, 127, 153, 154, 156; travels in Europe, 27, 73; woodlot at Walden Pond, 24, 26, 47, 74
Emerson, Ralph Waldo, works of: "The American scholar," 2, 107; "Art," 82, 98–99; "Biographical Sketch" of Thoreau, 21, 110, 115; "Experience," 106–7; "History," 105; journal, 127; *Nature*, 88; "Ode to Beauty," 84; "Self-Reliance," 82
Emerson, William, 47
environmentalism, 36
Essex Institute, Salem, Massachusetts, 129–30
ethics, xii, 4, 6–7, 93
Exhibition of the Industry of All Nations, New York, 1853–54, 129

Fagus Werk factory, Alfeld, Germany, 42
Farmer, Jacob, 113
Fedorko, Kathy, 116
Female Anti-Slavery Society, 24
Fichte, Johann Gottlieb, 80
Field, John and Mary, 71
Flannery, Michael, 27–28
Foucault, Michel, 132, 136
Freeman, Brister, 23
Freeman, Fenda, 23
Fruitlands, "consociate family," Harvard, Massachusetts, 36, 132–33, 173n62
Fruitlands Museum, Harvard, Massachusetts, 158
Fugitive Slave Act, 1850, 23, 24, 25, 76, 77
Fuller, Margaret, 56, 81–82; *Summer on the Lakes, in 1843*, 56–57, 59
Furtak, Rick Anthony, 4

Garrison, William Lloyd, 24, 208n1
Gelderen, Martin van, 158
Gensler, 42
Gibbon, Edward, xiii
Gillender Building, New York, 44
Gilpin, William, 3, 69, 73, 90, 91, 92, 93, 94
Gilpin, William, works of: *An Essay on Prints* (1768), 91; *Observations on the River Wye* (1782), 90, 91; *Three Essays* (1792), 91; *Three Essays*, (3rd ed., 1808), 69
Glaeser, Edward, 7, 36
Gleason, Herbert W., *Map of Concord*, 11
Gochberg, Reed, 116, 117, 158
Godwin, Parke, 29

Goff, Lisa, 67
Golahny, Amy, 84
Goodman, Nelson, 108
Gookin, Daniel, 58
graphite, 114–16
Gray, Asa, 110, 111, 125
Gray Herbarium, Harvard University Herbaria, 131
Great Wall of China, 38
Greeley, Horace, 129
Greene, Calvin, 75
Gropius, Walter, 42
Gross, Robert, 12, 22

Haeckel, Ernst, 180n91
Harding, Walter, 125
Harding's Gallery, Boston, Massachusetts, 81–82, 83
Hardy, Manly, 140
Harper, Stephen, 30
Harris, Thaddeus William, 5, 110
Harvard College, 1, 5, 83, 110, 127, 154
Harvard University Herbaria, 131
Hauser, Tobias, 77–78
Hawai'i, US annexation of, 30
Hawthorne, Nathaniel, 84, 117
Hayden, Lewis, 24
Hegel, Georg Wilhelm Friedrich, 80
Heidegger, Martin, 78
Hepburn, Ronald, 3, 104–5
Higginson, Thomas Wentworth, xiii, 55, 62
historical taxonomy, 7, 32, 33, 34, 37, 46, 52–53
historical understanding, 9, 21, 120, 121
history, 2, 3, 6, 13, 14, 17, 21, 25, 26, 32, 37, 40, 52, 59, 60, 72, 75, 84, 105, 120, 122, 130, 135, 156
Hitchcock, Edward, 114
Hoar, Edward, 20, 33, 103, 131, 151
Homer, 141
Horticultural Hall, Boston, Massachusetts, 84
Hosmer, Edmund, 60
Hosmer, Joseph, 66, 101–2
Hosmer, Lydia, 130
Humboldt, Alexander von, 109–10, 123, 127, 159n1

Hunt house, Concord, Massachusetts, 60, 72–73
Huntington Library, San Marino, 117

idealism, German, xi, 4, 107, 127, 157
immigrants, 7, 12, 26, 29, 31, 135; African enslaved, 12, 26; Canadian, 12; Irish, 12, 26–29, 31, 51
India, "denotified tribes," 48–49
Ingraham, Cato, 23
Ingraham, Duncan, 23
Inka Empire (Tawantinsuyu), 38
Ise Jingū shrine, Japan, 43
Ishtar Gate, Babylon, 38

Jackson, Charles T., 115, 131
James, William, 5
Jefferson, Thomas, *Notes on the State of Virginia*, 18
Jersey, Channel Island of, 7, 19
J. Pierpont Morgan Library and Museum, New York, 20

Kaag, John, 4
Kansas-Nebraska Act, 169n91
Kant, Immanuel, 80
Keats, John, 153
Keillor, Garrison, xiii
Kemal, Salim, 158
King Philip's War (1675–78), 16
Know Nothings. *See* American Party (Know Nothings)
Krishna, 152, 153

landscape, 58, 121, 132; in art, 86, 91, 95, 97; in nature, 67, 86, 91, 93
Lane, Charles, 36–37, 132, 173n62
Latour, Bruno, 5, 132, 136
Laugier, Marc-Antoine, *Essai sur l'architecture* (2nd ed., 1755), 69, *70*, 71
Lehmann, Ann-Sophie, 158
Lemire, Elise, 21–22, 23
Leutze, Emmanuel, 83
Liberator, 24, 76, 208n1
Lincoln, Abraham, 169n91
Little Crow (Thaóyate Dúta), 37
Livingston, Goodhue, 44
log cabin, 56, 57, 45, 61

Lojek, Helen, 26
Lowell, James Russell, *My Study Window* (1871), 62

MacDonald, William, 42
Maine, 9, 19, 20, 57, 60, 124, 131, 135, 138, 139–40, 141, 151, 154
Malafouris, Lambros, 5
Maliseet (Wəlastəkwewiyik), 140
Marshall, Megan, 158, 185n38
Martha's Vineyard, Massachusetts, 16
Mashantucket Pequot Museum and Research Center, 17
Mashantucket Pequot Tribal Nation, 17
Mashpee Wampanoag Tribe, 16, 17
Massachuset(t) (Muhsachuweesut), 14, 17, 140
Massachusetts Anti-Slavery Society, 24
Massachusetts Bay Colony, 13, 21, 59
Massachusetts Enfranchisement Act, 1869, 16
Matthiesson, F. O., xii
Mausoleum of Halicarnassus, 44
Maynard, Barksdale, 55, 56, 60, 61, 75
Medford, Massachusetts, 21
Melville, Herman, 129
Metropolitan Museum of Art, New York, 82, 134
Meyer, Adolf, 42
Michelangelo (Michelangelo Buonarotti), 40, 44, 83
Middlesex County Fair, 27
Miller, Hugh, 87
Miller, Peter N., 158
mindprint, xii, 1, 2, 6, 7, 8, 9, 10, 76, 80, 102, 105, 108, 119, 121, 136, 139, 141, 150, 151, 154, 156, 158
Minnesota, 19, 20, 37, 50
Mohegan Indian Tribe, 17
Monk, Ray, xiii
Moosehead Lake, Maine, 139
moose lure, 138–39
Morgan, Lewis H., 35
Mount Katahdin, 57, 103
Muhsachuweesut (Massachuset[t]), 14, 17, 140
Museum of Comparative Zoology, Harvard University, 125, *126*, 127, 132, 133

Museum of Science, Boston (formerly New England Museum of Natural History of the Boston Society of Natural History), 127, 132, 158
music, 9, 60, 110, 141, 143–50, 152, 153
Musketaquid, 12, 14, 15, 18, 30, 31, 59, 130, 135
Musketaquid River. *See* Concord (Musketaquid) River; Sudbury River

Nanepashemet, 14
Nantucket Athenaeum, 129
National Academy of Design, New York, 83
National Association of Building Owners and Managers, 43
Native American Graves Protection and Repatriation Act, 1990, 135
Native Americans, 1, 9, 12, 13–14, 15, 16, 19, 20, 21, 30, 31, 58, 102, 109, 120, 121, 135, 137, 139–41; artifacts, 1, 8, 18–19, 102, 109, 113, 117, 120, 121, 139, 150–51; languages, 17, 19, 139–41
natural history, 1, 5, 8–9, 106, 110, 111, 113, 114, 116, 122, 125, 130, 154
nature, 3, 4, 5, 8, 9, 33, 58, 61, 62, 63, 67, 71, 74, 76, 78, 79, 80, 86, 87, 88, 90, 91, 92, 93, 94, 95, 96, 97, 98, 100, 103, 104–5, 106, 107, 109, 111, 114, 122, 124, 127, 128, 141, 142, 143, 147, 148, 156
Neolithic Revolution, 34
New Bedford, Massachusetts, 19, 33, 129, 130
New England Botanical Club, 131
Newton, Isaac, xi, xiii
Nietzsche, Friedrich, 5
Nipmuc, 17
Noepe, 16
nomadism, 7, 12, 35, 36, 37, 40, 45, 47, 48–50, 51, 52, 53
Nʉmʉnʉʉ (Comanche), 40
Nutting, Wallace, 73

Obama, Barack, 30
Oglála Lakȟóta (Oglala Lakota), 50, 169n93
Oken, Lorenz, 80

Old Manse, Concord, Massachusetts, 84, 117
Old Summer Palace (Yuanming Yuan), Beijing, China, 43
ornament, 54, 82, 83, 133
Osgood, Ellen, née Sewall, 116, 117
Osgood, Joseph, 116
Oxford, UK, 41–42

Pan, 153
Panawáhpskewi (Penobscot), 9, 19, 20, 33, 57, 135, 138, 140, 151
Pantheon, Rome (Basilica of St. Mary and the Martyrs), Italy, 42, 43
paragone, 94
Parker, Theodore, 125
Parkman, Francis, Jr., 50
Paugus (Pekquawket leader), 139, 204n15
Peabody, Elizabeth Palmer, 81, 141; *Æsthetic Papers*, 80
Peabody, George, 133
Peabody, Mrs. R. P., 51
Peabody, Sophia, 84
Peabody Museum of Archaeology and Ethnology, Harvard University, 102, *103*, 118, *118*, 127, 133, *134*, 135, 158
Penobscot (Panawáhpskewi), 9, 19, 20, 33, 57, 135, 138, 140, 151
Penone, Giuseppe, 187n63
pestle, 101–2, *103*, 135
Petrovski, Henry, 115
Pevsner, Nikolaus, 41
Phidias, 40
picturesque, 69, 73, 90, 91, 92, 93, 95
Pilgrim Hall, Plymouth, Massachusetts, 128
Plato, 62; *Republic*, 88; *Sophist*, 88
poetry, 72, 81, 82, 97, 107, 108, 111, 154, 156
Polis, Joseph, 9, 20, 21, 151
Polk, James K., 177n51
"Praying Indians," 16, 17, 19, 58
Price, Uvedale, *An Essay on the Picturesque* (1794; expanded ed., 1796), 93, 94
"Primitive Hut," *70*, 71
Punkatasset Pond, Concord, Massachusetts, 150
Putnam, Frederic Ward, 133

Putnam's Monthly, 28, 29
Pyramids of Giza, 39

racial prejudice, 34
Rader, Karen, 132
railroad, 39, 45, 50, 51, 63, 65–66, 67, 89, 130, 142, 144; Fitchburg Railroad, 12, 25, 26, 51, 64, 145
Ramsay, Alexander, 37
Raphael (Raphael Sanzio), 83
Ray, Robert, 73
Reni, Guido, *Aurora*, 84, 85–86, *85*, 106
Rice, Reuben, 100–101, 111
Richardson, Robert, 96
Ricketson, Anna, 75
Ricketson, Daniel, 19, 33, 75, 130, 152
Ricketson, Walton, 75
Ripley, Sarah Alden Bradford, 125, 127
Robbins, Caesar, 25–26
Robbins, Hannah Simonds, 62
Robbins, Roland Wells, 55, *55*
Roma and Sinti, 49, 50
Rose, Jonathan, 35
Roxbury Female Academy, 117
Royall, Isaac, 21
Rubens, Peter Paul, 179n78
Ruskin, John, 95, 96, 97; *The Elements of Drawing* (1857), 96; *Modern Painters* (1843–56, 1860), 95; *The Seven Lamps of Architecture* (1849), 95

Saito, Yuriko, 3, 46, 105, 117, 155, 158
Salviati, Francesco, *The Three Fates*, 83
Sanborn, Franklin, 18–19, 20, 21, 37, 73 125, 127, 132, 133, 178n74, 181n105, 198n104
savagery, 35
Sayre, Robert, 20, 21
Schelling, Friedrich, 80
Schlegel, Friedrich, 80
Schneider, Richard, 83–84, 96, 107
science, 2, 9, 28, 86, 111, 112, 114, 124, 132
science studies, 131
Scott, James C., 36, 48
Scribner, Ira, 60
Scythians, 35
Sears, Clara Endicott, 132
sedentism, 7, 33, 34, 36, 37, 41, 51, 54

Sedgwick Museum of Earth Sciences, University of Cambridge, 116
Selldorf, Annabelle, 43
Sewall, Ellen. *See* Osgood, Ellen, née Sewall
Shattuck, Ben, 20
Shattuck, Lemuel, *History of the Town of Concord* (1835), 14, 15, 17, 59, 114
shelter, 7, 33, 34, 38, 39, 40, 46, 48, 49, 53, 54, 56, 57, 58, 59, 61, 62, 63, 67, 71, 72, 76, 77, 78, 79, 80, 98
Sherwood, Jennifer, 41
Simons, Martha, 19, 33
Sinclair, Murray (Mizanay [Mizhana] Gheezhik), 30
slavery, 21–22, 24, 26, 30–31, 35, 71, 76, 77, 154
Smail, Daniel Lord, 158
Smithsonian Institution, 107, 123
social evolution, 35
song, 9, 142, 143
soul, 9, 63, 69, 98, 143, 147, 148, 149, 150, 152, 153
sound, 9, 136, 137–53
Spirn, Anne Whiston, 67, 69
Spooner, James, 75
Stallo, John (Johann), *General Principles of the Philosophy of Nature* (1848), 80
St. John shipwreck, 28–29
Stockwell, Samuel, *Mississippi River*, 84
Sudbury River, 15, 57, 134, 146
Sullivan, Daniel, 75

Tagore, Maharaja Bahadur Sir Jatindramohan, 46
Tagore Castle, Kolkata, India, 46
Tahatawan, 14, 120
Tahmont, Swasin, 140, 141, 151
Taj Mahal, Agra, 39
Tawantinsuyu (Inka Empire), 38
"telegraph harp," 144, 145
Tempesta, Antonio, 85
Texas, 177n51
Thatcher, George, 33, 57, 124, 138, 140
Thebes, 41
Thomas, Nicholas, 5, 158
Thoreau, Cynthia, 1, 24, 64, 131
Thoreau, Helen, 1, 24
Thoreau, Henry David: and abolitionism, 22, 23, 24–25, 29; and aesthetics, 3, 4–5, 8, 9, 10, 39, 54, 57–58, 61, 72, 76, 80–81, 82, 89, 93, 102, 103, 104, 105, 112, 117, 120, 136, 148, 150, 153, 154–55, 156; collection, botanical, 8, 109, 110–11, 131; collection, mineralogical and geological, 8, 109, 110, 112, 114, 115, 116, 117, 132; collection, Native American artifacts, 8, 17, 18–19, 29–30, 102, *103*, 117, *118*, 118–21, 133, *134*, 135, 136; collection, ornithological, 8, 109, 113, 130, 132; collections, 8–9; correspondence, 27, 33, 37, 50, 63–64, 73, 74, 83, 91, 96, 115, 123, 124, 132, 152–53; as ethicist, xii, 4, 30, 41, 61–62, 92, 93–94, 98, 103, 105, 108, 114, 146, 147, 154; flute, 149, 151–52, 153, 154; house at Walden Pond, xi, xii, 1, 2, 7, 8, 19, 22, 24, 26, 27, 32, 35, 41, 45, 47, 51, 54, 55–57, *55*, 59, 60–64, 65–67, *68*, 69, 72, 73, 77, 78–79, 80, 88, 107, 108, 109, 123, 137, 142, 144; house at Walden Pond, replicas, 55, *55*, 77–78; house at Walden Pond after abandonment, 27, 32, 73, 74–76; in Maine, 1846, 19, 57; in Maine, 1853, 135, 138–41, 151; in Maine, 1857, 21, 131, 135, 151; as mystic, 4–5; and Native Americans, 1, 6, 7, 8, 9, 12, 13–14, 17, 18–21, 29, 37, 58, 59, 101–2, *103*, 109, 112, 117, 118–21, *118*, 122, 123, 125, 128, 130, 133–34, *134*, 135–36, 137, 138–41, 150–51, 154; as pencil manufacturer, 1, 51, 64, 99, 114–16; as poet, 81, 84–86, 97, 107–8, 154; spyglass (telescope), 113; on Staten Island, 83, 129; study (in Yellow House), 109; surveying, 1, 59, 63, 67, 99–100, 101, 115; and turtle, 114, 125, *126*
Thoreau, Henry David, works of: "An Address on the Succession of Forest Trees," 178n75; "The Aurora of Guido," 84–86; "Autumnal Tints," 87, 97; *Cape Cod*, 7, 13–14, 28, 129; "Cape Cod," *Putnam's Monthly*, 1855, 28–29; "Indian Books," 19–20; Journal, xi, xii, 1, 3, *11*, 17–18, 19, 24–25, 27, 33, 57, 58, 60, 61, 65, 69, 80, 84, 86, 87, 88, 89, 90, 91, 93–94, 95, 96, 97, 100–3, 104, 107–8, 111, 112, 117–18,

Thoreau, (*continued*)
119, 120, 121–22, 127–28, 129, 130, 134, 135, 137, 138, 142, 143, 145, 146–47, 148, 49, 150–51, 152, 156, 198n110; "Ktaadn and the Maine Woods," 57, 103; "Life without Principle," 208n1; *The Maine Woods*, 9, 20, 45, 57, 135, 138–40; "A Plea for Captain John Brown," 22; "Resistance to Civil Government" ("Civil Disobedience"), 22, 76; "The Service," 186n46; "Slavery in Massachusetts," 22, 76, 154; *Walden; Or Life in the Woods*, xii, xiii, 1, 2, 4, 5, 18, 22, 23, 24, 29, 33, 36, 41, 54, 55, 56, 61, 63, 65, 66, 67, *68*, 69, 71–72, 73, 76–77, 78, 88, 89, 90, 92, 98, 99, 107, 109, 111, 116, 137, 142, 144, 146, 147, 149–50, 151, 152; *A Week on the Concord and Merrimack Rivers*, xii, 5, 14, 87, 105, 115, 124–25, 129, 141, 144–45, 146, 150; "Wild Apples," 3; "A Winter Walk," 36

Thoreau, Jean, 7, 19

Thoreau, John, Jr., 1, 5, 18, 116, 117, 120, 121, 150, 152, 205n38

Thoreau, John, Sr., 1; as pencil manufacturer, 1, 51, 64, 114; Texas house, 50, 64

Thoreau, Sophia, xii, 1, 24, 25, 28, 67, 75, 83, 99, 116, 130, 131; *Walden* title page illustration, 7, 8, 67, *68*, 69, 76

Thorson, Robert, 114, 119

Titian (Tiziano Vecellio), 93, 94

Titon, Jeff Todd, 142, 143

tools, 8, 63, 87, 99, 101, 118, 157

transcendentalism, xi, 110, 116, 132, 154

Trowbridge, Samuel Breck Parkman, 44

Truth and Reconciliation Commission of Canada, 30

Turner, J. M. W., 95

Ulrich, Laurel Thatcher, 158

underground railroad, 23–24

United State Constitution, Thirteenth Amendment, 30, 169n91

urbanism, 34, 36, 41

Vasari, Giorgio, 94, 95

Vedas, 141

Vignola, Giacomo (or Jacopo) Barozzi da, 52

Vincent, Patrick, 124

Visnu Purāna, 99

vitalism, 196n87

Vitruvius, 39, 52, 71

Waagen, Gustave, 83

Walden Pond, xi, xii, xiii, 1, 2, 7, 19, 23, 24, 26, 27, 32, 34, 35, 39, 41, 45, 47, 51, 53, 54, *55*, 55, 56, 57, 60, 61, 63, 64, 65, 67, 72, 73, 74, 75, 77, 79, 88, 89, 90, 101, 103, 107, 109, 123, 137, 141, 142, 145, 146, 152, 154, 155, 158

Walls, Laura Dassow, 25, 71, 77, 109, 151, 152

Wampanoag Tribe of Gay Head (Aquinnah), 16

Ward, David, 158

Ward, Samuel Gray, 81, 82, 83

Warren, Henry, 18, 19

Wəlastəkwewiyik (Maliseet), 140

Wheeler, Abiel, 27

Whelan, Hugh, 27, 74

White, John, Sr., 22

White, Zilpah, 22

Whiteread, Rachel, 78

Whitman, Walt, 166n43

wigwam, 18, 36, 58, 63, 151

Wilkinson, C. P. Seabrook, 82

Willard, Simon, 15

Williams, Henry, 24–25

Wilson, Alexander, 113

Winckelmann, Johann Joachim, 95

Wittgenstein, Ludwig, xi, xii, xiii; house near Skjolden, Norway, 56

Wittgenstein, Ludwig, works of: *Philosophical Investigations*, xiii; *Tractatus Logico-Philosophicus*, xii, 61

Wollheim, Richard, 158

Wood, David, 4, 158

Woodward, John, 116

Wôpanâak Language Reclamation Project, 17

Wordsworth, William, xi, 72, 109, 162n17

Wulf, Andrea, 110

Wyman, Jeffries, 133

Wyman, Thomas, 47

Zengzi (Zeng Shen, Thseng-tseu), 147